Curriculum Studies Worldwide

Series Editors
William F. Pinar
Department of Curriculum and Pedagogy
University of British Columbia
Vancouver, BC, Canada

Janet L. Miller
Teacher's College
New York, NY, USA

This series supports the internationalization of curriculum studies worldwide. At this historical moment, curriculum inquiry occurs within national borders. Like the founders of the International Association for the Advancement of Curriculum Studies, we do not envision a worldwide field of curriculum studies mirroring the standardization the larger phenomenon of globalization threatens. In establishing this series, our commitment is to provide support for complicated conversation within and across national and regional borders regarding the content, context, and process of education, the organizational and intellectual center of which is the curriculum.

More information about this series at
http://www.palgrave.com/gp/series/14948

Elise L. Chu

Exploring Curriculum as an Experience of Consciousness Transformation

palgrave
macmillan

Elise L. Chu
University of British Columbia
Vancouver, BC, Canada

Curriculum Studies Worldwide
ISBN 978-3-030-17700-3   ISBN 978-3-030-17701-0 (eBook)
https://doi.org/10.1007/978-3-030-17701-0

© The Editor(s) (if applicable) and The Author(s), under exclusive licence to Springer Nature Switzerland AG 2019
This work is subject to copyright. All rights are solely and exclusively licensed by the Publisher, whether the whole or part of the material is concerned, specifically the rights of translation, reprinting, reuse of illustrations, recitation, broadcasting, reproduction on microfilms or in any other physical way, and transmission or information storage and retrieval, electronic adaptation, computer software, or by similar or dissimilar methodology now known or hereafter developed.
The use of general descriptive names, registered names, trademarks, service marks, etc. in this publication does not imply, even in the absence of a specific statement, that such names are exempt from the relevant protective laws and regulations and therefore free for general use.
The publisher, the authors, and the editors are safe to assume that the advice and information in this book are believed to be true and accurate at the date of publication. Neither the publisher nor the authors or the editors give a warranty, express or implied, with respect to the material contained herein or for any errors or omissions that may have been made. The publisher remains neutral with regard to jurisdictional claims in published maps and institutional affiliations.

Cover illustration: © Masahiro Noguchi/Moment/gettyimages

This Palgrave Macmillan imprint is published by the registered company Springer Nature Switzerland AG
The registered company address is: Gewerbestrasse 11, 6330 Cham, Switzerland

To my profoundly beloved parents.

In memory of my dearly adored husband.

And, for all my teachers, embodied and bodiless, who have touched me deeply and changed me.

Foreword

When Elise L. Chu invited me to supervise her master's thesis, I had little idea of the conversation that would ensue. As someone who had excised questions of spirituality from my own consideration of curriculum, Elise's work compelled me to acknowledge the "moreness"—otherness and transcendence—that characterizes our human being in the world (Huebner, 1999). I learned that this did not require that I shun reason but rather that I acknowledge those reasons for living that reason knows nothing of. Inspired by Huebner's evocation to "dwell faithfully in the world" (p. 403), she invited me to consider the ways in which the languages offered by religious and spiritual traditions, with all their various idiosyncrasies, could contribute to the rich and "complicated conversation" that is curriculum (Pinar, 2012).

This text that would eventually become her outstanding master's thesis and shortly thereafter this book issues a similar invitation to its readers. Elise not only engages in a conversation between science and religion—between contemporary thought and ancient wisdom—but also illustrates the significance of that conversation for a rich understanding of curriculum as consciousness transformation. Beginning with powerful stories of early spiritual experiences, she guides us through her own journey of consciousness transformation via the study and practice of Buddhism. It is a path full of tension and possibility—ultimately involving a conversation between Buddhism and quantum physics—a language, she believes, that integrates ancient wisdom and contemporary science. We need both, she argues, for the "re-spiritualization of curriculum." In hermeneutic fashion, she understands the importance of preserving and nurturing such "a double vision"—"keeping both the whole and its parts, faith and reason, wisdom and method, or the ultimate and phenomenal aspects of reality in sight." It is only in the middle or the in-between, she asserts, that multiple meanings of life, and their interplay, can emerge and be engaged.

In so arguing, Elise embraces and advocates for a form of life that lives alongside the dominant rational norm—driven by the either/or thinking of faith *or* reason—but which refuses to succumb to or be actualized within its terms. Refusing—as in I'd prefer not to—to impose a new norm on any life—as is often the case with religious or scientific enculturation—Elise gestures toward a way of living that in its in-between-ness gives itself and makes itself a form (Agamben, 2000, p. 105). It is an experimental way of living as it keeps the question of truth, and our relationship to it, open. It is a form of life that might be characterized as elliptical—an experience of movement and of the provisional (Berlant, 2015)—precisely because of its openness and potentiality. An ellipsis indicates a gap where meaning may be implied but remains unspoken; it may signal something that is beyond words (a plenitude or 'moreness'); and it may gesture toward the yet unfinished (Clarke & Phelan, 2017).

Real conversations, in Jardine's (2008) sense, are also elliptical. They leave us lost for words as we "hesitate" and "cup our ears" to hear the other, but also to listen to those ghostly discourses that haunt our thinking and being (p. ix). We become self-conscious, "sensitive and sympathetic readers," as Elise expresses it, of the limits and possibilities of an array of languages and symbol categories that shape our encounter with one another and the world. In real conversations we sacrifice a little of our long-held prejudices and expose ourselves to the influence of something other, even if temporarily.

When Elise first entered my office I had little idea of the gifts she bore; nor in her humility, I wager, did she. Cut from the cloth of Western rationality, I was confronted by a student with "an open and appreciative mind" who had the courage to think in spaces I had long ignored. With Elise, I learned so much more than I ever taught...

University of British Columbia Anne M. Phelan
Vancouver, BC, Canada

REFERENCES

Agamben, G. (2000). *The Highest Poverty: Monastic Rules and Form-of-Life*. Stanford, CA: Stanford University Press.

Berlant, L. (2015). *Living in Ellipsis: On Biopolitics and the Attachment to Life*. Keynote Presentation at the Affect Conference: Memory, Aesthetics, and Affect, University of Manitoba, Winnipeg, Canada, September.

Clarke, M., & Phelan, A. M. (2017). *Teacher Education and the Political: The Power of Negative Thinking*. London, UK: Routledge Press.

Huebner, D. E. (1999). Curriculum as Concern for Man's Temporality. In V. Hillis (Ed.), *The Lure of the Transcendent: Collected Essays by Dwayne E. Huebner* (pp. 131–142). New York, NY: Routledge. (Original work published 1967).

Jardine, D. (2008). Foreword. In C. Eppert & H. Wang (Eds.), *Cross-Cultural Studies in Curriculum* (pp. 74–127). New York, NY: Routledge.

Pinar, W. F. (2012). *What Is Curriculum Theory?* (2nd ed.). New York, NY: Routledge.

ACKNOWLEDGMENTS

This book is an expansion of my MA research. I want to pay special thankfulness, warmth, and appreciation to the persons who made this book possible.

Firstly, I wish to express my profound gratitude, love, and respect to my supervisor Prof. Anne Phelan for her continuous warm support, caring encouragement, open-minded listening, and illuminating guidance during my MA and current PhD studies. This book would not have been possible without her. I feel so blessed to have the good fortune to learn from an educator who knows profoundly what education is and is all about and, in many respects, knows my works deeper than myself. Her being and teaching inspire me joyously toward being an educator alike even if I know that there is still a very long way for me to go.

My special gratitude and respect go to Prof. William Pinar for his inspiring teaching and various warm support, and also for his encouragement to seek the possibility of publishing this book. I am deeply touched and inspired by his commitment and immense contribution to the curriculum field. His playful and liberal language, as well as his thought-provoking responses and questions, significantly broadened my horizons and cultivated in me new visions. It's a blessing and pleasure having him in my current PhD supervisory committee. I would also like to say a sincere thanks to my MA supervisory committee member, Dr. Susan Gerofsky, for her insightful feedback on my thesis and patient guidance during the earliest stage of my studies at UBC.

Throughout my life, I have had the good fortune to learn from many respectable and caring teachers. My gratitude to my father-like mathematics teacher, the late Prof. Guan-Aun How, is immense and can hardly be expressed well in words. Prof. How has been highly esteemed and adored by his students. His compassion and thoughtfulness were reflected in his teaching that featured turning highly obscure and complicated mathematics into step-by-step illuminating and intriguing reasoning which guided us through various conceptual barriers and burst open the beauty and power of mathematics—leaving us with awe, wonder, and profound joyousness. His fabulous teaching aroused my enthusiasm in Abstract Algebra and shaped my ways of thinking and teaching. From my university days onward, he had constantly encouraged me to do further studies and to ask him questions. Every time I visited him to ask questions, I was moved by his delightful, welcoming, and thoughtful tutoring and inspired by his uplifting encouragement. Just after I had graduated, I was working as an administrative assistant within the department of which he was the chairperson. He always tried to take on as many works as possible on his own in order to give me more time to study, and when he did require my help, he always came to my office in person instead of calling me to his office. I remember one occasion on which he came to my office. I was too busy concentrating on a math proof to notice his presence, so he just waited patiently until I noticed him on my own as he was so caring and thoughtful and did not want to interrupt my thinking process. Without him, I would never have fully appreciated the profound beauty of mathematics and nor would I have grasped the essence of great teachers when I was learning to become a teacher.

In addition to Prof. How, my gratitude to my MSc supervisor, the late Prof. Seong-Nam Ng, is equally profound. I admire his integrity and excellent mathematics capacity and deeply appreciate the expanding experience of delving, with his guidance, into Non-Associated Rings (a branch of mathematics related to quantum theory)—extremely complex and abstruse, yet stunningly beautiful and powerful. While Prof. Ng was a taciturn man, he had a deep concern for his students. I gratefully appreciate his encouragement to advance to a PhD program and his offer to recommend me to another professor at National Taiwan University to continue my study. I also cherish in mind his kindness in managing to write a reference letter to UBC for me while he was in hospital, and he only let me know his condition after he had submitted the reference letter. While, to his disappointment, I did not continue my math study due to health problems, I know, with faith, that he must be very happy to know that I am currently in a doctoral program learning from many great teachers. As does Prof. Phelan, both Prof. How and Prof. Ng held equality as a presupposition to be verified and elegantly demonstrated emancipatory teachers' will (in Jacques Rancière's words). Their influences on me are profound. In addition, I wish to show my great appreciation to Prof. Wheijen Chang, my university physics teacher, for raising a philosophical issue in the form of a short "digression" in one of my first-year Physics classes (the philosophical seed she planted in my mind eventually sprouted and grew into a tree) and for her encouragement for me to investigate into educational issues when I became a first-year Calculus lecturer.

In addition to the above teachers, my unique and immense gratitude goes to my most significant spiritual teachers, the late Miao-Zong Shifu (Shifu means a father-like teacher) and Guanyin bodhisattva of Sheng En Temple. I cherish their profound love, compassion, wisdom, and teachings and sincerely hope that I will never fail to live up to their expectations. My profound gratitude also goes to my longtime family-like mentor, Mr. Jun-Hau Lai, a great I-Ching Master—although he is so modest that he would never accept such a title—for his compassionate and insightful guidance over the past three decades. I also want to present my profound appreciation to my qigong teacher, Master Xue-Zhong Zhao, and his wife, Mrs. Zhao. It was thanks to Master Zhao's teaching of Informatics Qigong that I learnt to feel and guide the Qi (although I remain an awkward practitioner), and thanks to Master Zhao's and Mrs. Zhao's caring qigong healing and encouragement that I was able to regain my feet and continue my studies. My heartfelt gratitude also goes to CJ and Jun for their selfless and generous sharing of qigong experiences and their warm care, tutoring, and encouragement.

My immense love, affection, and gratitude to my parents are beyond words; I can never thank them enough. Their profound and endless love and care is always the most significant source of my courage and perseverance. I also wish to express my profound gratitude to my parents-in-law, my brother, sister, and siblings-in-law for their heartwarming care and support. My heartfelt gratitude also goes to my family-like friends Dick and Lina for their constant warm care and support; to Ru-You Dharma Master and Ling-Yin of Huizhong Temple for their beautiful demonstration of the union of compassion and wisdom in daily life, I am very grateful for having wise and caring mentors like them on my way to learning to walk the Bodhisattva Path; to my late husband's faithful friends Blake, Yong-Long, Yao-Wei, and Chang-Yong for their warm friendships; to my young but sage friend Alexis for his constant encouragement and heartwarming friendship; also to Bruce for his generous sharing of publication experiences, and to all my other warmhearted PhD program cohorts for their various support; to Yuliana for her warm friendship and selfless sharing of thoughts—the first time I heard of Nietzsche's three metamorphoses was from her; and to my many other respectable teachers and friends in Taiwan and Canada. My heartfelt gratitude also goes to the reviewer of this book for his/her very kind encouragement, penetrating reading, and insightful suggestions for improvement. I also want to express my heartfelt gratitude to Linda, Hemalatha, and the whole editorial and production team of Palgrave Macmillan for their professional insights, brilliant work, patient guidance, and warm support.

Finally, my immense and most affectionate love, gratitude, and respect go to my dearly adored late husband. I can never thank him enough for his loving confidence in me and his firm belief in the significance of this research long before it was well written. I deeply cherish his continual reminders of my vocation and his affectionate determination to protect me from interference during the process of doing this research. His profound love and wisdom have continued to give me courage and strength in the face of the various challenges that arose during the process of conducting this research and will, I know, accompany and support me unceasingly throughout my lifetime.

Prologue: An Autobiographical Note

I am currently a PhD student in Curriculum Studies at the University of British Columbia under the supervision of Prof. Anne Phelan. My major in university was Applied Mathematics, my study and research interest in MSc program was Abstract Algebra, precisely Group Theory, Coding Theory, and Non-Associative Rings. This book is a revised and extended version of my MA thesis, also under the supervision of Prof. Phelan. During my study in the MA program, Prof. Phelan's profound wisdom, as well as her pedagogical thoughtfulness and watchfulness, had opened for me a nurturing space that allows all aspects of myself—including my interest in mathematics and science—to unfold and reintegrate, and made this educational research process simultaneously a playful and meaningful self-transformative journey. While the readers would not consider the main body of this book to be autobiographical, I agree with Smith (1999) that "all writing is in a sense autobiographical" (p. 43), and hope that this autobiographical note would provide the readers a glimpse of my own *currere*—my "running of the course" (Pinar, Reynolds, Slattery, & Taubman, 2008, p. 515)—regarding how my life history and experiences, academic training, intellectual development, and spiritual growth shape each other, and shape this book.

I was born and raised in a sedate country town in Taiwan, where the local folk religion—which comprises a blend of Taoism, Buddhism, and Confucianism—is the most popular system of belief. At the core of this folk religion are: reverence for the transcendent source of Nature and for the gods and ancestors; a belief in the moral reciprocity, the law of karma, the energy (Qi) that animates the universe, personal destiny, fateful coincidence and potential relationships, and the existence of the six realms—six directions of reincarnation that include hell, hungry ghost, animal, *asura* (malevolent nature spirits), human existence, and deva (heavenly existence). My father was an elementary schoolteacher, and my mother was a kindergarten teacher, and both of them had come from farming families. In the countryside villages where my grandparents lived, as in many other rural villages in Taiwan, the majority of the inhabitants worship Guanyin bodhisattva (*Avalokiteśvara*, or Goddess of Mercy) in their home. Guanyin, meaning "perceiving the sounds (of the world)," is well known as a constant listener and a compassionate giver of fearlessness. During my childhood, I heard many touching miraculous stories of the manifestation of Guanyin bodhisattva during World War II.

Before my parents formally worshipped Guanyin bodhisattva at home, they worshiped Tudigong (Lord of the Soil and the Ground) as the guardian of the family, at their elders' suggestion. When I was attending elementary school, although my mother had been piously offering incense and fruits to Tudigong daily for many years, she experienced a crisis of faith when she prayed in vain for a cure to my father's health problems. Deeply frustrated, she addressed Tudigong, saying: "Do you really exist? Do gods really exist?" The next morning, at around 5 a.m., while my mother was sweeping the ground of the backyard while my six-year-old younger sister played nearby, my sister looked up to see a semi-transparent elder smiling at her; the figure, dressed resplendently in ancient clothes, bore a striking resemblance to the picture my sister had seen of Tudigong at the family altar, and she immediately called to my mother: "Mom, look! An elder!" When my mother turned around and saw the figure, she was severely startled and dropped her broom in shock. The elder looked at her kindly and said simply, "Devout lady, I am the Tudigong," before fading away. This dramatic event greatly reinforced my entire family's belief in religious doctrines and had a profound influenced on our worldview.

However, in the educational context of Taiwan, religious language is forbidden, eliminating superstitions has long been a campaign, and existential inquiries are largely ignored. When I was a high school student, I strongly questioned the worldly values imposed on us. In my own efforts to seek out alternative values, what I found most appealing were biographies of enlightened monks, Buddhist poetry, D. T. Suzuki's works on Zen, and William Blake's poems. It seemed to me that these works suggested not only the existence of transcendental realities beyond our ordinary perception, but also different ways of being in the world. Yet, at that time, the nature of human existence and the meaning of life remained vague to me.

Another experience that further reshaped my worldview occurred in my third year of university when my mother was introduced to a prestigious and compassionate Taoist abbot, Miao-Zong Shifu, who had then been a medium of Guanyin bodhisattva for around 20 years, since 1968. Being famous for his omniscience and prophetic insights, in trance states, this selfless abbot was multilingual and could respond to people from around Taiwan and the world (including politicians, entrepreneurs, merchants, educators, agriculturalists, scientists, and astronomers) in their own languages and gave highly specialized guidance as well as prophetic insights. In my first encounter with this embodied Guanyin bodhisattva, I was awed and touched by his precise description of an unspoken prayer I had raised for my parents a few days earlier when I was in another city.

During the following two decades, my family and I were profoundly grateful for having countless similar awe-inspiring and heartwarming experiences of being heard, understood, cared for, and guided. One typical story took place around 15 years ago. One morning, when my mother stepped into the Taoist temple, the abbot, our deeply respected and adored Shifu, came to her and asked her if she had an elder sister who had passed away when she was still a middle school student. My mother was surprised and answered, "Yes! What happened?" Shifu continued, "Your sister came to my vision last night wearing a middle school uniform. She told me that she is your elder sister and she comes to seek bodhisattva's help because your third elder brother, a government officer, is currently falsely accused of taking bribes and is going to be sentenced, but he can hardly redress the injustice." My mother was startled because my uncle, who lived in another county, had never mentioned this to her. After experiencing this vision, however, Shifu arranged a meeting with my uncle. In that meeting, Guanyin bodhisattva came and drew a picture of the man who actually took bribes and had used my uncle as a scapegoat and then told my uncle that the last name of this person was Huang. My uncle could hardly believe it because it turned out that the person who framed him was someone he would never suspect—a colleague, his best friend. It was thanks to the compassion and wisdom of Guanyin bodhisattva that my uncle was finally able to effectively refute this unjust accusation.

Like many other believers, gradually my family and I developed wholehearted faith and learnt to decode the wisdom implied in prophetic stanzas written specifically for each person by Guanyin bodhisattva, and learnt to recognize various forms of callings and responses from Guanyin bodhisattva and from the universe in everyday life (e.g., surprising coincidences; striking words, scenes, and encounters; lucid dreams, intuition, and insights) which would later be reaffirmed by Guanyin bodhisattva who spoke through Shifu. I deeply appreciate this sort of training for maintaining faith and connection with Guanyin bodhisattva and am profoundly grateful for various heartwarming experiences after Shifu passed away. Foreseeing the supports I would need later in my life, Shifu and Guanyin bodhisattva thoughtfully gave me in advance many significant written prophetic stanzas and oral guidance that I did not fully understand their profound meanings and wisdom until many years later when I was facing challenging situations and having to make difficult decisions. I cannot thank Shifu and Guanyin bodhisattva enough for these crucial support that helped me adhere to my vocation and aspiration and persevere in my studies amidst all difficulties.

Throughout my transformation from a critical spectator to a respectful witness of this embodied Guanyin bodhisattva's awe-inspiring manner, deeds, compassion, wisdom, and supernormal knowledge (*Abhijñā*) far beyond human capacity, I developed a certain degree of spiritual discernment and a preliminary understanding of spiritual concepts and language, such as equanimity, selflessness, omniscience, prophecy, *bodhicitta*, great compassion, and transcendental wisdom. No longer did I consider spiritual narratives in the context of various religions as merely mythic fabrication, exaggerated rhetoric, unattainable ideals, or groundless superstition. In my university days and teaching career, my personal spiritual experiences motivated me toward texts such as Buddhist and Taoist scriptures and treatises, Jane Roberts' Seth books, Brian Weiss' books on past lives and reincarnation, Raymond Moody's research on near death experiences, Si-Chen Lee's research on finger reading and psychokinesis, Michael Talbot's book *The Holographic Universe*, and texts on various breakthroughs in contemporary physics. The knowledge acquired from the aforementioned literature, along with my corresponding personal experiences, greatly broadened my horizons and allowed me to contemplate the nature of consciousness and human existence, the meaning of life, and the essence and purpose of education from new perspectives.

The texts that are particularly worth mentioning are Seth books and *The Holographic Universe*. While some scholars might question the integrity of the whole Seth material due to its alleged origin through channeling, and personally I do keep some of Seth's ideas in suspension of judgment, overall, Seth material was illuminating as it opened up an expanded mental playground for me to freely and joyfully play with various liberating ideas regarding the nature of human existence and reality. One interesting anecdote happened when I read about the advent of "the future Seth" and was puzzled by the mystery of time that suggested the coexisting of past, present, and future. In the same week when I was meeting with Shifu, unexpectedly I witnessed the debut of "the future bodhisattva" as if Guanyin bodhisattva was following my study progress and playfully responded to my confusion and curiosity. Years later, I joyfully learnt about Einstein's special relativity, which suggests that "reality embraces past, present, and future equally and that the flow [of time] we envision bringing one section to light as another goes dark is illusory" (Greene, 2004, p. 132). Quantum physicist Brian Greene (2004) added that "all the physical laws that we hold dear fully support what is known as *time-reversal symmetry*" (p. 145), meaning, "in theory, events can unfold in reverse order" (p. 145).

My first encounter with *The Holographic Universe* was in 1997 when the Chinese translation of this book was published in Taiwan. As I read, I was extremely excited by the holographic paradigm of the universe (a prototype of the holographic principle of string theories), not only because of its theoretical beauty and its resonance with Buddhist philosophy, but also because it was reminiscent of a special experience I had in Grade 4 when I unusually woke up at midnight and found that the whole bedroom was stunningly filled with uniformly distributed floating and glittering clusters of light-flowers in shapes akin to enlarged 3D snow-crystals and in colors of green and purple. The clusters of light-flowers were flashing in a constant and peaceful rhythm, yet when I reached out my hands to touch them, they were empty, similar to the holographic projection of objects that I saw some years later in movies and other videos. After observing these gorgeous light-flowers for a while, I decided to wake my father and ask him what these were. My father soon woke up my mother too, but strangely, while I pointed here and there to show them the light-flowers, neither of them saw any. Even so, my parents looked very composed, and in their efforts to comfort me and to figure things out, they took me to the living room and then went outside to the courtyard, and I only found that the beautiful light-flowers were everywhere. As my parents didn't see anything, they soon took me back to bed. The next morning when I woke up anticipating seeing the light-flowers, disappointedly they had all gone. Not long ago when I mentioned this event again to my parents, interestingly they confessed that in actuality they both were terribly frightened by me in that night; yet thanks to their love and wisdom, I have a lovely memory of gorgeous clusters of light-flowers glittering stunningly in the rooms, in the tranquil moonlight, in my whole experiential world.

This experience made me realize that people could not only interpret the world differently, but also could literally see or sense the world differently. With this realization, I cultivated an open and appreciative mind toward various extra-sensory and spiritual experiences of others from diverse spiritual and religious traditions. One of the examples is Canadian indigenous law scholar John Borrows' (2010) work *Drawing Out Law: A Spirit's Guide*. In this book, he skillfully weaved theories and stories regarding how he was guided by spirits in drawing out law. The stories start from his recurring dream about four hills—a metaphor of four hills of life or life's seasons—that "represented many teachings about how to live in balance with the world" (p. 4). In ways much like Borrows', on the affection level, my "holographic light-flowers" experience and other spiritual experiences have guided me through my scientific and existential inquiries that conjointly shaped my educational thinking. Yet, in the current educational landscape, particularly in "curricula immunized from the human condition and devoid of story, attachment and meaning" (Phelan, 2004, p. 12), too often we easily dismiss "lived experience that [does] not fit inside the dominant molds of rationalism" (p. 11); such experience could be "the lure of the transcendent" (Huebner, 1985a/1999, p. 360) which points to "the fissure in human knowing, the openness" (Huebner, 1985b/1999, p. 349) that signifies infinite transformative possibilities. In such a curriculum, we also become oblivious to the wisdom that in our authentic existence as being-in-the-world (Heidegger, 1927/2010), the observer and the observed are equal (Bohm, 1980; Greene, 2004; Kumar, 2013), and that in this undivided dynamic wholeness (Bohm, 1980), the individual–world dialectic—wherein the world and the individual calls forth new responses from each other, wherein the observer is the observed and the observed is the observer, wherein cause is effect and effect is cause (Huebner, 1967/1999)—is one of the most significant sites for meaning-making.

During my career as a full-time teaching assistant and then a lecturer for first-year university Calculus, due to the absence of spiritual wisdom in the educational context, I encountered hundreds of freshmen every year who were struggling on their own in search of meaning both inside and outside the classrooms. While I was concerned about students' academic performance in their studies of Calculus, I was more profoundly concerned about how the relentless power of the machinery of the education system drove everyone forward and left deeper questions of meaningfulness to the individual youngsters as "their own business." As an educator, I questioned: Is this really none of our business?

In 2011, while personally practicing Buddhist philosophy and engaging with the holographic perspective of the universe, I enrolled in the MA program in Math Education at UBC. Despite my enthusiasm for existential inquiries, given my professional background as a Calculus teacher, at first I saw no alternative but to direct my research focus toward Calculus Reform. Fortunately, taking the course Introduction to Curriculum Issues and Theories taught by Prof. Phelan changed my conditioned impressions of what curriculum and education are and could be; the transformative power of this course also renewed my aspiration and changed my compromised life. With a new vision, I made the momentous decision to alter my program of study from Math Education to Curriculum Studies. To this day, I deeply appreciate Prof. Phelan, who opened for me new possibilities of pursuing my genuine research interests, articulating the formerly silenced voice, and living with authenticity.

As a beneficiary of the existential tradition of curriculum, I deeply appreciate the opportunity to undertake an investigation into the profound curriculum scholarship of Dwayne Huebner—"one of the most important minds the field of curriculum has known,… [and] may well be judged by future historians of the field as *the* most important" (Pinar, 1999, p. xxiv)—as well as the works of other significant curriculum theorists. In the essay "Education and Spirituality," Huebner (1993/1999) asked that if one dwells faithfully in the world, "what images of education, specifically curriculum, are possible?" (p. 403). He indicated that he spoke as one who tries to dwell as a Christian because it is his religious tradition and because he is more familiar with its many qualities, quirks, and its language (Huebner, 1993/1999, p. 403). He invited those in other traditions "to attempt the same, thereby enriching the ensuing conversation" (Huebner, 1993/1999, p. 403). As a response to Huebner's invitation, I make such an attempt in this book and sincerely hope that this book will contribute to the curriculum field by enriching it with the language of Buddhism and quantum physics, a language that integrates ancient wisdom and contemporary science, informed by my personal spiritual experiences.

References

Bohm, D. (1980). *Wholeness and the Implicate Order.* New York, NY: Routledge.
Borrows, J. (2010). *Drawing Out Law: A Spirit's Guide.* Toronto, ON: University of Toronto Press.
Greene, B. (2004). *The Fabric of the Cosmos: Space, Time, and the Texture of Reality.* New York, NY: Alfred A. Knopf.
Heidegger, M. (2010). *Being and Time* (J. Stambaugh, trans.). Albany, NY: State University of New York Press. (Original work published 1927).
Huebner, D. E. (1999). Curriculum as Concern for Man's Temporality. In V. Hillis (Ed.), *The Lure of the Transcendent: Collected Essays by Dwayne E. Huebner* (pp. 131–142). New York, NY: Routledge. (Original work published 1967).
Huebner, D. E. (1999). Religious Metaphors in the Language of Education. In V. Hillis (Ed.), *The Lure of the Transcendent: Collected Essays by Dwayne E. Huebner* (pp. 358–368). New York, NY: Routledge. (Original work published 1985a).
Huebner, D. E. (1999). Spirituality and Knowing. In V. Hillis (Ed.), *The Lure of the Transcendent: Collected Essays by Dwayne E. Huebner* (pp. 340–352). New York, NY: Routledge. (Original work published 1985b).
Huebner, D. E. (1999). Education and Spirituality. In V. Hillis (Ed.), *The Lure of the Transcendent: Collected Essays by Dwayne E. Huebner* (pp. 401–416). New York, NY: Routledge. (Original work published 1993).
Kumar, A. (2013). *Curriculum as Meditative Inquiry.* New York, NY: Palgrave Macmillan.
Phelan, A. M. (2004). Rationalism, Complexity Science and Curriculum: A Cautionary Tale. *Complicity: An International Journal of Complexity and Education,* 1(1), 9–17.
Pinar, W. F. (1999). Introduction. In V. Hillis (Ed.), *The Lure of the Transcendent: Collected Essays by Dwayne E. Huebner* (pp. xv–xxviii). New York, NY: Routledge.
Pinar, W. F., Reynolds, W. M., Slattery, P., & Taubman, P. M. (2008). *Understanding Curriculum: An Introduction to the Study of Historical and Contemporary Curriculum Discourses.* New York, NY: Peter Lang. (Original work published 1995).
Smith, D. G. (1999). *Pedagon: Interdisciplinary Essays in the Human Sciences, Pedagogy, and Culture.* New York, NY: Peter Lang.

CONTENTS

Part I Significant Issues Regarding Spirituality and Education   1

1 The Issue of De-Spiritualization in Education   3
    1.1 Classical Science, De-Spiritualization, and Global Crises   3
    1.2 New Science and Spiritual Wisdom   7
    1.3 Overview of the Chapters   9
    References   15

2 Spirituality, Truth, and Education   17
    2.1 Introduction   17
    2.2 The Concepts of Spirituality in the Educational Literature   20
    2.3 Significant Epistemological Concerns Over Education   25
    2.4 Plato's Allegory of the Cave: The Relationship Between Truth and Education   31
    References   37

Part II The Nature of Consciousness, Self, and Reality 39

3 A Dialogue Between Buddhism and Quantum Physics 41
3.1 Introduction 41
3.2 The Concepts of Truth in Buddhism 42
3.3 A Dialogue Between Buddhism and Quantum Physics 53
3.4 The Implications of This Dialogue for Education 66
References 74

Part III Consciousness Transformation 77

4 The Concepts and Process of Consciousness Transformation 79
4.1 Introduction 79
4.2 The Two Barriers to Consciousness Transformation 80
4.3 The Transformation of Consciousness into Four Transcendental Wisdoms 81
4.4 The Five-Stage Gradual Path of Consciousness Transformation in Buddhism 82
4.5 The Union of Wisdom and Method 85
4.6 The Approach of Negation 90
4.7 The Implications 93
References 97

Part IV Curriculum as an Experience of Consciousness Transformation 99

5 Understanding the Nature of Consciousness, Self, and Reality 101
5.1 Introduction 101
5.2 The Limitations of Scientific Method and Rational Analysis 103
5.3 The Imperative of Integrating Existential Knowledge and Spiritual Wisdom into Curriculum 107
References 113

6	Learning to Appreciate Human Temporality	115
	6.1 Time and Human Existence	115
	6.2 Death and Authenticity	118
	6.3 Learning to Appreciate Human Temporality	120
	References	123

7	Cultivating Impartiality and *Bodhicitta*	125
	7.1 Introduction to Impartiality and Bodhicitta	125
	7.2 The Axioms of Equality and Inequality	128
	7.3 Bodhicitta *as an Alternative to the Market Logic and Global Competitiveness*	132
	References	135

8	Becoming Responsibly Responsive	137
	8.1 Introduction	137
	8.2 Cultivating Spiritual Discernment in Language and Reality	140
	8.3 The Injunctions of the Four Noble Truths and the Awakening to Responsibility	143
	8.4 Identity, Appropriational Circuit, Movie Consciousness, and Responsibility	145
	References	151

9	Cultivating Selflessness	153
	9.1 Introduction	153
	9.2 The Concepts of Self and Selflessness	154
	9.3 The I-Me-Mine Complex	158
	9.4 Meditative Stabilization and Selflessness	160
	References	163

10	Learning to Embody a Non-Dualistic Worldview	165
	10.1 Introduction	165
	10.2 The Six Perfections and the Embodiment of a Non-Dualistic Worldview	166
	10.3 The Meanings, Practices, and Educational Implications of the First Four Perfections	168
	10.4 The Curriculum of Witnessing	171
	References	176

Part V Conclusion Without Conclusion   177

11 The Metamorphosis and the Confounded Speech   179
    11.1 Retrospection   179
    11.2 Three Metamorphoses of the Spirit: Camel, Lion, and
          Child   181
    11.3 The Blind Men and the Elephant   187
    11.4 The Tower of Babel   193
    References   196

Index   199

PART I

Significant Issues Regarding Spirituality and Education

CHAPTER 1

The Issue of De-Spiritualization in Education

1.1 CLASSICAL SCIENCE, DE-SPIRITUALIZATION, AND GLOBAL CRISES

Intrinsic in human temporality, there exist existential questions about the meaning, purpose, and significance of life. While generations of curious youngsters enter into education systems anticipating acquiring the answers to these questions, school and university curricula generally fail to provide sufficient wisdom to address such inquiries. This might be attributed to the fact that the cultural framework for approaching such existential questions is largely considered to be *religious* in nature, and is therefore excluded from the scope of school curriculum as a consequence of intentional distancing of education from religion. For example, in the United States, the Lemon Test, formalized in 1971, had been "employed by the Court to determine whether laws, policies, and practices related to religion in the public sector were constitutional" (Pinar, Reynolds, Slattery, & Taubman, 1995/2008, p. 613). According to Pinar et al. (1995/2008), the three parts of the Lemon Test are: "(1) the government act that bears on religion must reflect a secular purpose, (2) it may neither advance nor inhibit religion as its primary effect, and (3) it must avoid excessive government entanglement with religion" (p. 613); and "it has affected not only specific legal decisions but a more general perception of public education in the United States" (p. 613). In such a context, educators in the USA have made efforts over several decades to distance their work from its

© The Author(s) 2019
E. L. Chu, *Exploring Curriculum as an Experience of Consciousness Transformation*, Curriculum Studies Worldwide,
https://doi.org/10.1007/978-3-030-17701-0_1

origins in Christian traditions, and the place of religious traditions in education has been gradually replaced by scientific and technical enterprise, as exhibited in the symbiotic relationship of the testing industry and schooling (Huebner, 1985b/1999c, p. 340). Huebner (1985b/1999c) observed that the questions of values and ends, despite not possibly being suppressed, has altered the rhetoric and increasingly cloaked it in scientific or developmental language (pp. 340–341). As he pointed out, despite the fact that Western and Eastern religious traditions "all acknowledge the spiritual as an integral aspect of human life,… [and] human beings participate in a spiritual dimension of existence, something more than the material, the sensory, and the quantitative" (Huebner, 1985b/1999c, p. 342), and that the "questions of life's meaning and significance loom large within the religious traditions, the dependency of education upon those traditions appeared to yield to dependency upon the traditions of science" (Huebner, 1985b/1999c, p. 340). Looking back, the main problem of this substitution is that, during the period when the educational and scientific traditions were merging, positivism—with its root in classical (Newtonian) physics—and its associated absolutistic and objectivistic worldview as well as materialist social values were assuming a dominant role. As a result, the spiritual wisdom of long-standing religious traditions was largely rejected.

Formally founded and named by the sociologist and philosopher August Comte (1798–1857) in the 1830s as a distinctive movement, positivism maintains the Newtonian world-as-machine worldview (Nickle, 2005, p. 1854), rejects "the possibility of knowledge of unobservable physical objects… [and regards] metaphysical speculation as failing to keep imagination limited by observation" (Sullivan, 2009, p. 395). Because of the rejection of spiritual speculation and wisdom, human beings become forgetful of the grand source that give life profound meaning and purpose. The exclusion of spiritual language and wisdom from education also hides from us "what we are really about when we educate" (Huebner, 1985a/1999b, p. 359). In the absence of spiritual wisdom in education, we forget that "knowing is a relation between the person and the other" (Huebner, 1985a/1999b, p. 365). Huebner (1985a/1999b) suggested,

> [by failing to recognize knowledge] as an invitation to join hands with someone else in their involvement with earth,… [and] an invitation to establish a relationship of care and being cared for—a relationship of duty,

love, and reverence,... we make the objects of the world care for us. We harness these objects, their qualities and characteristics, to our needs and wants, frequently destroying them, and gradually the earth, so they can serve us. (p. 366)

Huebner (1985a/1999b) lamented that "the mutuality of love and reverence is broken in technical communities, for we no longer care for that which cares for us" (p. 366). This mutuality of duty, love, and reverence became gradually replaced by the absolutistic and objectivistic worldview which assumes the mind-independence of reality (Bryman, 2004) and a sharp distinction between the observer and the observed, and by Charles Darwin's theory of evolution, which is often interpreted or misinterpreted as connoting the *life as war* metaphor to represent human experiences (McTaggart, 2011, p. xxi).

In the educational context, in the absence of spiritual wisdom and the mutuality of duty, love, and reverence, students are either blindly accepting of the absolutistic and objectivistic worldview, seeing competition among humans as human nature, viewing the doctrine of virtues as mere platitudinous and hypocritical dogma for social control, or to the contrary, struggling strenuously to maintain their deep beliefs and values that are contradictory with, and confused by, the prevailing absolutistic and objectivistic worldview. On the societal and political levels, the absolutistic and objectivistic worldview and the materialist social values are reflected in the formulaic logic of The Market and the language of global competitiveness along with the formula of "Unless we do X, we will fall behind" (Smith, 2000, p. 18). Smith (2000) commented that this becomes "a simple and powerful recipe for the creation of Loser Culture" (p. 18), for winning implies losing, and that "any social and educational planning motivated by the sheer desire to win of necessity breeds not only hypercompetitiveness in the social realm, but also its adjunct effects of heightened social paranoia and the turning of friends into enemies" (p. 18). Also, since there must, by definition, only be a few winners, more and more people feel as if they are losers and that life is a race (Smith, 2000, p. 18). He quoted remarks by the Canadian philosopher of technology Franklin that "the language of global competitiveness is the language of war" (p. 18), and remarked that, as educators, we might ask: "Who can survive it, and how?" (p. 18). Smith (2000) foresaw that the increasing forms of resistance against the radical commercialization of human values on a global scale might prefigure a global conversation regarding "what it means to live well humanly speaking" (p. 16), and indicated that "discussions regarding shared futures must inevitably involve religious questions, that is, questions about meaning, purpose, and what is truly required to nurture and sustain human life in its most noble and dignified senses" (p. 16).

Since the rise of classical science, the excessive desire to gain and win nurtured by the absolutistic and objectivistic worldview and materialist social values has gradually blinded humankind to the interconnectedness and interdependence of everything on the Earth, and to the existence of infinite transcendental possibilities. Such blindness can lead to dire consequences for not only human beings, but also the planet as a whole. In his lecture to the Nobel Peace Prize Committee at Oslo, Norway in 2007, Al Gore (2008) addressed the issue of global warming, cautioning: "We, the human species, are confronting a planetary emergency—a threat to the survival of our civilization that is gathering ominous and destructive potential" (p. 55). Moreover, climate change is not the only global crisis we face today. According to Lomborg (2004), the 2004 Copenhagen Consensus conference identified more than 30 major global challenges, including conflicts and arms proliferation, terrorism, corruption, deforestation, chemical pollution and hazardous waste, depletion of the ozone layer and water resources, loss of biodiversity, vulnerability to natural disasters, malnutrition and hunger, etc.

Underscoring the interdependence of various elements for the diversity of life on Earth, indigenous law scholar Borrows (2010) reminded us that "to look just on the surface, and think that what you see from horizon to horizon is all that is need to survive, is to misunderstand your place on the ground which you stand" (p. 72); he continued that "to scale its heights—to learn its lessons—one must be alive to the underlying structures that support the visible and non-so-visible world around you" (p. 72). Borrows' insights echo with Huebner's, and I am convinced that the key to the realization of the nature of human existence and reality as "more than the material, the sensory, and the quantitative" (Huebner, 1985b/1999c, p. 342) and to a resolution of the present global crises lies in the transformation of consciousness into wisdom, and this could be facilitated by curriculum that is well informed by the resonances between new science and ancient spiritual wisdom of religious traditions, particularly the resonances between the phenomena, theories, and philosophies of quantum physics and the spiritual wisdom of Buddhism regarding the nature of consciousness, self, and reality.

1.2 NEW SCIENCE AND SPIRITUAL WISDOM

Taking into consideration "the strange world of electromagnetic frequencies, matter and anti-matter, particles and waves" (Huebner, 1993/1999d, p. 401) uncovered by contemporary physics, Huebner (1993/1999d) emphasized that "our sensory system, and social/political systems, are in touch with but a small part of the reality of the universe" (p. 401), and that the "embodied images are no more a reality than are unembodied images a mere figment of an 'unreality'" (p. 401). However, over the last 300 years, while the development of physics has moved from classical to relativistic, and into quantum physics and the exploration of unified theory (Greene, 2004, p. 22), which differ "profoundly from classic[al] physics on the important matter of how the consciousness of human agents enters into the structure of empirical phenomena" (Schwartz, Stapp, & Beauregard, 2005, p. 1309), "until recently, virtually all attempts to understand the functional activity of the brain have been based, at least implicitly, on some principles of classic[al] physics that have been known to be fundamentally false for three-quarters of a century" (Schwartz et al., 2005, p. 1310).

Schwartz et al. (2005) therefore proposed an alternative conceptual framework for analyzing brain dynamics that is able to "represent [these mechanisms] more adequately than classic[al] concepts" (p. 1309), and they concluded that "the causal efficacy of mental effort is no illusion" (p. 1325). In the same vein, psychiatrist Bruce Greyson (2010) advocated for expanding "models of mind to accommodate extraordinary experiences such as NDEs [near-death experiences]" (p. 43). The development of quantum physics has inspired many researchers from various realms to conduct research and experiments on consciousness (McTaggart, 2007). In 2008, a surprising level of agreement as to the nature of consciousness emerged in a multidisciplinary meeting on Neuroscience, Spirituality and Consciousness in Freiburg, Germany (Forman, 2011, p. 279). In contrast to the reigning epiphenomenal model of consciousness, this new hypothesis suggests:

(i) Consciousness is a fundamental element of reality. (ii) Consciousness is mediated by the brain... Brains are transducers of consciousness. (iii) Consciousness is independent of the brain..., though it remains so far unobservable unless transduced by brains. (iv)... The ability to sense "something larger" (which cannot itself be observed), a mystical ability, may be the skill distinguishing human beings from other hominids. (Forman, 2011, p. 279)

The development of contemporary physics and the emerging new models of consciousness not only remind us of the profundity and believability of spiritual wisdom conveyed by religious traditions but also shed light on a new direction of educational thinking.

As an undeniable fact, breakthroughs in contemporary physics have forced, and continue to force, dramatic revisions to our picture of reality (Greene, 2004, p. 5). To our surprise, these revisions bear a strong resemblance to the spiritual wisdom of various religious traditions that have been taught for thousands of years. In the face of pressing global crises, thanks to the development of quantum physics and new science, humankind is simultaneously granted profound opportunities for getting closer to the ultimate truth of reality and the nature of human existence. In his contemplation of the ultimate question of life's value, theoretical physicist and string theorist Brian Greene (2004) concluded that "an informed appraisal of life absolutely required a full understanding of life's arena—the universe" (p. 4). However, in sharp contrast to the absolutistic and objectivistic viewpoint, the "overarching lesson that has emerged from scientific inquiry over the last century is that human experience is often a misleading guide to the true nature of reality" (Greene, 2004, p. 5), therefore, "assessing existence while failing to embrace the insights of modern physics would be like wrestling in the dark with an unknown opponent" (Greene, 2004, p. 5). Greene (2004) asserted that only by "deepening our understanding of the true nature of physical reality, [do] we profoundly reconfigure our sense of ourselves and our experience of the universe" (p. 5). The power of truth was demonstrated in Mahatma Gandhi's *Satyagraha*, meaning "truth force", which Gore (2008) explicated that "in every land, the truth—once known,... has the power to unite us and bridge the distance between 'me' and 'we', creating the basis for common effort and shared responsibility" (p. 57). Based on my belief in this truth force, I am convinced that the truths of the nature of consciousness, self, and reality uncovered by the implications of quantum physics and the spiritual wisdom of Buddhism and other religious traditions are conducive to both the realization of the ultimate nature of human existence that is beyond our everyday perception and the resolution of present global crises.

In his concern for human temporality, or historicity, Huebner (1967/1999a) posited the role of an educator as that of a "historian in reverse" (p. 133) and contended:

History, not sociology, is the discipline which seems the most akin to the social study of education. The historian can be interpreted as looking back to where a society has been to determine how it arrived at a given point. In so doing, he[1] identifies certain threads of continuity to unite diverse moments in time. In contrast, the educator looks forward. He, too, seeks to identify threads of continuity to unite diverse moments in time, but these are moments of yesterday and tomorrow, not of two yesterdays. It might be said that an educator is an historian in reverse. The curriculum person deserves to be chided for his ahistoricalism—not only is he ignorant of where his own field has been or is going, but he may also be missing a possibility that historical modes of thought might lead to more powerful tools for use in curriculum design. (p. 133)

It is due to the identification of threads of continuity between the ancient spiritual wisdom of religious traditions and the phenomena, theories, and philosophies of new science, particularly between Buddhism and quantum physics—the moments of yesterday and tomorrow—that I seek the possibility that the historical modes of thought of various religious traditions in tandem with the phenomena, theories, and philosophies of quantum physics might provide a broadened perspective for deliberating the nature of human existence, the meaning and significance of life, as well as the essence and purpose of education, and might lead to more powerful tools for use in curriculum design. Based on this contemplation, I explore the potentiality of curriculum as an experience of consciousness transformation.

1.3 Overview of the Chapters

This book addresses the issue of de-spiritualization in education through an interdisciplinary lens. It includes five parts: Part I Significant Issues Regarding Spirituality and Education (Chaps. 1 and 2), Part II The Nature of Consciousness, Self, and Reality (Chap. 3), Part III Consciousness Transformation (Chap. 4), Part IV Curriculum as an Experience of Consciousness Transformation (Chaps. 5, 6, 7, 8, 9 and 10), and Part V Conclusion Without Conclusion (Chap. 11).

Moved by a deep concern over education's de-spiritualization and inappropriate reliance on classical science along with its corresponding absolutistic and objectivist worldview, which I believe have contributed to the radical commercialization of human values, in Parts I and II (Chaps. 1, 2 and 3) of this book, I argue for curriculum imbued with spiritual wisdom. My argument is in three parts. First, drawing on the curriculum scholarship of Dwayne Huebner, I identify openness to the transcendent and a non-dualistic worldview as two of the most prominent aspects of spiritual truth that can counter absolutism and objectivism. Secondly, I explore the relationship between truth and education in light of Martin Heidegger's interpretation of Plato's allegory of the cave and assert that the essence and purpose of education can be found in the four-stage transition of the essence of truth assumed by an individual—from taking the mere shadows as the ultimate reality to suspecting and penetrating the pretended and disguised, and then returning for the ultimate liberation of all the others. In order to verify the truthfulness of Plato's allegory of the cave and its existential significance for human beings, my third move is to conduct a dialogue between Buddhism and quantum physics and to demonstrate a startling convergence of the two branches of thought regarding the ultimate nature of consciousness, self, and reality. On the basis of Huebner's and other curriculum theorists' works, Heidegger's explication of Plato's allegory of the cave, the dialogue between Buddhism and quantum physics, I propose the transformation of consciousness as the essence and purpose of education.

In Part III (Chap. 4), drawing specifically on the concepts and process of Buddhist spiritual practices for educational use, I explore the two barriers to consciousness transformation, four transcendental wisdoms, the five-stage gradual path of consciousness transformation in Buddhism, the union of wisdom-side and method-side practices for consciousness transformation, and the approach of negation.

In Part IV (Chaps. 5, 6, 7, 8, 9 and 10), I explore how we might understand curriculum as an experience of consciousness transformation through an examination of six key elements, including: understanding the nature of consciousness, self, and reality; learning to appreciate human temporality; cultivating impartiality and *bodhicitta*; becoming responsibly responsive; cultivating selflessness; and learning to embody a non-dualistic worldview.

In Part V (Chap. 11), I envision the coming of the historical moment for human beings to complete the metamorphosis toward a new spirit of faith, or a new religion that is not a religion, and propose the requirement of faith with reason and reason with faith as the way to move toward this new kind of faith. Through the lens of the hermeneutic circle, I demonstrate how the exclusion of spiritual wisdom and lived experiences from curriculum have undermined human beings' capacities for understanding and creating meanings of life. Then, I address the topic of confounded speech and highlight the inherent openness of the meanings of different languages and traditions by means of drawing on philosophical hermeneutics.

Below I offer an overview of the book's chapters.

Chapter 1 The Issue of De-Spiritualization in Education: This introductory chapter firstly explores education's de-spiritualization, its roots in the inappropriate reliance on classical science and the associated worldview, and its dire consequences. The development of new science reminds us of the profundity and believability of spiritual wisdom and sheds light on a new direction of educational thinking. Identifying the threads of continuity between Buddhism and quantum physics, this book asserts that the intersection of these two branches of thought might provide a broadened perspective for deliberating the nature of human existence, the meaning and significance of life, and the essence and purpose of education, and might lead to the identification of powerful tools for curriculum design. Based on this contemplation, this book explores the potentiality of curriculum as an experience of consciousness transformation.

Chapter 2 Spirituality, Truth, and Education: This review of literature explores significant issues related to spirituality, truth, and education, including emerging spiritual tensions in society, the concepts of spirituality, the distinction between religion and spirituality, significant epistemological concerns over education, and the concept of truth and its relationship to education. Drawing mainly on the works of Dwayne Huebner, Parker Palmer, and John Miller, openness to the transcendent and a non-dualistic worldview are identified as two of the most prominent aspects of spiritual truth that can counter absolutism and objectivism. The relationship between truth and education is then explored in light of Martin Heidegger's interpretation of Plato's allegory of the cave.

Chapter 3 A Dialogue between Buddhism and Quantum Physics: This conversation is conducted in order to explore how quantum physics and its implications resonate with the spiritual wisdom of religious traditions, particularly the wisdom of Buddhism regarding the nature of consciousness, self, and reality, and what the resonances between Buddhism and quantum physics mean for education and educational purposes. Firstly, an exploration is made of the concepts of truth in Buddhism and the ways in which these concepts resonate with the notions of spirituality and spiritual truth found in the educational literature. Secondly, by means of examining various phenomena, theories, and philosophies of quantum physics and their corresponding concepts in Buddhism, this dialogue demonstrates how these two branches of thoughts resonate with each other. Finally, on the basis of this deepened and extended understanding of spirituality, spiritual truth, the whole spiritual path, and the relationship between education and truth, the implications of this dialogue for education and educational purposes are explored.

Chapter 4 The Concepts and Process of Consciousness Transformation: This chapter seeks answers to the following questions: How might we further understand the concepts and process of consciousness transformation? What are the main barriers to be overcome in that process? What are the characteristics of various stages of progress? What disciplines and practices are necessary in various stages? What are the features of these disciplines and practices? How might we facilitate the transformation of consciousness in educational contexts? For this purpose, the main concepts and process of Buddhist spiritual practices of consciousness transformation are explored. These concepts and process include the two barriers to consciousness transformation, the transformation of consciousness into four transcendental wisdoms, the five-stage gradual path of consciousness transformation in Buddhism, the union of wisdom-side and method-side practices for consciousness transformation, and the approach of negation.

Chapter 5 Understanding the Nature of Consciousness, Self, and Reality: Part IV explores how we might understand curriculum as an experience of consciousness transformation by means of examining six key elements (Chaps. 5, 6, 7, 8, 9 and 10). This chapter firstly addresses the issues of the overreliance on science and rationalism in the educational landscape, including the (in)validity of scientific knowledge, frozen futurism, and the diminished half-life, and explores the limitations of scientific method and rational analysis in answering the existential inquiries. Uncovering the fundamental differences between the approach of negation and the approach of science, the author then argues for the imperative of integrating existential knowledge and spiritual wisdom regarding the nature of consciousness, self, and reality into curriculum. The significance of the union of method and wisdom, or the analytical and the intuitive, for consciousness transformation is supported with experimental evidence.

Chapter 6 Learning to Appreciate Human Temporality: Human temporality is one of the most significant features of human existence. This chapter examines the concept of time and its relationship with the nature of human existence; on this basis, it then proceeds to explore Heidegger's concept of authenticity in relation to the certainty of death. Given the fact that the upholding of objective and impersonal knowledge of death, particularly the biomedical one, had hindered us from seeing death as it is, the existential significance of the subjective and experiential views of dying and death is emphasized. This chapter concludes that learning to appreciate human temporality can be understood as learning to appreciate the ultimate nature of human existence and learning to appreciate the present based on the reverence of human mortality and the right view that sees death as it is.

Chapter 7 Cultivating Impartiality and *Bodhicitta*: *Bodhicitta* is the aspiration to attain the highest spiritual goal of the omniscience of enlightenment for the liberation of all sentient beings, it requires the cultivation of impartiality. Without taking the antidote to partiality, our compassion and love will be discriminatory, and the result of our practices for consciousness transformation will be inferior. This chapter explores the concepts of impartiality and *bodhicitta*, and then, through the lens of the Buddhist Middle Way, discusses the philosophical differences between the axioms of equality and inequality, as explicated by Rancière (2010). In contrast to the formulaic logic of The Market and the language of global competitiveness that instigate social and educational planning inspired by the sheer desire to win, the altruistic motivation of *bodhicitta* provides us an alternative logic for educational planning, teaching, learning, and studying, and for sustaining human life in a noble and dignified way.

Chapter 8 Becoming Responsibly Responsive: This chapter explores the concept of being responsibly responsive and examines how we might become responsibly responsive from three different perspectives. Firstly, drawing on the practices of the four reflections and four exact realizations, the author examines the role of language in dominating our worldview and how the habitual force of hypostatization and reification might hinder us from seeing things as they really are—which is the moral basis for becoming responsibly responsive. Secondly, the author explores the educational significance of the injunctions of the four noble truths for overcoming the stultifying effects of passivity brought about by pain. Thirdly, drawing on Lusthaus's (2002) analysis of the appropriational circuit between the grasper and the grasped as well as Pinar's (1974) analysis of dehumanization and movie consciousness, the author shows that becoming responsibly responsive is first and foremost an inner work of overcoming the sharp subject–object dichotomy.

Chapter 9 Cultivating Selflessness: With an emphasis on the view component (wisdom-side) of spiritual practices for overcoming the sharp subject–object duality, this chapter firstly explores the concepts of self and selflessness. Drawing on Thompson (2015), the self is understood as an enacted I-ing process and is dependent on the conceptual schema and the scale of observation. For the purpose of recognizing and overcoming our attachment to the self as an independent existence, the author examines how the I–Me–Mine complex could be a useful conceptual tool. Finally, based on various experimental evidences, the author reveals how meditative stabilization can facilitate the cultivation of selflessness.

Chapter 10 Learning to Embody a Non-Dualistic Worldview: This chapter explores the deeds component (method-side) of spiritual practices for overcoming the dualistic worldview by means of drawing on the practices of the six perfections. Firstly, this chapter explores the order and interrelationships of the six perfections for embodying a non-dualistic worldview, and then explores the meanings, practices, and educational implications of the first four perfections. Finally, the embodiment of a non-dualistic worldview is understood through the concept of witnessing. Throughout this chapter, the dependently co-arising nature of self and world, the approach of negation, and the union of wisdom and method play crucial roles in clarifying significant concepts and practices.

Chapter 11 The Metamorphosis and the Confounded Speech: Drawing on Quinn's (2001) illumination of humanity's history with the sacred through Nietzsche's allegory of On the Three Metamorphoses and Ricoeur's essay on religion, atheism, and faith, the author envisions the coming of the historical moment for human beings to complete the metamorphosis toward a new spirit of faith, or a new religion that is not a religion, and proposes the requirement of faith with reason and reason with faith on the way toward this new kind of faith. Then, through the lens of the hermeneutic circle, the author demonstrates how the exclusion of spiritual wisdom and lived experiences from curriculum has undermined human beings' capacities for understanding and creating meanings of life. Finally, the author addresses the topic of confounded speech and highlights the inherent openness of the meanings of different languages and traditions by means of drawing on philosophical hermeneutics.

Note

1. In this book, the usage of masculine gendered language, such as "man" for humankind, "he" for s/he, etc., in direct quotations from Huebner's and Heidegger's and Pinar's works has been left unaltered only to prevent the loss of meanings specific to the corresponding historical context. No gender discrimination is intended.

REFERENCES

Borrows, J. (2010). *Drawing Out Law: A Spirit's Guide.* University of Toronto Press.

Bryman, A. (2004). Fallacy of Objectivism. In M. S. Lewis-Beck, A. Bryman, & T. F. Liao (Eds.), *Encyclopedia of Social Science Research Methods* (p. 377). Thousand Oaks, CA: Sage Publications.

Forman, R. K. C. (2011). An Emerging New Model for Consciousness: The Consciousness Field Model. In H. Walach, S. Schmidt, & W. B. Jonas (Eds.), *Neuroscience, Consciousness and Spirituality* (pp. 207–288). Dordrecht: Springer.

Gore, A. (2008). Finding the Moral Resolve to Solve the Crisis of Global Climate Change. *Vital Speeches of the Day, 74*(2), 55–58.

Greene, B. (2004). *The Fabric of the Cosmos: Space, Time, and the Texture of Reality.* New York, NY: Alfred A. Knopf.

Greyson, B. (2010). Implications of Near-Death Experiences for a Postmaterialist Psychology. *Psychology of Religion and Spirituality, 2*(1), 37–45.

Huebner, D. E. (1999a). Curriculum as Concern for Man's Temporality. In V. Hillis (Ed.), *The Lure of the Transcendent: Collected Essays by Dwayne E. Huebner* (pp. 131–142). New York, NY: Routledge. (Original work published 1967).

Huebner, D. E. (1999b). Religious Metaphors in the Language of Education. In V. Hillis (Ed.), *The Lure of the Transcendent: Collected Essays by Dwayne E. Huebner* (pp. 358–368). New York, NY: Routledge. (Original work published 1985a).

Huebner, D. E. (1999c). Spirituality and Knowing. In V. Hillis (Ed.), *The Lure of the Transcendent: Collected Essays by Dwayne E. Huebner* (pp. 340–352). New York, NY: Routledge. (Original work published 1985b).

Huebner, D. E. (1999d). Education and Spirituality. In V. Hillis (Ed.), *The Lure of the Transcendent: Collected Essays by Dwayne E. Huebner* (pp. 401–416). New York, NY: Routledge. (Original work published 1993).

Lomborg, B. (2004). Introduction. In B. Lomborg (Ed.), *Global Crises, Global Solutions* (pp. 1–9). New York, NY: Cambridge University Press.

Lusthaus, D. (2002). *Buddhist Phenomenology: A Philosophical Investigation of Yogacara Buddhism and the Ch'eng Wei-shih Lun.* New York, NY: RoutledgeCurzon.

McTaggart, L. (2007). *The Intention Experiment: Using Your Thoughts to Change Your Life and the World.* New York, NY: Free Press.

McTaggart, L. (2011). *The Bond: How to Fix Your Falling-Down World.* New York, NY: Simon & Schuster.

Nickle, T. (2005). Positivism. In M. C. Horowitz (Ed.), *New Dictionary of the History of Ideas* (Vol. 5, pp. 1852–1857). Detroit, MI: Charles Scribner's Sons.

Pinar, W. F. (1974). Heightened Consciousness, Cultural Revolution, and Curriculum Theory: An Introduction. In W. F. Pinar (Ed.), *Heightened Consciousness, Cultural Revolution, and Curriculum Theory* (pp. 1–15). The Proceedings of the Rochester Conference (Rochester, New York, May 3–5, 1973).

Pinar, W. F., Reynolds, W. M., Slattery, P., & Taubman, P. M. (2008). *Understanding Curriculum: An Introduction to the Study of Historical and Contemporary Curriculum Discourses.* New York, NY: Peter Lang. (Original work published 1995).

Quinn, M. (2001). *Going Out, Not Knowing Whither: Education, the Upward Journey, and the Faith of Reason.* New York, NY: Peter Lang.

Rancière, J. (2010). On Ignorant Schoolmasters. In C. Bingham & G. J. J. Biesta (Eds.), *Jacques Rancière: Education, Truth, Emancipation* (pp. 1–24). London: Continuum Publishing Group.

Schwartz, J. M., Stapp, H. P., & Beauregard, M. (2005). Quantum Physics in Neuroscience and Psychology: A Neurophysical Model of Mind–Brain Interaction. *Philosophical Transactions of the Royal Society B: Biological Sciences, 360*(1458), 1309–1327.

Smith, D. G. (2000). The Specific Challenges of Globalization for Teaching and Vice Versa. *The Alberta Journal of Education Research, XLVI*(1), 7–26.

Sullivan, L. E. (2009). Positivism (Education). In L. Sullivan (Ed.), *The SAGE Glossary of the Social and Behavioral Sciences* (p. 395). Thousand Oaks, CA: Sage Publications.

Thompson, E. (2015). *Waking, Dreaming, Being: Self and Consciousness in Neuroscience, Meditation, and Philosophy.* New York, NY: Columbia University Press.

CHAPTER 2

Spirituality, Truth, and Education

2.1 Introduction

Over the past several decades, as Tara Fenwick (2001) indicated, we have witnessed "an unusual and significant outpouring of deep human longing, expressed in what Charles Taylor (1996) described as a 'wild' explosion of spirituality" (p. 10). In the 1950s and 1960s, the interest in higher or deeper consciousness had pointed to popular concerns or even needs to acknowledge the supra-sensory, and these concerns or needs were supported by a variety of scholarly or popular works (Huebner, 1985b/1999d, p. 343). For instance, in *Beyond the Post-Modern Mind* published in 1972, Huston Smith "called attention to the increasing body of scientific and philosophical literature that questions today's prevailing mind-set… and acknowledged a sacred consciousness or spirit" (Huebner, 1985b/1999d, p. 343).

In the educational context of the United States, after decades of efforts to distance educational works from its Christian (primarily Protestant) origins, a chapter titled "Spirituality and Knowing" in the *National Society for the Study of Education Yearbook* of 1985 suggested "a new direction in the continuing dialogue between traditions of education and traditions of religion" (Huebner, 1985b/1999d, p. 340). This new concern for the spiritual also provides new perspectives for considering issues of values and ends (Huebner, 1985b/1999d, p. 342). In the realm of curriculum studies, starting in the 1960s, curriculum reconceptualists posed significant philosophical questions

© The Author(s) 2019
E. L. Chu, *Exploring Curriculum as an Experience of Consciousness Transformation*, Curriculum Studies Worldwide,
https://doi.org/10.1007/978-3-030-17701-0_2

17

concerning the search for meanings, the purpose of life, and authenticity of the self (Koetting & Combs, 2005, p. 85). One of the most important minds among them was Dwayne Huebner (Pinar, 1999, p. xxiv). As a "seminal educational thinker who pointed the way beyond positivist and technological theories of pedagogic planning and evaluation" (Alexander, 2003, p. 231), Huebner gestured "beyond what can be expressed discursively to an ineffable 'other'" (p. 231) and "foreshadowed the spiritual revolution in late-twentieth century thought" (p. 231).

Growing concerns about the spiritual in educational context were also reflected in the emergence of holistic education. The term "holistic education" was created at the first National Holistic Education Conference, which was held at the University of California, San Diego in July 1979 (Miller, 2005). As one of the most important holistic educators, John Miller based the holistic curriculum on the perennial philosophy, which constitutes the core wisdom underlying various spiritual traditions and teachings (Miller, 2007, p. 16). He explored spirituality in education from various perspectives in his book *The Holistic Curriculum* (1988), and also in his later works, including *Education and the Soul* (Miller, 2000), *Educating for Wisdom and Compassion* (Miller, 2006), and *Whole Child Education* (Miller, 2010). Holistic education flourished in the late 1980s and the early 1990s (Miller, 2007, p. vii). One survey showed that by 1994, there were at least 7500 alternative schools in the USA which included holistic values in their philosophies of education (Forbes, 1996, p. 1; Mintz & Muscat, 1994). While the values and vision of humanity in the holistic education movement became increasingly popular during the 1990s, Forbes (1996) observed with some regret that "the insights of this vision are often clouded by misty-eyed New Ageism, and a great deal that is valuable is dismissed because of this association" (pp. 1–2)—despite the fact that certain fundamental aspects of the New Age Movement are profound. Since the late 1990s, the intimate relationship between spirituality and education has grown and this has seen the publication of many books on the topic; significant publications include Parker Palmer's *The Courage to Teach* and Rachael Kessler's *Soul in Education* (Miller, 2007, p. vii).

In recent years, in response to a variety of critiques of school practices, a number of educational scholars have turned their attention to the exploration of spirituality and related issues (Koetting & Combs, 2005, p. 83). These concepts and issues include: the necessity of distinguishing between spirituality and religion (Fenwick, 2001; Koetting & Combs, 2005; Palmer, 2003b; Walton, 1996); connectedness to a life force; the inner search for wholeness and the realization of interconnectedness to the others; an ongoing moving toward one's more authentic identity; healing; altruistic and emancipatory learning (Koetting & Combs, 2005); the search for a deeper philosophical meaning and purpose of life (Iannone & Obenauf, 1999; Koetting & Combs, 2005); the change of mind (Vella, 2000); and the emerging spiritual tensions (Fenwick, 2001). In the newly formed fields of contemplative education, mindfulness-based education and art-based research, there has also been considerable recognition of the significance of the spiritual and the embodied spiritual practices for education (Park, 2014, pp. 52–54).

The explosion of spirituality as a phenomenon of interest is also reflected in the dramatically increasing number of specialized graduate courses which deal with the connections between spirituality and religion (Hodge & Derezotes, 2008, p. 103). For instance, according to Hodge and Derezotes (2008), in 1990 in the USA, there were only a couple of social-work graduate programs that offered elective courses on spirituality. However, Hodge and Derezotes' (2008) research revealed that the number of programs rose steadily, from 17 in 1995 to at least 50 programs in 2000; by 2005, there were approximately 75 graduate programs offering courses on spirituality and religion. In addition, in 2014 the first Master of Education Degree program in Contemplative Inquiry and Approaches in North America offered by Simon Fraser University was granted approval (Johnson, 2014).

While the explosion of spirituality represents a reaffirmation of the significance of spirituality for human beings, the popularity of spiritual practices, such as the practice of mindfulness, is coupled with the potential danger of spirituality being appropriated and trivialized as what Anderson has termed "a quick fix to ease the stresses of modern life" (as cited in Johnson, 2014, para. 8), in which event the underlying existential significance and wisdom behind such practices could easily be neglected. In other words, spiritual practices are at risk of being deprived of their existential significance and becoming just another set of tools for instrumentalists. As Fenwick (2001) emphasized, spirituality is not merely a shallow "hurry-up-and-feel-good" practice which focuses on only "an inner journey of healing, personal peace and exploring the self" (p. 11). Fenwick discussed four emerging spiritual tensions in our society which have been recognized by religious studies scholar Elizabeth Dreyer (p. 11). The first is "the collapse of the 'wall separating church and state,' represented most dramatically in the current international conflict, but also evident in the movement of private spiritual experience to the public stage" (Fenwick, 2001, p. 11). The second is "the lack of interiority, where a superficial society caught in a bricolage of postmodern images, and desperately seeking authentic self-awareness, somehow is still unable or unwilling to nurture a contemplative interior life" (Fenwick, 2001, p. 11). The third is "a split between spirituality and religion related to a perceived failure of mainline religions to connect with the needs of a postmodern people yearning for meaning" (Fenwick, 2001, p. 11). The last "is the pluralism among different spiritualities which don't necessary listen to or work with one another to address common problems" (Fenwick, 2001, p. 11). These are issues that deserve careful consideration by educators who seek the potentiality of the revival and renewal of the intimate relationship between spirituality and education.

In the following sections, in an attempt to identify critical issues regarding spirituality and education, particularly issues pertaining to the integration of the resonances between quantum physics and the wisdom of Buddhism into curriculum, and the ongoing conversation about spirituality in relation to education, I review the educational literature, particularly the works of Huebner, Palmer, and Miller. In doing so, I draw on Martin Heidegger's interpretation of Plato's allegory of the cave and explore the relationship between truth and education.

2.2 The Concepts of Spirituality in the Educational Literature

Spirituality and religion are so intimately related that some people regard them as almost synonymous concepts. However, in educational contexts, many researchers emphasize the necessity of distinguishing between spirituality and religion. In inquiring what distinctions among spiritualities are significant for educators, Fenwick (2001) expressed her concern and stated that "'spirituality' in educational literature is too often essentialized as some sort of monolithic force blending deep cultural, political, and epistemological divides" (p. 11). She therefore stressed the significance of multiple delineations of spirituality (Fenwick, 2001, p. 11). Likewise, Koetting and Combs (2005) stated that it is impossible to understand spirituality in terms of a single simple definition, and emphasized the importance of distinguishing between religion and spirituality. They asserted that in "reviewing writings on spirituality and education, it is important to establish at the very beginning of our discussion that spirituality does not mean organized religious beliefs as found in present day political discourse" (Koetting & Combs, 2005, p. 83). Palmer (2003b) also contended that the distinction between religion and spirituality is essential in public education if we want to "raise spiritual topics in a way that respects the vast diversity of people's deeply held traditions and beliefs" (p. 380). The distinction between religion and spirituality is effectively explicated by Walton (1996):

> Religion may or may not play a role in individual spirituality and is quite distinct from spirituality... Religion is described as a framework for beliefs, values, traditions, doctrine, conduct, and rituals... Whereas spirituality is a much more encompassing term... a spiritual individual may or may not be religious. (pp. 238–239)

Yet Beck (1986) reminded us that while one need not be religious to be spiritual, "large questions" of life have been explored for millennia by religious traditions; as such, religious traditions are bound to have a great many profound insights to offer regarding images, perspectives and principles of living, and these can be discerningly drawn on even by nonreligious people (p. 156).

The issues regarding the distinction between religion and spirituality and their corresponding places in education are well addressed by Huebner. For Huebner (1985b/1999d), "to speak of the 'spirit' and the 'spiritual' is not to speak of something 'other' than humankind, merely 'more' than humankind as it is lived and known" (p. 343), and "talk of the 'spirit' and the 'spiritual' in education need not, then, be God talk... Rather the talk is about lived reality, about experience and the possibility of experiencing" (p. 344). Nevertheless, Huebner (1985b/1999d) maintained that the veins of language regarding the spiritual within various religious traditions should be mined for educators, although interpretation of the experiences that are stored in histories, stories, myths, and poems requires sufficient care and hermeneutic skill to ensure that no single religion is consulted or ignored. Huebner (1985b/1999d) recognized the histories, stories, myths, and poems in various religious traditions as symbols of "moreness," of otherness, and of the transcendent, and as symbols that life as lived can be different. These symbols may be "stories of relationships—of struggle, conflict, forgiveness, love—during which something new is produced: new life, new relationships, new understandings, new forms of power and political control" (Huebner, 1985b/1999d, p. 344). There may be symbols that signify the wholeness and unity of body–mind, of self–others, of the human–natural world, and of the past–present–future (Huebner, 1985b/1999d, p. 344). There are also "symbols of at-oneness when the inchoate and disturbing cohere in new meanings" (Huebner, 1985b/1999d, p. 344), and the "symbols of liberation, of exodus from various forms of enslavement and domination: personal, interpersonal, or social" (Huebner, 1985b/1999d, pp. 344–345). For Huebner (1985b/1999d), these are "symbols of more than the present; more than current forms for life. These are the symbols of the spirit and the spiritual and how life as lived is, and can be, informed, reformed, and transformed" (p. 345). Huebner (1985b/1999d) suggested that these symbols of the spirit and the spiritual point not only to dimensions of human experience which are beyond our sensory systems but also to the fact that encountering, experiencing, and acknowledging the spiritual is possible. These symbols are of great significance for education. He contended:

> Everyone experiences, and continues to have the possibility of experiencing the transcending of present forms of life, of finding that life is more than is presently known or lived. This is what education is about. Education is only possible because the human being is a being that can transcend itself. (Huebner, 1985b/1999d, p. 345)

Nevertheless, being blinded by social and cultural systems, educators and students often "do not recognize their participation in the transcendent, in their ever open future" (Huebner, 1993/1999e, p. 405), and do not realize that "we dwell in a near infinite world, that our possibilities are always more than we realize, and that life is a movement, change, or journey" (Huebner, 1993/1999e, p. 404). Huebner (1993/1999e) thus underscored that "the question that educators need to ask is not how people learn and develop, but what gets in the way of the great journey— the journey of the self or soul" (p. 405) and that education should be a way of attending to, and caring for, this journey.

Moreover, in addressing the issue of spirituality and knowing, Huebner (1985b/1999d) emphasized that the questions that are of primary interest to educators should be the relationship between knowing and the spiritual, rather than "knowing the spiritual" or "spiritual modes of knowing," for these two expressions cannot exhaust the possible relationships between spirituality and knowing (pp. 345–346). While the vitality or power of life that makes people experience moments wherein present forms of behavior are somehow transcended are commonly labeled as "spiritual," Huebner (1985b/1999d) elucidated that what is important is the experience itself, rather than the source, reasons, or labels, and that "what is known from personal experience is not the spiritual, but the stories of one's life, its many transforming and transcending moments" (Huebner, 1985b/1999d, p. 346). What follows and accompanies these experiences, thus, is not knowledge of the spiritual, but rather knowledge of one's self (Huebner, 1985b/1999d, p. 346). Additionally, as records of those who have been transformed or have experienced the transcending moments (e.g., the originators and sages of major religions in the world), the language or symbols of religious traditions make it possible to know about other people (Huebner, 1985b/1999d, pp. 346–347). These "are not modes of knowing the spiritual, but ways to know others, and consequently also ways to know one's self" (Huebner, 1985b/1999d, p. 347). The moments of transforming and transcending are also stored by religious traditions in the spiritual disciplines (Huebner, 1985b/1999d, p. 347). These are not knowledge-producing disciplines; rather, these are "disciplines by which persons keep themselves open, available, and vulnerable so that they can be transformed and participate in experiences of transcendence" (Huebner, 1985b/1999d, p. 347). Therefore, "there are no modes of knowing the spiritual" (Huebner, 1985b/1999d, p. 348); the phrasing of knowing the spiritual in actuality refers to knowing one's self and others, and the disciplines for knowing one's self and others (Huebner, 1985b/1999d, p. 347). From this point of view, the denial or rejection of the spiritual in current education is, in effect, equivalent to the rejection of genuine knowing of one's self and others, and the disciplines for knowing one's self and others.

Huebner (1985b/1999d) continued his critique, asserting that there are no spiritual modes of knowing either, for claiming spiritual modes of knowing "is to assume privileged access to realms of experience" (p. 348), and if this is accepted, centuries of efforts to free diverse forms of knowing from the dogmas of particular religious traditions would be compromised. However, Huebner (1985b/1999d) underscored that

> an active dialectic between religious traditions and the many and diverse modes of knowing must be maintained... The understanding of religious traditions is usually enriched by new developments in the various fields of knowledge. The reverse is also true. To the extent that various modes of

knowing are separated from religious traditions they become closed in upon themselves and lose their vitality, their "spirit," their creativity, and the possibility of being transcended. (p. 348)

As Huebner pointed out, "the qualities associated with the spiritual are foundational in every mode of knowing" (Huebner, 1985b/1999d, p. 349). In the case of the scientific mode of knowing, for example, Einstein (1930/1954) maintained that "the cosmic religious feeling is the strongest and noblest motive for scientific research" (p. 39); it is this feeling that gives a person the strength to remain true to their purpose, and that "only those who realize the immense efforts and, above all, the devotion,... are able to grasp the strength of the emotion out of which alone such work... can issue" (Einstein, 1930/1954, p. 39). Since various modes of knowing, even everything that is done in schools and in preparation for school activities (e.g., the everyday teaching and study of various disciplines), in depth, are already infused with the spiritual despite the fact that traditional religious symbols may not be employed explicitly, what is needed is not to see the spiritual as something special that lies outside of the school curriculum and activities (Huebner, 1985b/1999d, p. 348; Huebner, 1993/1999e, p. 414), but "to probe deeper into the educational landscape to reveal how the spiritual... is being denied in everything" (Huebner, 1993/1999e, p. 414).

In the educational literature, the concepts of spirituality are often delineated by means of a list of personal characteristics or descriptions of certain aspects of spirituality without deeper examination of the nature of human existence. For example, Beck (1986) has attempted to approach the concepts of spirituality through a listing of specific characteristics typical of spiritual people, including awareness, breadth of outlook, a holistic outlook, integration, wonder, gratitude, hope, courage, energy, detachment, acceptance, love, and gentleness (pp. 151–153). In the preceding section, I have identified some aspects of spirituality addressed by various researchers, including: connectedness to a life force; the inner search for wholeness and the realization of interconnectedness to others; an ongoing moving toward one's more authentic identity; healing; altruistic and emancipatory learning; the search for a deeper philosophical meaning and purpose of life; and the change of mind. While the identification of these characteristics or aspects related to the concepts of spirituality is undoubtedly valuable, the full meaning of spirituality remains elusive.

One reason for the failure of these characterizations of spirituality to give us an integral perception of spirituality is that spirituality, rather than being merely some desirable human qualities or special capabilities to be pursued, is, as discussed earlier, "about lived reality, about experience and the possibility of experiencing" (Huebner, 1985b/1999d, p. 344). It is a foundational aspect of human knowing and an integral aspect of human life, and every aspect of human life is already infused with it. From this perspective, the attempt to understand or cultivate spirituality might be futile if it is undertaken simply by means of focusing upon certain aspects of its phenomenal manifestation without probing deeply into the nature of human existence. Huebner's elucidation of the significance of veins of religious language for education discussed in this section unveils the intimate relationship between spirituality and the nature of human existence, and makes clear why education needs to be grounded on the acknowledgement of the transcendent nature of the human being. His suggestion that the need is not to see the spiritual as something special that lies outside ordinary school curricula and activities, but rather to probe into how the spiritual is being denied in everything in the educational landscape points to the significant spiritual approach of *negation* that will be explored in Chap. 4. Following Huebner's suggestion, in order to explore how the spiritual is being denied in everything in the educational landscape, the following section examines significant epistemological concerns about education.

2.3 Significant Epistemological Concerns Over Education

As discussed in Chap. 1, during the period when the educational and scientific traditions were merging, the philosophical outlook was dominated by positivism and its associated absolutistic and objectivistic worldview. As a result, the spiritual wisdom of long-standing religious traditions were largely rejected. Through the introduction of the concept of "the transcendent," Huebner suggested a spiritual alternative to positivism (Alexander, 2003, p. 236). While tying education closely to spirituality, and to transcendent and religious symbols, Huebner did not rule out the connection between education and knowing. Rather, this tying merely transforms what we mean by knowledge, and what are ruled out in this epistemological change are the absolutism and objectivism that often associated with positivist science (Alexander, 2003, p. 237).

In contrast to absolutism, Huebner (1985b/1999d) argued that

> present forms of knowing are always incomplete, always fallible. Behind every confidence and certainty is residual doubt. As scientists have pointed out, the only thing known for certain is what is not true, what has been disproved. There is always a better way of being in the world, more complete prediction, more perfect expression of experience and feeling, more just meetings with others, better techniques and instrumentalities. (p. 349)

For Huebner, the possibilities of knowing, feeling, being, doing, and speaking are always greater than we realize. His emphasis on the dwelling of the transcendent within human beings dismissed absolutism. As he said, "the human being dwells in the transcendent, or more appropriately, the transcendent dwells in the human being. To use more direct religious imagery, the spirit dwells in us. Our possibilities are always before us" (Huebner, 1993/1999e, p. 404).

Contrary to objectivism, Huebner holds that knowledge entails subjective engagement (Alexander, 2003, p. 237); for him, "every mode of knowing is also a mode of being in relationship. It is a relationship of mutual care and love" (Huebner, 1985b/1999d, p. 349). He illustrated that, like the land, as the modern ecology movement suggested, will care for those who care for it, the knowledge between two people (e.g., parent and child, or two people in love) also points to such dialectic between knowing and loving (Huebner, 1985b/1999d, p. 349). This dialectic is manifested in the Biblical Hebrew word for "to know," which also means an intimate or sexual relationship (Huebner, 1985b/1999d, p. 349). Huebner (1985b/1999d) explicated that only by "letting one's self be in the care of a part of the world one is informed by it" (p. 349), and that "the distortion of this relationship of mutual care and love occurs only when caring is for the self and knowing becomes an act of control, often an act of violence" (Huebner, 1985b/1999d, p. 349). Knowledge as a symbolic and referential system, therefore,

> points to something beyond those using it, [and] is a twofold relationship. It depicts our love, or lack thereof, for the earth and those of us who people it. Thus, knowledge is also... a manifestation of love and its distortions. (Huebner, 1985b/1999d, p. 365)

Likewise, drawing on the philosophy of science, Palmer (1983/2003a) criticized objectivism as wrongly "assuming a sharp distinction between the knower and the objects to be known" (p. 63). Citing Fritjof Capra, Palmer (1983/2003a) explains:

> The electron does not have properties independent of my mind. In atomic physics, the sharp Cartesian split between mind and matter, between I and the world, is no longer valid. We can never speak of nature without, at the same time, speaking about ourselves. (p. 64)

Knowledge, therefore, is neither subjective nor objective, but something transcendent of both (Palmer, 1983/2003a, p. 65). Despite the fact that objectivism is no longer convincing, Palmer (1983/2003a) noted that it "is institutionalized in our educational practices, in the ways we teach and learn… through the power of 'hidden curriculum'" (p. 65). Through our conventional ways of teaching, "we form students in the objectivist worldview" (Palmer, 1983/2003a, p. 65). Palmer (1983/2003a) criticized some pedagogical experiments for dealing only with techniques while leaving the underlying epistemology unexamined and unchanged, emphasizing that to "find new ways of transmitting knowledge, we must first find a new knowledge. To find a better medium, we must find a better message" (Palmer, 1983/2003a, p. 66). The message that education should convey, Palmer argued, is truth. He traced the Germanic root of truth that is also the origin of the word "troth," as in the vow "I pledge thee my troth" (Palmer, 1983/2003a, p. 66). With this troth, he said, "one person enters a covenant, a pledge to engage in a mutually accountable and transforming relationship, a relationship forged of trust and faith" (Palmer, 1983/2003a, p. 66). Therefore, "truthful knowing weds knower and the known… We find truth by pledging our troth, and knowing becomes a reunion of separated beings whose primary bond is not of logic but of love" (Palmer, 1983/2003a, p. 67). Truth demands the acknowledgement of the interdependence of the knower and the known that co-participate in a community of faithful relationships (Palmer, 1983/2003a, p. 67). While advocating the imperative to educate toward the truth, Palmer (1983/2003a) emphasized that this "does not mean turning away from facts and theories and objective realities" (p. 67). Devoting ourselves to truth does not necessarily change the facts; what is changed "is our relation to the facts, or to the world that the facts make known" (Palmer, 1983/2003a, p. 67).

Both Huebner's and Palmer's philosophies reflect a non-dualistic or non-objectivistic worldview which weds the knower and the objects to be known, and espouses truthful knowing as being in a relationship of mutual care and love that is forged of trust and faith when we pledge our troth to engage in a mutually accountable and transforming relationship. For both of them, knowledge does not always mean truth. Rather, in the absence of mutual care and love, knowledge can be mere distortions of truth, and knowing becomes an act of control or violence. As a manifestation of mutual love and care that weds the knower and the objects to be known, this non-dualistic worldview is what education should convey.

This non-dualistic worldview can also be understood in terms of the subject–subject attitude proposed by Huebner. For Huebner (1963/1999b), although the dichotomization of the world into subject and object has been essential for the progress of classical science, it is also a barrier to conversation (p. 88). He proposed instead a subject–subject attitude, or what Buber called the I–Thou relationship in contrast to the I–It relationship, as an alternative to the objectivistic dichotomy of the subject–object attitude (Huebner, 1963/1999b, pp. 88–89). Within this subject–subject or I–Thou mode, the "butterfly and the fellow traveler and the rainbow and the pebble are no longer just objects and you a subject. They too become subjects which cannot be completely grasped. They have an existence alongside your existence" (Huebner, 1959/1999a, p. 5). Thus, the world of nature and people is no longer something to be studied, predicted, controlled, and used, but rather to love, to live with, to communicate with, and to participate with (Huebner, 1963/1999b, pp. 88–89).

However, for a communication to be a real dialogue or true conversation, it requires our willingness to be influenced by others, and this willingness to be influenced demands openness toward the world of nature and people (Huebner, 1963/1999b, p. 78). Drawing on Heidegger, who speaks of truth as openness to being, Huebner (1985b/1999d) maintained that truth "acknowledges the incompleteness and expects to uncover something else. This is the fissure in human knowing, the openness that is part of the spiritual" (p. 349). In other words, truth involves the openness to the transcendent that connotes infinite possibilities. Huebner (1963/1999b) underscored, however, that real dialogue or true conversation also requires love, and in an ongoing helical process of true conversation, "man attempts to break through his solitude, affirm the existence of the other, and meet him as an equal—free, alone, and of infinite value" (p. 78).

Speaking from a practical perspective, Huebner's proposal of the subject–subject attitude and the concept of true conversation expand our understanding of the non-dualistic worldview and the concept of the transcendent. Together, the openness to the transcendent that connotes infinite possibilities and a non-dualistic worldview as a manifestation of mutual love and care that wed the knower to the objects to be known constitute two prominent aspects of spiritual truth and two of the most significant spiritual epistemologies that rule out absolutism and objectivism. As such, they resonate not only with the characteristics of nature, but also with the core wisdom common to various religious and spiritual traditions which is often referred to as the *perennial philosophy*. In Aldous Huxley's book on perennial philosophy, written in 1970, perennial philosophy is defined as

> the metaphysic that recognizes a divine Reality substantial to the world of things and lives and minds; the psychology that finds in the soul something similar to, or even identical with, divine Reality; the ethic that places man's final end in the knowledge of the immanent and transcendent Ground of all being—the thing is immemorial and universal. (as cited in Miller, 2007, p. 16)

Miller (2007) identified the elements of the perennial philosophy as:

1. There is an interconnectedness of reality and a mysterious unity… in the universe.
2. There is an intimate connection between the individual's inner self, or soul, and this mysterious unity.
3. Knowledge of this mysterious unity can be developed through various contemplative practices.
4. Values are derived from seeing and realizing the interconnectedness of reality.
5. This realization can lead to social activity designed to counter injustice and human suffering. (pp. 17–18)

Huxley's brief definition of the perennial philosophy and the elements of perennial philosophy identified by Miller (2007) provide us with a glimpse of the essential consensus of various religious and spiritual traditions that recognize a divine Reality as the immanent and transcendent Ground of all beings, the interconnectedness of reality, and the intimate connection of one's inner self to the mysterious unity. This essential consensus reveals the fact that the openness to the transcendent and a non-dualistic worldview, as two of the most prominent aspects of spiritual truth, are common to various religious and spiritual traditions.

Grounding his holistic thinking upon the perennial philosophy, Miller (2007) explored spirituality and its relationship with education from a holistic point of view (p. 16) and strove to "bring education into alignment with the fundamental realities of nature. Nature at its core is interrelated and dynamic" (Miller, 2007, p. 3). He argued that if "nature is dynamic and interconnected and our education system is static and fragmented, then we only promote alienation and suffering" (Miller, 2007, p. 5). Being dynamic and interrelated as characters of nature are in resonance with the aforementioned spiritual truth that features the openness to the transcendent and the non-dualistic worldview. The dynamic and interrelated features of nature are also found in the perennial philosophy, which "acknowledges diversity and the fact that the universe is in process; however, underlying diversity and change is unity. This unity is not monistic; instead, the emphasis is on the [dynamic] relationship between the whole and the part" (Miller, 2007, p. 18) and "it is this relationship that is at the heart of the perennial philosophy" (Miller, 2007, p. 18). Despite the fact that the existence of a mysterious unity is essential to various religions, however, just as Huebner asserted that what is important about the transcendent moments is the lived experience itself rather than the source or labels of the spiritual, Miller, drawing on Gandhi, also emphasized that this unity or interconnectedness of reality is evident in everyday life and "should not be relegated to remote forms of mysticism" (Miller, 2007, p. 18). As two of the most prominent aspects of spiritual truth, the openness to the transcendent and the non-dualistic worldview must thus be understood from the perspective of the everydayness and can well be mined by educators for educational purposes.

The foregoing exploration of significant epistemological concerns related to education, including absolutism and objectivism, not only reveals how the spiritual is being denied in everything in the educational landscape, but also extends our understanding of the relationship between spirituality and knowing as well as the conception of spiritual truth and its relationship with education. This extended understanding of the conception of truth and its relationship with education is discussed in greater detail in the following section.

2.4 PLATO'S ALLEGORY OF THE CAVE: THE RELATIONSHIP BETWEEN TRUTH AND EDUCATION

As discussed earlier, the openness to the transcendent and a non-dualistic worldview are recognized as two of the most significant aspects of spiritual truth, and two significant spiritual epistemologies for education that rule out absolutism and objectivism. Based on this understanding, in the following, I explore the conception of truth and its relationship with education.

On one hand, spiritual truth as "openness to being" acknowledges the dwelling of the transcendent or the spirit in the human being and the transcendental possibilities of human lives. It is the openness to the transcendent that makes possible various modes of knowing, and in turn, education. As Huebner (1985a/1999c) articulated eloquently,

> education is the lure of the transcendent—that which we seem is not what we are for we could always be other. Education is the openness to a future that is beyond all futures. Education is the protest against present forms that they may be reformed and transformed. Education is the consciousness that we live in time, pulled by the inexorable Otherness that brings judgment and hope to the forms of life which are but the vessels of present experience. (p. 360)

Nonetheless, the lure of the transcendent is threatening (Huebner, 1985a/1999c, p. 363). Huebner (1985a/1999c) indicated that in the face of the threats of the unknown and the stranger outside and inside of us, we need the assurance that life can be whole again and will be enhanced rather than destroyed—and love is that assurance (pp. 363–364). He maintained that "the power of love can acknowledge weakness. Love heals the differences within us. It reconciles the new tensions and divergences in our life" (Huebner, 1985a/1999c, p. 364). As reconciliation, love and care

> provide the patience, trust, collective memories and hopes, and conversation to heal the social body—to bring wholeness to the family, class, organization, or gathering which appeared to be disrupted by the newness. Love and care provide the assurance that the family or social gathering will not be destroyed if it gives up some of what it has come to value, but will find new life and new meaning. (p. 365)

A non-dualistic worldview as a manifestation of omnipresent love and a significant aspect of spiritual truth that embraces truthful knowing as being in a relationship of mutual care and love, therefore, is crucial for the real occurrence of education. In tandem, the openness to the transcendent and a non-dualistic worldview—as two of the most prominent aspects of spiritual truth and two of the most significant spiritual epistemologies for education that rule out absolutism and objectivism—constitute a fecund ground that enables the possibilities and real occurrence of education.

On the other hand, however, assumptions and understandings of the "truth" vary from individual to individual. Sometimes, "truth" takes the form of static, absolute, and objective knowledge. For Huebner (1985b/1999d), however, this constitutes deadened knowledge rather than truth. Similar to Palmer's (1983/2003a) concern over the institutionalization of objectivism in our educational practices (p. 65), Huebner (1985b/1999d) addressed the same issue and asserted that the problem is that our schools and other educational institutions are not places of knowing, but rather places of knowledge—which is a fallout of the knowing process and is a form separated from life (p. 351); he underscored that, until the present forms of knowledge are once again brought into the process of truthful knowing, the knowledge is dead (p. 351). Additionally, "if the student is brought into the deadness of inert knowledge, the student is also deadened, alienated from the vitality that co-creates the worlds of self and others. By enlivening knowledge, the student is also empowered" (Huebner, 1985b/1999d, p. 351). The way to enliven knowledge, Huebner (1985b/1999d) indicated, is "to accept it with doubt and to place it back into the eternal cycle of openness, love, and hope" (p. 351) which is "the story of human life as celebrated in religious traditions" (p. 350). In other words, the enlivening of knowledge requires us to educate toward spiritual truth based on the openness to the transcendent that connotes infinite possibilities and a non-dualistic worldview as a manifestation of mutual love and care that weds the knower and the objects to be known. Education, as the lure of the transcendent, therefore, entails the examining, overcoming, transforming, reforming, shifting, and transcending of the presently assumed "truth" grasped by an individual.

The perspective on education described above is not new, but has been "articulated and used by educators and philosophers for centuries" (Miller, 2007, p. 67). Miller (2007), referring to Hadot's 2002 book *What is Ancient Philosophy*, stated that "Platonic dialogues were not just an intellectual exercise but a form of spiritual practice that demanded self-inquiry and self-transformation" (p. 68). According to Miller (2007), in *The Republic*, Plato contended that education "should teach the person to see beyond the impermanence of the material world to intuit the 'real world' of ideas" (p. 69). Heidegger (1942/1962) also noted that Plato opened Book VII of *The Republic* with the allegory of the cave, stating: "Next, said I, here is a parable to give us an aspect (of the essence) of education as well as of the lack of it, which fundamentally concerns our Being as men" (Heidegger, 1942/1962, p. 257). For Heidegger (1942/1962), Plato's allegory of the cave as a metaphor for education that concerns "our Being as men" also depicted a four-stage transition of the essence of truth presumed or realized by an individual (Heidegger, 1942/1962, pp. 251, 257).

As explicated in Heidegger's (1942/1962) work on Plato's doctrine of truth, Plato's cave allegory, in the first stage, likens human beings to a strange sort of prisoners in an underground cave who are chained and prevented from moving their legs and heads throughout their whole lives (pp. 251–252). Being so confined, they "would have seen nothing of themselves or of one another, except for the shadows (constantly) thrown by the fire-light on the wall of the cave facing them" (Heidegger, 1942/1962, p. 252), and would suppose the passing shadows to be the real beings. Then, in the second stage, were one of prisoners to be set unchained, forced suddenly to turn his head and eyes around, and told that what he had formerly seen was only nothingness and pretense, he would certainly be "perplexed and believe what he formerly saw ... to be [more real and] more unhidden than the objects now shown to him" (Heidegger, 1942/1962, p. 252), and he would try to escape and turn back if he were forced to look at the firelight itself that made eyes ache (Heidegger, 1942/1962, pp. 252–253). In the third stage, were the unshackled prisoner to be dragged up along the steep and rugged ascent to the upper world outside of the cave, he would need to grow accustomed to the sunlight before he could see things in this upper world illuminated by it; finally, he would look up the sun as it is in itself and come to the realization that the sun is "the cause of all that he and his companions (who are remaining down in the cave) used to see" (Heidegger, 1942/1962, p. 253), and the sun as the highest and the primary first cause is termed by Heidegger (1942/1962) as the divine, the Idea of the Good, the Idea of all ideas, or the Highest Idea (pp. 262, 264, 268), which are the supra-sensuous and can only be sighted in the non-sensuous[1] glance (p. 268). At that time, when the former prisoner remembered the cave and his fellow prisoners, he would surely be happy for himself in the change and feel sorry for them, and would never "be likely to covet the prizes or envy the men exalted to honor or power in the cave"; indeed, he would likely "endure anything rather than go back to his old beliefs and live in the old way" (Heidegger, 1942/1962, p. 253). Finally, when he returned to the cave and managed to free the other prisoners, he would face the ridicule of these prisoners and also risk being killed by those who were so obsessed with their own "opinions" and rejected to surmise even the possibility that what they considered as real "is only real in a shadowy sense" (Heidegger, 1942/1962, p. 255).

On one hand, Heidegger (1942/1962) argued that the significant force of Plato's allegory of the cave is that it makes the essence of education visible and knowable by virtue of illustrating the transitions from one stage to another that always demand a reorientation of the soul (pp. 255–256). At the same time, Heidegger (1942/1998) reasoned that Plato also wanted to show that the essence of education

> does not consist in merely pouring knowledge into the unprepared soul as if it were some container held out empty and waiting. On the contrary, genuine education takes hold of our very soul and transforms it in its entirety by first of all leading us to the place of our essential being and accustoming us to it. (p. 217)

On the other hand, Heidegger maintained that "what underlies Plato's thinking is a change in the essence of truth" (p. 257). Given that this allegory can show both education and truth, Heidegger (1942/1962) reasoned that there must be an essential relationship between them (p. 257). Similar to Huebner's (1985b/1999d) assertation that "education is only possible because the human being is a being that can transcend itself" (p. 345), Heidegger (1942/1962) indicated that this relationship between education and truth "is found in the fact that the essence of truth and the manner of its change first made 'education' in its fundamental structure possible" (p. 257). In resonance with previous discussion regarding how education entails the overcoming and shifting of the presently assumed truth grasped by an individual, Heidegger (1942/1962) also maintained that what links education and truth into an essential unity is the fact that the transplantation of man into the region of his essence which takes place in pure education "is only possible if everything commonly known to man up to this time and the way it was known become different" (p. 257). In other words, "that which is persistently unhidden to man and the manner of this unhiddenness has to change" (Heidegger, 1942/1962, p. 257). According to Heidegger (1942/1962), in Plato's allegory, the word "unhiddenness" in Greek (*aletheia*; ἀλήθεια) can also be translated as truth, and the change of the definition or essence of truth or unhiddenness presumed or realized by an individual always involves steady overcoming of a hiddenness of the hidden (i.e. the pretended and the disguised) (pp. 257, 260–261).

Heidegger's standpoint not only underpins Huebner's (1985a/1999c) contention that "education is the lure of the transcendent" (p. 360), but also suggests the imperative of an epistemological conversion—a conversion from absolutism and objectivism to the openness to the transcendent and a non-dualistic worldview—for the possibility and real occurrence of education. As revealed in the above brief account of the allegory of the cave, in the first stage, the prisoners "would have seen nothing of themselves or of one another, except for the shadows (constantly) thrown by the fire-light on the wall of the cave facing them" (Heidegger, 1942/1962, p. 252). Seeing no interrelationship among themselves, each other, the fire, and more real things that create the shadows, the prisoners presumed what is presented in the shadowy phenomena as the only truth. This lack of awareness regarding these interrelationships and the hidden possibilities intrinsic in these relationships is what traps the prisoners and what hinders real education.

In the first three stages, which represent three different levels of realization of the truth or unhiddenness, it is worth noting that the transitions from one stage to another require being unchained, told, forced, and dragged by *others*. However, as depicted in the final stage, the human beings who have remained chained in the cave might be so reluctant to listen to the "others" who return from outside of the cave and so obsessed with their own opinions that they reject to surmise even the possibility that what they consider to be real is only real in a shadowy sense. Although Heidegger (1942/1962) declared that this allegory not only deals with truth, but also contains Plato's doctrine of truth, questions that arise are: What is the extent of the truthfulness of Plato's doctrine of truth in the allegory of the cave? What is the significance of the transitions of the essence of truth for human beings?

While the relationship between education and truth is well illuminated in Plato's allegory of the cave, the two questions posed above suggest the necessity of an in-depth exploration of spiritual truth and the panorama of the whole spiritual path from different perspectives. As discussed earlier, a consideration of the truthfulness of the allegory as well as the significance of the transitions of the essence of truth for human beings are crucial to the contemplation and comprehension of the essence and purpose of education. In other words, before we proceed to deliberate how we might educate toward the truth, we need to make clear why Plato likened human beings to shackled prisoners who view the shadows on the wall of the cave as the truth and reality, and to ascertain the significance of the transitions of presumed truth depicted in the allegory. Otherwise, for those who, either consciously or unconsciously, embrace classical science and take for granted absolutism and objectivism as unquestionable truth, spiritual truth may never be considered as more truthful truth than what they have had in mind, and the whole discourse regarding truth, spirituality, and education may be easily neglected or dismissed as having neither truthfulness nor significance. In light of my religious background as a Buddhist and my identification of the threads of continuity between spiritual wisdom in Buddhism and the phenomena, theories, and philosophies of quantum physics, I now turn to these systems of thought to further explore the questions regarding truthfulness and significance articulated above. In the next chapter, I develop a dialogue between Buddhism and quantum physics which is conducive to the deliberation of the essence and purpose of education set forth in this chapter.

Note

1. The supra-sensuous and the non-sensuous glance refer to the experience outside of the cave as depicted in the third stage of Plato's cave allegory. According to Heidegger (1942/1998), in Plato's depiction of the adaptation of the gaze to the ideas outside of the cave, he said: "Thinking goes... 'beyond' those things that are experienced in the form of mere shadows and images, and goes... 'out toward' these things, namely, the 'ideas'" (p.180). Heidegger (1942/1998) explicated:

    These are the suprasensuous, seen with a nonsensuous gaze; they are the being of beings, which cannot be grasped with our bodily organs. And the highest in the region of the suprasensuous is that idea which, as the idea of all ideas, remains the cause of the subsistence and the appearing of all beings. Because this "idea" is thereby the cause of everything, it is therefore also "the idea" that is called "the good." This highest and first cause is named by Plato and correspondingly by Aristotle... the divine. (p. 180)

    In Chap. 3, I explore how the concept of the "ideas" might be understood as information carried by particles and radiation.

References

Alexander, H. A. (2003). Education as Spiritual Critique: Dwayne Huebner's Lure of the Transcendent. *Journal of Curriculum Studies, 35*(2), 231–245.
Beck, C. (1986). Education for Spirituality. *Interchange, 17*(2), 148–156.
Einstein, A. (1954). Religion and Science. In A. Einstein (Ed.), *Ideas and Opinions* (S. Bargmann, trans., pp. 36–54). New York: Crown. (Reprinted from *The New York Times Magazine*, pp. 1–4, November 9, 1930).
Fenwick, T. J. (2001). Critical Questions for Pedagogical Engagement of Spirituality. *Adult Learning, 12*(3), 10–12.
Forbes, S. H. (1996, June). Values in Holistic Education. Paper presented at the Third Annual Conference on Education, Spirituality and the Whole Child at the Roehampton Institute, London. Retrieved from http://www.holistic-education.net/articles/values.pdf.
Heidegger, M. (1962). Plato's Doctrine of Truth (J. Barlow, trans.). In B. William & D. A. Henry (Eds.), *Philosophy in the Twentieth Century* (Vol. 3, pp. 251–270). New York, NY: Random House. (Original work published 1942).
Heidegger, M. (1998). Plato's Doctrine of Truth (T. Sheehan, trans.). In W. McNeill (Ed.), *Martin Heidegger: Pathmarks* (pp. 155–182). Cambridge, UK: Cambridge University Press. (Original work published 1942).
Hodge, D. R., & Derezotes, D. S. (2008). Postmodernism and Spirituality: Some Pedagogical Implications for Teaching Content on Spirituality. *Journal of Social Work Education, 44*(1), 103–123.
Huebner, D. E. (1999a). The Capacity for Wonder and Education. In V. Hillis (Ed.), *The Lure of the Transcendent: Collected Essays by Dwayne E. Huebner* (pp. 1–9). New York, NY: Routledge. (Original work published 1959).
Huebner, D. E. (1999b). New Modes of Man's Relationship to Man. In V. Hillis (Ed.), *The Lure of the Transcendent: Collected Essays by Dwayne E. Huebner* (pp. 74–93). New York, NY: Routledge. (Original work published 1963).
Huebner, D. E. (1999c). Religious Metaphors in the Language of Education. In V. Hillis (Ed.), *The Lure of the Transcendent: Collected Essays by Dwayne E. Huebner* (pp. 358–368). New York, NY: Routledge. (Original work published 1985a).
Huebner, D. E. (1999d). Spirituality and Knowing. In V. Hillis (Ed.), *The Lure of the Transcendent: Collected Essays by Dwayne E. Huebner* (pp. 340–352). New York, NY: Routledge. (Original work published 1985b).
Huebner, D. E. (1999e). Education and Spirituality. In V. Hillis (Ed.), *The Lure of the Transcendent: Collected Essays by Dwayne E. Huebner* (pp. 401–416). New York, NY: Routledge. (Original work published 1993).
Iannone, R. V., & Obenauf, P. A. (1999). Toward Spirituality in Curriculum and Teaching. *Education, 119*(4), 737–743.

Johnson, G. (2014, January 22). Get a Degree in Mindfulness at Simon Fraser University. *The Georgia Straight.* Retrieved from http://www.straight.com/life/571946/get-degree-mindfulness-simon-fraser-university

Koetting, J. R., & Combs, M. (2005). Spirituality and Curriculum: The Need to Engage the World. *Taboo: The Journal of Culture & Education, 9*(1), 81–91.

Miller, J. P. (2000). *Education and the Soul: Toward a Spiritual Curriculum.* Albany, NY: State University of New York Press.

Miller, J. P. (2006). *Educating for Wisdom and Compassion: Creating Conditions for Timeless Learning.* Thousand Oaks, CA: Corwin Press.

Miller, J. P. (2007). *The Holistic Curriculum* (2nd ed.). Toronto, ON: University of Toronto Press.

Miller, J. P. (2010). *Whole Child Education.* Toronto, ON: University of Toronto Press.

Miller, R. (2005). Philosophical Sources of Holistic Education. *Değerler Eğitimi Dergisi [Journal of Values Education], 3*(10), 1–9.

Mintz, J., & Muscat, A. (1994). *The Handbook of Alternative Education.* New York, NY: Macmillan Publishing Company.

Palmer, P. J. (2003a). Education as Spiritual Formation. *Educational Horizons, 82*(1), 55–67. (Reprinted from *To Know as We Are Known: Education as a Spiritual Journey,* pp. 17–32, 1983, New York, NY: HarperCollins).

Palmer, P. J. (2003b). Teaching with Heart and Soul: Reflections on Spirituality in Teacher Education. *Journal of Teacher Education, 54*(5), 376–385.

Park, S. R. (2014). *Embodied Inner Work: An Educator's Journey of Body-Mind-Heart Integration.* Unpublished doctoral dissertation, Simon Fraser University, Burnaby, Canada.

Pinar, W. F. (1999). Introduction. In V. Hillis (Ed.), *The Lure of the Transcendent: Collected Essays by Dwayne E. Huebner* (pp. xv–xxviii). New York, NY: Routledge.

Taylor, C. (1996). Spirituality of Life–and Its Shadow. *Compass, 14*(2), 10–13.

Vella, J. (2000). A Spirited Epistemology. In L. English & M. Gillen (Eds.), *Addressing the Spiritual Dimensions of Adult Learning* (pp. 7–16). San Francisco, CA: Jossey-Bass.

Walton, J. (1996). Spiritual Relationships: A Concept Analysis. *Journal of Holistic Nursing, 14*(3), 237–250.

PART II

The Nature of Consciousness, Self, and Reality

CHAPTER 3

A Dialogue Between Buddhism and Quantum Physics

3.1 Introduction

In this chapter, in order to verify the truthfulness of the doctrine of truth in Plato's allegory of the cave and the concepts of spiritual truth—particularly the transcendent and the non-dualistic worldview—found in the previous chapter, and to explore the significance of the transitions of the essence of truth for human beings, I first investigate the concepts of truth in Buddhism and demonstrate how they resonate with the concepts of spiritual truth and the significance of educating toward the truth found in Chap. 2. By means of conducting a dialogue between Buddhism and quantum physics, I then display how the concepts of truth in Buddhism are supported and enriched by various phenomena, theories and philosophies of quantum physics. Finally, on the basis of this dialogue, I explore how these enriched veins of thought, along with the increased confidence in the truthfulness of spiritual truth and the reaffirmed recognition of the significance of the transitions of the essence of truth for human beings, might lead to deeper insights into the essence and purpose of education identified in the preceding chapter and provide powerful tools for educational thinking and curriculum design.

3.2 The Concepts of Truth in Buddhism

In Buddhism, "truth" refers to the true nature of self and reality, and the concepts of truth are multifold. This section explores the Buddhist concepts of the two truths, the four noble truths, and an overview of the spiritual path as revealed in the four noble truths, and how these resonate with the concepts of spiritual truth and the significance of educating toward the truth found in Chap. 2.

3.2.1 The Two Truths

In Buddhism, a distinction is made between two truths—the ultimate truth (absolute truth) and the phenomenal truth (conventional truth, relative truth, or commonsensical truth). The ultimate truth is "the object known by a mind discerning the final nature of things—emptiness" (Newland, 2009, p. 131); the phenomenal or conventional truth refers to "objects found by conventional minds that are not analyzing the ultimate nature of things. This includes everything that exists except emptiness" (Newland, 2009, p. 125). The *right view*[1] (*sammā-diṭṭhi*, or *samyag-dṛṣṭi*) of the ultimate truth, which refers to the correct seeing of the ultimate nature of things, is understood as the realization of emptiness. The right view of the phenomenal truth is a proper understanding of the cause and effect of karma and its results (Sopa, 2005, p. 22); it refers to the confidence in the certainty of the process of cause and effect that "positive karma definitely produces happy results and negative karma will definitely produce suffering results" (Sopa, 2005, p. 22). According to Sopa (2005), the right view of both truths is "the basis of all white dharmas, meaning that all positive, happy, and blissful experience arises from that right view" (p. 22). Thus, a correct understanding of both truths is crucial for Buddhist spiritual practices.

In the doctrine of Buddhism, consciousness, self, and reality are inseparable. All phenomena, including the inner self and external reality, are perceived to have an illusionary and projective nature and only exist in consciousness. This view is rooted in the central doctrine of *Yogacara*[2] (the Consciousness-Only school of Buddhism), which maintains that "nothing exists except in the consciousness" (Wei, 1973, p. 1). According to Wei (1973), Vasubandhu[3] indicated in his "Thirty Verses on Consciousness-Only" that the concepts of self and reality do not imply the existence of an ultimately real self and reality; they are merely fictitious constructions, and the phenomena of self and reality are based on the manifestation and transformation of consciousness (p. lvii). Regarding this point, Hsuan-Tsang (also translated as Xuanzang) (596–664 C.E.), the founder of the Chinese Consciousness-Only Buddhism, explained:

> The inner consciousness manifests itself in what seems to be an external sphere of objects... [The] phenomena of [self and reality]... lie within the consciousness, yet, because of wrong mental discrimination or particularization, they are taken to be external objects [that are distinct from consciousness]. (Wei, 1973, p. lviii)

Hsuan-Tsang illustrated this conception by employing the analogy of "a man in a dream, who in that state believes all the images he sees to be real external objects, whereas actually they are only the projections of his own mind" (Wei, 1973, p. lviii). As illuminated by Buddha in the King of Concentrations Sutra, "all phenomena are empty of absolute reality, illusory like the moon reflected in the lake. They appear one way, but that is not their ultimate mode of existence" (Sopa, 2005, p. 139). This illusory and projective nature of all phenomena is in accordance with the implications of Plato's allegory of the cave, and is the common ground of both ultimate and phenomenal truths taught by Buddha.

As the ultimate nature of self and reality, emptiness is a profound insight attained by an "ultimate mind," a mind that gets at the basis of things, through both inferential reasoning and introspective meditation (Newland, 2009, pp. 17, 58). In Buddhist terminology, the Tibetan and Sanskrit words which are translated as emptiness[4] do literally mean "emptiness" (Newland, 2009, p. 6). However, rather than suggesting the lack or absence of meaning, hope, or existence, in this context it refers to the lack of an exaggerated and distorted kind of existence—a false absolute,[5] essential, and independent existence—that we have projected onto things and onto ourselves (Newland, 2009, p. 6; Sopa, 2005, p. 138). At first, it can be frightening to doubt about the substantiality of reality, and we might feel that persons and things cannot exist at all if they do not exist in a substantial way we are accustomed to seeing them (Newland, 2009, p. 7). Yet, according to Newland (2009), "if it were our essential nature to be as we are, we would always be exactly that. We would be locked into existence-just-as-what-we-are-now. There could be no life—everything would be static and frozen" (p. 7). Thus, "our utter lack of a self-existent self—an independently existing self, an ultimately real self—does not mean that we do not exist at all. Persons and other phenomena do exist interdependently" (Newland, 2009, p. 8).

According to Buddha, the meaning of emptiness is coterminous with dependent origination or dependent arising, which means that all that exists comes into being in dependence upon causes and conditions (Newland, 2009, p. 32; Yin-shun, 1998, p. 132). Based on the causality that "in dependence upon this, that arises" (Newland, 2009, p. 125), we see that things exist and appear due to causes and conditions (Yin-shun, 1960/1998, p. 166), and that

> since those causes and conditions are existent and have arisen, they naturally depend on other causes and conditions... Where there is a cause, there is an effect... Apart from causes and conditions, nothing can exist. (Yin-shun, 1960/1998, p. 166)

On one level, the doctrine of dependent origination reveals "how everything that exists in the world is relative, dependent on other parts" (Sopa, 2005, p. 359). While persons and things appear to us to be independent and have their own self-existence or essential reality, in actuality they are empty of such an independent, absolute and intrinsic nature. On this level, Buddha "is revealing the final nature of all things—the emptiness of all phenomena" (Sopa, 2005, p. 359). As Sopa (2005) explained, "the meaning of emptiness is dependent arising" (p. 138). In his *Fundamental Treatise*, Nagarjuna[6] illuminated that whatever arises dependently we explain as emptiness (Newland, 2009, p. 32). From this perspective, we see that phenomena "exist only through their interconnections with other (equally empty) phenomena" (Newland, 2009, p. 69). Indeed, "it is just empty things that exist and are active in cause and effect relations" (Newland, 2009, p. 37). Thus, not only are emptiness and dependent arising fully compatible, but they are in actuality two ways of talking about the same view of the nature of reality (Newland, 2009, p. 32). Buddha's way of teaching emptiness and dependent origination as an integrated, unified view of the true nature of things is highly praised by Tsong-kha-pa[7] (Sopa, 2005, p. 359).

On another level, as demonstrated in the theory of the twelve links of dependent origination, the doctrine of dependent origination is also taught by Buddha to reveal the process of cause and effect by which the circumstances of *samsara*[8] arise (Sopa, 2005, p. 325). According to *Yogacara* doctrine, each of our actions of body, speech, and mind deposits "a [karmic] seed or impression [or information] on the consciousness, which carries that seed forward as a potential, will eventually ripen and yield a result in the form of some type of future life experience" (Sopa, 2005, p. 328). Precisely speaking, in *Yogacara* doctrine, the karmic seeds are deposited in the eighth consciousness, also known as the *Alaya* or storehouse consciousness[9] (Choi, 2011, pp. 53–54). Before ripening, the karmic seeds carried by consciousness will never get lost, and become the causes of various forms of reincarnation (Choi, 2011, pp. 55–56). There are twelve links of dependent origination: ignorance, formative activity, consciousness, name and form, the six sense bases, contact, feeling, craving, grasping,[10] existence, birth, aging and death (Sopa, 2005, pp. 324–360). As the very first of this causal chain, ignorance—meaning being ignorant of the ultimate truth of emptiness—is the most fundamental root of *samsara* (Sopa, 2005, p. 325). It "is a fundamental inability to recognize the infinite potential, clarity, and power of our own minds" (Mingyur, 2007, p. 117). The very point of the twelve links of dependent origination is that "all the causes that give rise to cyclic existence are *within* the individual" (Sopa, 2005, p. 352). As a description both of the empty nature of all experiences and phenomena and of the causal chain that perpetuates the cyclic forms of life process, dependent origination thus unites the right view of both truths—the doctrine of emptiness and the law of cause and effect of karma.

The concept of dependent origination appears easy to understand. Nevertheless, Buddha said to Ananda that the "true meaning of 'all things arise interdependently' is very profound" (Yin-shun, 1960/1998, p. 165), and since the meaning of emptiness is dependent arising, so is the true meaning of emptiness. By means of observing school buildings, for instance, we can easily conclude that they do not have an intrinsic existence because if they did, they would not depend on causes and conditions and would not change. Yet Newland (2009) reminded us that "we should not therefore conclude that the very meaning of emptiness—things' lack of intrinsic existence—is simply that things are impermanent or that things depend on causes" (p. 67). He explained:

> Often we speak of dependent arising as though it was shorthand only for the dependence of effects upon causes and conditions. However, dependent arising also includes the idea that wholes depend upon their parts as well as the idea that *all things depend upon being designated or imputed by consciousnesses*. For example, fire arises in dependence upon fuel as a causal

condition; but fuel is something that a mind identifies as burnable and on that basis thinks, "There is fuel." Likewise, cars are physically built up out of auto parts, but auto parts are recognized and imputed by the mind in consideration of their connection with real or potential cars. (Newland, 2009, pp. 69–70)

In *Madhyamaka* (the Middle Way school of Buddhism), "the term 'dependent arising' includes the notion that all things exist in dependence upon conceptual designation"[11] (Newland, 2009, p. 70). Nevertheless, Thompson (2015) emphasized that "such conceptual dependence doesn't mean that nothing exists apart from our words and concepts, or that we make up the world with our mind" (p. 331). It means, rather, that upon a basis of designation, the identity of something as a single whole depends on how we cognitively conceptualize this basis and refer to it with a term (Thompson, 2015, pp. 330–131). This is the subtlest level of dependent arising and is crucial for attaining a proper understanding of emptiness. It is also the type of dependent arising that is of the greatest significance for education and as such will be discussed in further detail in Parts III and IV.

A proper understanding of emptiness involves a precise identification of the object of negation without either refuting too much (by denying production) and thus undermining ethics and negating the conventional existence altogether, and falling prey to the extreme of nihilism, or refuting too little (by affirming intrinsic nature) and thus slipping into the other extreme of eternalism or reificationism, and leaving our ignorance intact (Newland, 2009, pp. 28–38). This point is crucial in Buddha's teaching of the Middle Way. Following Buddha's Middle Way doctrine,

> Tsongkhapa identifies this actual object of negation as *things having their own way of existing without being posited through the force of consciousness*. This is what we mean by "self" or "intrinsic nature" [or *svabhāva*, in Sanskrit]. The sheer absence of this is emptiness. Therefore, at bottom, to understand emptiness means understanding that things have no way of existing apart from minds that impute them. (Newland, 2009, p. 70)

In other words, to understand emptiness properly means understanding the profound meaning of dependent origination and the central doctrine of Consciousness-Only that maintains nothing exists except in consciousness. Moreover, from this perspective, "even emptiness is itself empty; that is, when one searches for the ultimate essence of emptiness, it too is unfindable. One finds only the emptiness of emptiness" (Newland, 2009,

p. 31). However, this does not mean that emptiness does not exist at all. While "emptiness—as the ultimate nature—does not depend on causes or conditions, it still exists only in interdependence with other phenomena" (Newland, 2009, p. 63). For Tsong-kha-pa, Newland (2009) explained, "emptiness—like all other phenomena—depends on the mind that recognizes it and knows, 'Emptiness exists'" (p. 63).

Through the above exploration, we have attained a certain conceptual understanding of emptiness; however, the hidden meaning of emptiness is profound and cannot be fully grasped by analytical reasoning alone. As Newland (2009) said, while it is transformative to know with certainty by means of inferential reasoning that things do not exist as they appear to us, "it is still a conceptual and therefore a dualistic kind of understanding" (p. 17). It is not yet a direct and truthful knowing of the actual ultimate truth—emptiness itself. Aiming at refining the conceptual and dualistic understanding of emptiness into *nirvana*—a liberating and direct, nondualistic experience of emptiness—along the spiritual path, the bodhisattva[12] becomes more and more familiar with emptiness by means of introspective meditation that links analysis with serene one-pointed concentration (Newland, 2009, pp. 17, 64). According to Newland (2009),

> this culminates in the profound experience of direct, nondualistic mental perception of emptiness. For this ultimate mind, totally switched over to [another channel of reality]..., no conventional phenomena appear at all. This is what Tsong-kha-pa refers to as the actual ultimate truth. That is, the bodhisattva does not at that time think, "I am realizing emptiness," or "Oh, emptiness really does exist." Only emptiness appears. (p. 64)

When switching back to the conventional channel of reality from the ultimate channel experienced in deep meditation, bodhisattvas understand how our everyday reality is merely conventional and is not at all the only or final perspective (Newland, 2009, p. 42). Yet this direct and nondualistic experience of emptiness does not wipe out the conventional reality; instead, conventional reality has its own kind of validity as objects known by conventional consciousness (Newland, 2009, p. 42). What is wiped out by the profound direct experience of oneness is the dualistic egoistic view that hinders the realization of the true nature of human existence that signifies infinite possibilities and omnipresent love intrinsic in everything. This experience is identical to the realizing of a mysterious unity depicted in the perennial philosophy, which, as discussed in Chap. 2, is the core wisdom common to various religious and spiritual traditions. However, as revealed in Chap. 2, both Huebner and Miller emphasized that what is important about transcendent and non-dualistic moments is the lived experience itself rather than its label or source, and such moments should not be relegated to remote forms of mysticism. As underscored in the perennial philosophy, "this realization can lead to social activity designed to counter injustice and human suffering" (Miller, 2007, p. 18).

As mentioned earlier, the right view of both the ultimate and phenomenal truths is the basis of all positive, happy, and blissful experiences. While we have now attained a certain conceptual understanding of the ultimate truth of emptiness, Sopa (2005) reminded us that since the law of cause and effect of karma was categorized by Buddha as an extremely hidden phenomenon, and "the details of the relationship between karma and its results is extremely profound and subtle; they are much more difficult to understand fully than emptiness" (p. 23). The complexity of the relationship between karma and its results can be found in the Jataka stories, or in sutras, such as The Sutra of the Wise and the Fool, etc. For the purpose of gaining deeper insights into the law of cause and effect of karma, related phenomena and theories of quantum physics will be explored in the next section.

Due to misunderstanding regarding the meaning of emptiness, there has been a recurring quandary concerning the compatibility between emptiness and the law of cause and effect of karma: "If there is no 'I,' no 'mine,' and all dharmas are utterly empty, how can the law of karma prevail?" (Chang, 1983, p. 411). Chang (1983) inferred:

> It is precisely because everything is empty [of an independent, absolute nature] and there is no [absolute, essential and independent] self or 'I,' that everything can exist and the principle of karma can prevail. If things were truly existent, i.e., with a definite, enduring substance or entity, then no change or flow would be possible. Because nothing has self-nature (*svabhava*), everything is possible. (p. 411)

In other words, it is because all phenomena (including the inner self and external reality) are not ultimately real, but rather have a dependent arising nature that the law of the cause and effect of karma is able to function (Sopa, 2005, p. 139). Sopa (2008) stressed that "understanding causality and that things do not exist as they appear are not contradictory" (p. 219).

Therefore, not only does emptiness not mean nothingness, but on the contrary, in the words of the 12th Tai Situpa Rinpoche, "emptiness is described as the basis that makes everything possible" (Mingyur, 2007, p. 59). Mingyur (2007) further illuminated that "without emptiness, nothing could appear; in the absence of phenomena, we wouldn't be able to experience the background of emptiness" (p. 63). Emptiness, or infinite possibility, he continued, "is the *absolute* nature of reality. Everything that appears out of emptiness... is a *relative* expression of infinite possibility, a momentary appearance in the context of infinite time and space" (Mingyur, 2007, p. 63). From this perspective, the concept of emptiness and the concept of the transcendent are coterminous descriptions of the ultimate nature of self and reality that signify infinite possibilities. Besides, as the truthful knowing of the ultimate nature of self and reality, the direct, non-conceptual, and non-dualistic experience of emptiness attained through introspective meditation extends our understanding of a non-dualist worldview as a meditative insight that reveals the ultimate wholeness and interconnectedness of everything in the phenomenal world. Together, the conceptual understanding of emptiness attained through inferential reasoning and the non-conceptual and non-dualistic direct experience of emptiness attained through introspective meditation provide us with alternative perspectives for understanding the concepts of spiritual truth—particularly the openness to the transcendent and a non-dualistic worldview—found in Chap. 2.

Additionally, grounded in the Consciousness-Only doctrine which maintains that nothing exists except in the consciousness and suggests the illusory, projective, and dreamlike nature of all phenomena, the ultimate truth of emptiness echoes Plato's allegory of the cave wherein human beings are likened to a strange sort of prisoners who see the shadows cast on the cave wall as the only truth and reality. The integrated view of the ultimate nature of self and reality that combines the Consciousness-Only doctrine, the notions of emptiness and dependent origination, and the law of cause and effect of karma suggests that the key to infinite possibilities is in our consciousness. It also illuminates why to speak of the spiritual is not to speak of something other than humankind, why "knowing the spiritual" actually refers to knowing oneself and others and the disciplines for knowing oneself and others, and why various modes of knowing are already infused with the spiritual.

3.2.2 The Four Noble Truths

In addition to the two truths, for those who are ready to strive for the ultimate liberation from all *samsaric* suffering and cyclic forms of existence, Buddha also taught the four noble truths: the truth of suffering, the truth of the cause of suffering, the truth of the cessation of suffering, and the truth of the path (Sopa, 2005, p. 4). According to Sopa (2005), by teaching the truth of suffering as the first of the four noble truths, Buddha pointed to the significance of generating the desire for liberation. From the Buddha's perspective, most worldly beings are "deceived by the mistaken view that apprehends the attractions of *samsara* as sources of pleasure and happiness, when in fact they produce only dissatisfaction and suffering" (Sopa, 2005, p. 194). Being deceived by the attractive appearance of objects of desire, which are not the true causes of happiness and joy, sentient beings are entrapped in cyclic existence and therefore suffer (Sopa, 2005, p. 194). Sopa (2005) explained that when we are in the prison of cyclic existence, if we do not perceive our imprisonment as a problem, we will have no incentive to get out of it; instead, we grow used to it and become attached to it (p. 192). This is why we need to contemplate the truth of suffering. One of the ways of meditating on the truth of suffering is to contemplate the eight types of suffering, including the sufferings of birth, aging, sickness, death, encountering the unpleasant, separating from the pleasant, not getting what one wants, and the appropriating of aggregates (the combination of body and mind) (Sopa, 2005, pp. 198–224).

In order to achieve the cessation of suffering, we need to find out the cause of suffering. In Buddha's doctrine, *samsaric* suffering is caused by various forms of contaminated karma, produced by inner afflictions rooted in ignorance, which refers to being ignorant of the ultimate truth of the emptiness of self and reality, and as a result, "grasping at a false conception of self" (Sopa, 2005, pp. 195, 296, 326). On an essential level, "ignorance distorts the basically open experience of awareness into dualistic distinctions between inherently existing categories of 'self' and 'other'. Ignorance is thus a twofold problem" (Mingyur, 2007, p. 117). By means of perceiving the self as something permanent, essential and independent, we "impute upon the ever-changing aggregates a permanent sense of self—an egocentric, central 'I'" (Sopa, 2005, p. 195), and start to perceive whatever is not self as the *other* (Mingyur, 2007, p. 117). Mingyur (2007) analyzed that, as a result, "everything we experience becomes, in a sense, a stranger" (p. 117); by locking ourselves into a dualistic mode of perception, we become unable "to recognize the infinite potential, clarity, and power of our own mind" (p. 117), and "begin looking [outwardly] at other people, material objects, and so on, as potential sources of happiness and unhappiness, and life becomes a struggle to get what we need in order to be happy before somebody else grabs it" (p. 117). This egoistic view which grasps a false ultimately existent nature of the self and all phenomena is the root of *samsara* (Sopa, 2005, p. 299). However, ignorance—the root cause of suffering—can be eliminated; according to Tsong-kha-pa, the principle antidote to this ignorance is the wisdom that realizes the emptiness of self (Sopa, 2005, pp. 195, 299, 327). The key to the cessation of *samsaric* suffering thus lies in the right view of the ultimate truth: the realization of emptiness.

With this right view in mind, we still require the methods to actually attain liberation. The truth of the path that will lead to personal emancipation from all of the sufferings of cyclic existence is embodied in the *three trainings*, which include ethical conduct or discipline, meditative stabilization, and wisdom (*prajñā*) that realizes emptiness (Sopa, 2008, p. 4). While it is the training of wisdom that actually brings about the cessation of suffering, achieving that level of realization requires the training of meditative stabilization, and both goals rely on the firm foundation of ethical conduct (Sopa, 2008, p. 4). For those who have developed the bodhisattva's motivation—*bodhicitta*, meaning the aspiration to attain the highest spiritual goal of the omniscience of enlightenment for the liberation of all sentient beings in the same miserable situation—Buddha expanded the path of three trainings into the Mahayana practices of *six perfections* (*six paramitas*[13]): the perfections of generosity, ethical discipline, patience, joyous perseverance, meditative stabilization, and wisdom (Sopa, 2008, p. 8). According to Sopa (2008), each of the six perfections is a complex combination[14] of *methods* (particularly the first four or five perfections) based on *bodhicitta* and *wisdom* (particularly the last two perfections or the sixth perfection) based on the realization of emptiness, and "each perfection supports and is part of the practice of the others" (p. 8). Thus, in the explanation and application of generosity, for example, there is the generosity of generosity, the ethical discipline of generosity, ..., and the wisdom of generosity (Sopa, 2008, p. 209). Therefore, the six perfections are not fixed religious dogma to be observed mechanically within the framework of subject–object duality, but rather a dynamic and recursive matrix corresponding to vicissitudinary existential situations for cultivating "the *nonperceptual* and *with no object*" (Sopa, 2008, p. 213), for approaching the ultimate truth of self and reality and for the liberation of both oneself and all other sentient beings. Taking generosity as an example, "*generosity with no object* refers to understanding that the gift, the giver, and the recipient are empty of inherent existence" (Sopa, 2008, p. 214); "practicing giving with a realization of *sunyata* [emptiness] in the back of the mind is *nonperceptual* generosity" (Sopa, 2008, p. 214). The other perfections work in a similar way. The point of the six perfections is to cultivate the understanding that there are no ultimately existing objects or subjects; however, this does not mean there are no subjects and objects at all (Sopa, 2008, p. 213). Rather, the goal of these practices is to cultivate the realization that "the subject and object of any action are relative, dependent, and like illusions" (Sopa, 2008, pp. 213–214). Nevertheless, as Buddha emphasized in the Sutra *Gathering All the Threads*, this does not mean that one should practice the perfection of wisdom only (Sopa, 2008, p. 204). The requirement of both the wisdom-side practices and the method-side practices will be explored further in Chap. 4.

The truth of suffering and the truth of the cause of suffering provide us with deepened insights into why being ignorant of the ultimate truth of emptiness and attaching to a dualistic mode of perception are the sources of suffering. The truth of the cessation of suffering informs us that the key to the cessation of suffering lies in the cultivation and realization of the ultimate truth of emptiness, which signifies infinite transcendental possibilities and features a non-dualistic worldview. The truth of the path reveals the significant interrelationships between ethical conduct, meditative stabilization, and wisdom, and illuminates how each of these three trainings is indispensable to a spiritual pathway that will genuinely lead to positive, blissful life experiences and the achievement of various spiritual goals, whether these be "a better rebirth in our next life, personal liberation from cyclic existence, or perfect buddhahood for the sake of all sentient beings" (Sopa, 2005, p. 4).

The above exploration of the four noble truths provides us a glimpse of the essence of Buddhism's spiritual path that not only deepens our understanding of the metaphor of the four-stage transition depicted in Plato's allegory of the cave, but also, to a certain extent, offers answers to our question regarding the significance of the transitions of the essence of truth from one stage to another for human beings. Thus, the educational significance of the concepts of truth in Buddhism (including the two truths doctrine and the four noble truths) lies in that they make clear the existential significance of spiritual truths and spiritual practices for human beings that is intimately related to both the individual and collective experiences of genuine happiness and ultimate liberation. However, just as the extent of the truthfulness of Plato's doctrine of truth needs to be investigated, the educational significance of the concepts of truth in Buddhism need to be established based on the truthfulness of the Buddhist doctrine of truth. In the following section, therefore, a dialogue between the concepts of truth in Buddhism and their corresponding or supportive phenomena, theories, and philosophies in quantum physics is developed.

3.3 A Dialogue Between Buddhism and Quantum Physics

As discussed previously, in the doctrine of Buddhism, consciousness, self, and reality are inseparable, and the concepts of truth are established upon the doctrine of Consciousness-Only that maintains that nothing exists except in the consciousness. For the purpose of verifying the truthfulness of the Consciousness-Only doctrine and the Buddhist doctrine of truth, in this section, based on my identification of threads of continuity between the two systems of thought of Buddhism and quantum physics, I explore how we might understand the Buddhist concepts of truth—including emptiness, dependent origination, the law of cause and effect of karma, and the Consciousness-Only doctrine—from the perspective of quantum physics. The phenomena, theories, and philosophies of quantum physics to be explored are separated into three parts: the quantum measurement problem, uncertainty, and superstring theory; the holographic principle; and quantum entanglement, the theory of It from Bit, the participatory universe, and QBism.

3.3.1 The Quantum Measurement Problem, Uncertainty, and Superstring Theory and Buddhism

During the last 100 years, quantum mechanics is the most startling discovery in physics which undermines the whole conceptual schema of classical physics (Greene, 2004, p. 177). According to Greene (2004), the concepts of space and time in classical physics, established on Newton's equations of motion, are absolute, rigid, and immutable (pp. 7–8). However, in 1905, Einstein determined that space and time are not independent and absolute, but rather are enmeshed, relative, flexible, and dynamic (Greene, 2004, p. 9). By the 1930s, propelled by experimental results, physicists were forced again to introduce a whole new conceptual schema known as quantum mechanics (Greene, 2004, p. 10). In contrast to classical physics, quantum theory portrays a distinct reality "in which things sometimes hover in a haze of being partly one way *and* partly another. Things become definite only when a suitable observation forces them to relinquish quantum possibilities and settle on a specific outcome" (Greene, 2004, p. 11). According to the Copenhagen interpretation of quantum mechanics, it is not a question of a particle having a position that we do not know because we have not yet performed a measurement. Rather, in contrast to what we would expect, a particle "simply *does not have* a definite position before the measurement is taken" (Greene, 2004, p. 94); it "exists in a nether state, a sum of *all possible states*, until a measurement is made" (Kaku, 1994, p. 260), and therefore, prior to measurement, the coexisting possibilities move collectively, behaving like a wave. This is usually referred to as the quantum measurement problem. This phenomenon has been illustrated in a variety of double-slit experiments (Greene, 2004, pp. 84–88), culminating in a 1974 experiment wherein the Italian physicists Pier Giorgio Merli, Gian Franco Missiroli, and Giulio Pozzi successfully repeated Young's double-slit experiment using single electrons and showed that, when not being observed, even a single electron interferes with itself as predicted by quantum theory[15] (Rosa, 2012). Niels Bohr summarized that everything "has both wavelike and particle-like aspects. They are complementary features" (Greene, 2004, p. 185).

Moreover, "through the Heisenberg uncertainty principle, quantum mechanics claims that there are features of the world… that cannot simultaneously have definite values" (Greene, 2004, p. 112). For example, a particle cannot simultaneously have a definite a position and velocity, nor can it have a definite spin, either clockwise or counter-clockwise, about more than one axis (Greene, 2004, p. 112); "instead, particles hover in quantum limbo, in a fuzzy amorphous, probabilistic mixture of all possibilities; only when measured is one definite outcome selected from the many" (Greene, 2004, p. 112). This phenomenon echoes the doctrine of dependent origination and refutes the idea that particles have "*their own way of existing without being posited through the force of consciousness*" (Newland, 2009, p. 70). The mystic interrelationship between the observer's consciousness and the behavior of the observed electron is one of the most intriguing implications of this phenomenon. Since quantum theory is greatly at odds with our everyday experiences, at the time when quantum theory was first proposed by Niels Bohr and Werner Heisenberg, Einstein revolted against this concept and was fond of asking "Does the moon exist just because a mouse looks at it?" (Kaku, 1994, p. 260). Today, however, according to Greene (2004), the majority of physicists agree that particle properties only "come into being when measurements force them to" (p. 121), and when "they are not being observed or interacting with the environment, particle properties have a nebulous, fuzzy existence characterized solely by a probability that one or another potentiality might be realized" (p. 121).

Apparently, quantum physics negates absolutism and objectivism, and depicts a drastically different picture of reality than that portrayed by classical physics. Nevertheless, for decades, there has been a widespread impression that quantum mechanics is only applicable in the invisible microscopic realm (Vedral, 2011, p. 38). This assumption was overturned, however, in 2010, when Aaron O'Connell created the world's first quantum machine and performed the first quantum measurement visible to the naked eye (Cho, 2010, p. 1604). The journal *Science* honored it as the Breakthrough of the Year of 2010, and commented that this machine "might lead to tests of our notion of reality" (Cho, 2010, p. 1604). O'Connell's invention suggests that quantum mechanics is universally applicable to everything in both the microscopic and macroscopic realms. According to Greene (2004), if "quantum mechanics is a universal theory that applies without limitations to everything, [then] the observed and the observer should be treated in exactly the same way" (p. 203). This equal treatment of the observer and the observed convincingly suggests the inseparability of consciousness, self, and reality and a non-dualistic worldview. Furthermore, if quantum mechanics is applicable to the macroscopic realm, then the seemingly absolute, substantial, essential, and independent macroscopic material world, just like the microscopic realm depicted by quantum theory, when not being observed, would also be merely "a nebulous, fuzzy existence characterized solely by a probability that one or another potentiality might be realized" (Greene, 2004, p. 121), and thus be empty of any absolute, substantial, essential, and independent nature. This is exactly the meaning of emptiness.

The quantum measurement problem and the principle of uncertainty provide us with a scientific perspective for contemplating the doctrine of the truth of emptiness. Nevertheless, the true meaning of emptiness is more profound than we might think. According to superstring theory—a leading theory developed to unite general relativity and quantum mechanics—the particles (e.g., electrons, quarks, etc.) thought of as the smallest indivisible constituents of matter are not concrete dots at all (Greene, 2004, p. 17). Rather, "every particle is composed of a tiny filament of energy, some hundred billion billion times smaller than a single atomic nucleus... which is shaped like a tiny string" (Greene, 2004, pp. 17–18), and, much as different vibrational patterns of strings on a violin produce different musical notes, different vibrational patterns of the filaments of energy produce different particle properties (Greene, 2004, p. 18). Therefore, at the ultramicroscopic level, the universe described by superstring theory would be akin to a string symphony of pure energy vibrating matter into existence (Greene, 2004, p. 347). Moreover, for the fusion of general relativity and quantum mechanics to be mathematically sensible, superstring theory "requires *nine* spatial dimensions and one time dimension. And in a more robust incarnation of superstring theory known as M-theory, unification requires *ten* space dimensions and one time dimension" (Greene, 2004, p. 18). Superstring theory, thus, provides us with a novel framework for contemplating an eleven-dimensional space-time, to which the phenomenal world refers and which forms the basis of what is perceived in our daily life. From the perspective of superstring theory, the four-dimensional phenomenal world we have so far glimpsed is but "*a meager slice of reality*" (Greene, 2004, p. 18), and is far from being substantial, absolute, and permanent. Therefore, in his teaching regarding the emptiness of all phenomena, rather than denying the existence of the everyday physical world, what Buddha emphasized is that this is far from the ultimate reality (Choi, 2011, p. 90).

When viewed from the perspective of the quantum measurement problem, the principle of uncertainty, and superstring theory, the doctrine of the ultimate truth of emptiness becomes more sensible and conceivable. Additional theories in quantum physics that resonate with the concepts of truth in Buddhism include the holographic principle and parallel universes. In the following subsection, I explore how we might understand the central doctrine of Consciousness-Only, the concepts of dependent origination, and the law of cause and effect of karma from the perspective of the holographic principle and parallel universes.

3.3.2 *The Holographic Principle and Buddhism*

A hologram (or holographic film) of an object is a piece of two-dimensional etched plastic negative produced by the interference patterns of waves of two separate beams of a single laser light (Talbot, 2011, p. 14). When illuminated with appropriate laser light, a hologram will project a three-dimensional image by means of Fourier transforms, which are mathematical equations that are able to convert between three-dimensional images and waveform interference patterns (Greene, 2004, p. 482; Talbot, 2011, p. 27). In addition to the three-dimensionality of the projected image, another remarkable characteristic of holograms is the *whole in every part* property: Every fragment of a hologram contains all the information recorded in the whole. If a piece of a hologram containing the image of an apple is cut into pieces and then illuminated by a laser, each one of these pieces will still be found to contain the entire image of the apple (Talbot, 2011, pp. 16–17). Evolved from David Bohm's holographic model of the universe, which he called *the holomovement* (Bohm, 1980, pp. 190–197), and the parallel universe proposals, as well as "over thirty years of theoretical studies on the quantum properties of black holes" (Greene, 2011, p. 8), the holographic principle posits that "all we experience is nothing but a holographic projection of processes taking place on some distant surface that surrounds us" (Greene, 2011, p. 8).

As early as the 1970s, based on a long-term contemplation and an inspiration kindled by hologram, quantum physicist David Bohm became convinced that the universe was a kind of giant, flowing hologram (Talbot, 2011, p. 46). For Bohm, "the tangible reality of our everyday lives is really a kind of illusion, like a holographic image" (Talbot, 2011, p. 46). Underlying this tangible reality, there is a deeper order of existence—"a vast and more primary level of reality that gives birth to all the objects and appearances of our physical world" (Talbot, 2011, p. 46) in much the same way that a piece of hologram gives birth to a holographic image (Talbot, 2011, p. 46).

Bohm's idea of a holographic universe explains many puzzles in quantum mechanics, including the effect consciousness seems to have on the subatomic world (Talbot, 2011, p. 49). Bohm felt that "most physicists go about it the wrong way, by once again trying to fragment reality and saying that one separate thing, consciousness, interacts with another separate thing, a subatomic particle" (Talbot, 2011, p. 49). Bohm believed that it was meaningless to speak of the observing instrument and the observed object as interacting, because all such things are merely different aspects of an undivided wholeness, the holomovement (Bohm, 1980, p. 169; Talbot, 2011, p. 50). In addressing the issue of fragmentation between the observer and the observed, Bohm (1980) indicated that "one of the most difficult and subtle points about this question is just to clarify what is to be meant by the relationship between the content of thought and the process of thinking which produces this content" (p. 23). Employing the metaphor of a turbulent mass of vortices in a stream, Bohm (1980) explained:

> The structure and distribution of vortices, which constitute a sort of content of the description of the movement, are not separate from the formative activity of the flowing stream, which creates, maintains, and ultimately dissolves the totality of vortex structures... Similarly, when we really grasp the truth of the one-ness of the thinking process that we are actually carrying out, and the content of thought that is the product of this process, then such insight will enable us to observe, to look, to learn about the whole movement of thought and thus to discover an action relevant to this whole, that will end the "turbulence" of movement which is the essence of fragmentation in every phase of life. (Bohm, 1980, p. 24)

Bohm's metaphor of vortices in a stream effectively illuminates his point regarding how the observer and the observed—or the thinking process and its content, or consciousness and what is experienced—are merely different aspects of an undivided dynamic wholeness. His insights, in some ways, not only buttress the Consciousness-Only doctrine and the non-dualistic worldview, but also highlight the significance of the realization of the wholeness and interconnectedness of everything for guiding our actions and ending the fragmentation.

In the early 1990s, based on the theoretical studies of information storage of black holes, Nobel laureate Gerard't Hooft and Leonard Susskind began to envision a prototype of the holographic principle (Greene, 2004, p. 482). A consolidation of the holographic principle came in 1997 when the Argentinian physicist Juan Maldacena made a dramatic breakthrough (Greene, 2004, p. 483); by applying superstring theory mathematically, he convincingly argued that "everything taking place within the specified universe is a reflection of laws and processes acting themselves out on the boundary [surrounding this specified universe]" (Greene, 2011, p. 263). His results "realized explicitly the holographic principle, and in doing so provided the first mathematical example of Holographic Parallel Universes" (Greene, 2011, p. 263). "The holographic ideas have been subject to a great many stringent mathematical tests; having come through unscathed, they've been propelled into mainstream thought among physicists" (Greene, 2011, p. 269). In 2015, by means of calculating the value of entropy of entanglement, Arjun Bagchi, Rudranil Basu, Daniel Grumiller, and Max Riegler further theoretically confirmed the validity of the holographic principle (Vienna University of Technology, 2015).

According to Greene (2011), there has been exciting evidence that within the next few years the holographic ideas may well be able to be tested experimentally (p. 263).

While the holographic principle suggests that what we experience in daily life is but a reflection of a parallel process taking place in the universe that surrounds us "much as what we see in a holographic projection is determined by information encoded on a bounding piece of plastic" (Greene, 2004, p. 482), in reconfiguring our worldview, it is vital to bear in mind Bohm's caution against further fragmenting reality by saying that one separate thing interacts with another. The eleven-dimensional universe depicted in superstring theory, the four-dimensional phenomenal world experienced in our daily life, the hologram-like universe of information storing, processing, and projecting, and the consciousness should therefore be considered as merely different aspects of an undivided wholeness, and therefore inseparable.

Bohm's holographic paradigm resonates with neuroscientist Karl Pribram's brain theory. In the 1970s, when Pribram had collected enough experimental evidence for his holographic brain theory, he met, and collaborated with, David Bohm (Talbot, 2011, pp. 30–31). Together, they concluded that "our brains mathematically construct objective reality by interpreting frequencies that are ultimately projections from another dimension, a deeper order of existence that is beyond both space and time. The brain is a hologram enfolded in a holographic universe" (Talbot, 2011, p. 54). For Pribram, all that we perceive as *out* there—including our own brains and bodies—is but "a vast ocean of wave and frequencies, and reality looks concrete to us only because our brains are able to take this holographic blur [of waveform interference patterns] and convert it into the sticks and stones and other familiar objects that make up our world" (Talbot, 2011, p. 54). From this perspective, the seemingly objective world, which is usually deemed as separate from ourselves, is but a filtered interpretation by our consciousness out of one single undivided holographic universe, and the pertinent question regarding the two different aspects of reality—what we perceive in our everyday life (i.e., the phenomenal aspect of reality) and the other aspect of the holographic blur of waveform interference patterns (i.e., the ultimate aspect of reality)—would be: "Which one is real and which is illusion?" (Talbot, 2011, p. 55).

The central concept of the holographic principle is reified in Oxford philosopher Nick Bostrom's simple but curious philosophy that we are in a computer-simulated universe (Greene, 2011, p. 288). As a theoretical physicist and string theorist, Brian Greene (2011) totally agreed with Bostrom's deduction, stating that "logic alone can't ensure that we're not in a computer simulation" (p. 289), and that "after all, according to our belief, we're in one" (p. 289). In such a computer simulation, a "sufficiently well-structured program would keep track of the mental states and intentions of its simulated inhabitants, and so would anticipate, and appropriately respond to, any impending stargazing" (Greene, 2011, p. 287). At the very least, as Greene (2011) asserted, evidences for simulated worlds are grounds for rethinking the nature of our own reality (p. 293).

The holographic principle and Bostrom's philosophy of a computer-simulated universe provide us with a scientific framework for contemplating the central doctrine of Consciousness-Only that nothing exists except in the consciousness and Hsuan-Tsang's analogy of a man in a dream. This scientific framework not only expands our understanding of the doctrine of dependent origination, particularly regarding how things cannot have independent ways of existence without being posited through the force of consciousness, but also helps us realize the significance of consciousness in the creation of our own reality and how the division between inner self and external phenomena is merely illusionary in nature. In the West, the best-known philosopher to propound a similar idealism is George Berkeley (Butler, 2010, pp. 39–40; Siderits, 2007, p. 146). This is a sort of philosophy that not everyone will be persuaded to accept. One anecdote states that when Samuel Johnson first heard of Berkeley's claim that matter is a figment of the mind's conjuring, he kicked a stone and said "I refute it thus!" (Greene, 2011, p. 298; Siderits, 2007, p. 146). Johnson's reaction is a representative refutation built upon an objectivist worldview. Nevertheless, from the perspective of the holographic principle and Bostrom's computer-simulated universe, Johnson's experiences—including his thoughts, body, speech, and the stone he kicked in what he thought of as an external objective world—are but an abstraction, an interpretation by his own consciousness in a computer-simulated holographic universe, akin, in a sense, to the experiences of a man in a dream. As Lusthaus (2002) explicated, "even the notion that 'things exist external to my consciousness' is a notion conceived, affirmed, or denied in consciousness" (p. 5).

Given the *whole in every part* property of a hologram, Bohm (1990) developed the notions of the enfolded or implicate order and the unfolded or explicate order (p. 273):

The essential features of the [enfolded or] implicate order are... that the whole universe is in some way enfolded in everything and that each thing is enfolded in the whole. From this it follows that in some way, and to some degree everything enfolds or implicates everything, but in such a manner that under typical conditions of ordinary experience, there is a great deal of *relative* independence of things. The basic proposal is then that this enfoldment relationship is not merely passive or superficial. Rather, it is active and essential to what each thing is. It follows that each thing is internally related to the whole, and therefore, to everything else. The external relationships are then displayed in the unfolded or explicate order in which each thing is seen, as has already indeed been indicated, as relatively separate and extended, and related only externally to other things. The explicate order, which dominates ordinary experience as well as classical (Newtonian) physics, thus appears to stand by itself. But actually, it cannot be understood properly apart from its ground in the primary reality of the implicate order. (Bohm, 1990, p. 273)

Bohm's proposal of implicate order and explicate order harkens back to the Buddhist doctrine of two truths and demonstrates the profound meaning of dependent origination. In this holographic dependently arising relationship, everything actively implicates everything else and the whole. Therefore, the interdependency between things is much more complicated and immediate than we might have thought. Bohm's proposal also resonates with the poetic Buddhist metaphor of *Indra*'s net,[16] in which an infinite number of interconnected jewels strung together in a net reflect one another and themselves, thus illustrating the *whole in every part* concept embodied in holograms as well as the mysterious connections that exist between everything. Since the whole universe is enfolded or implicated in everything, whatever actions of mind, body, and speech we direct toward others must, in a holographic sense, reflect back upon ourselves much like the reflections of the jewels in *Indra*'s net. Philosophically speaking, the concept of implicit order suggests the likelihood of the law of cause and effect of karma.

In addition to Bohm's concept of implicate order, the phenomenon of quantum entanglement and the theory of It from Bit also suggest the dependently originating nature of the phenomenal world and the law of cause and effect of karma. In the following subsection, quantum entanglement and the theory of It from Bit and the ways in which both resonate with Buddhist concepts of truth are explored.

3.3.3 Quantum Entanglement, the Theory of It from Bit, the Participatory Universe, and QBism and Buddhism

Quantum entanglement is a bizarre state of interconnectedness between two particles (Greene, 2004, p. 116; Talbot, 2011, p. 36). According to various repeatable experiments, given a pair of appropriately prepared particles with common origin, no matter how far apart they are, if the measurement of a certain property of one particle is performed at a precise moment, the other particle (i.e., the one not measured) immediately relinquishes the fuzzy state of quantum limbo and takes on the identical or related property as if this measurement was performed directly on it (Greene, 2004, pp. 80, 116). According to Greene (2004), the phenomenon of quantum entanglement challenges a basic property of space that "it separates and distinguishes one object from another" (p. 122), and shows that two things "can be separated by an enormous amount of space and yet not have a fully independent existence" (p. 122). In 1935, Einstein, Podolsky, and Rosen proposed a thought experiment (now referred to as the EPR paradox) intended to attack quantum theory by showing that when the distance between two particles was enlarged to a certain extent, "no 'reasonable definition' of reality would permit such faster-than-light interconnections to exist" (Talbot, 2011, p. 37); yet, decades later, what they thought of as absurd was demonstrated experimentally to be true (Greene, 2004, p. 11). These experiments include the work of Alain Aspect and his collaborators in the early 1980s, and a refined version of Aspect's experiment carried out by Nicolas Gisin and his team in 1997 (Greene, 2004, pp. 113, 115; Theckedath, 1997, p. 64). Greene (2004) explained that space "does not distinguish such entangled objects. Space cannot overcome their interconnection. Space, even a huge amount of space, does not weaken their quantum mechanical interdependence" (p. 122). This phenomenon reveals how two particles that come from one origin in the microscopic realm are dependently arising and become the causes and conditions of each other. Furthermore, in 2011, experimental research on entanglement between two separated diamonds, visible to the naked eye, at room temperature, confirmed that "entanglement can persist in the classical context of moving macroscopic solids in ambient conditions" (Lee et al., 2011, p. 1253).

While the phenomenon of quantum entanglement reveals the most astonishing example of dependent origination and suggests the likelihood of the existence of the law of cause and effect of karma, in our everyday life, we rarely experience an immediate quantum entanglement phenomenon. The theory of *decoherence* provides an explanation that it is because particles, despite being too small to have any significant effect of quantum entanglement on a large object, are able to continually *nudge* the probability wave of a large object, meaning they disturb the coherence of the probability wave by blurring its orderly sequence of crests and troughs, and melt the quantum probabilities into the familiar probabilities of everyday life (Greene, 2004, pp. 209, 210). Nevertheless, Greene (2004) pointed out that "even though decoherence suppresses quantum interference..., each of the potential outcomes embodied in a wavefunction still vies for realization. And so we still left wondering how one outcome 'wins'" (p. 212).

Speaking from the perspective of the holographic principle, the theoretical physicist John Wheeler, who coined and popularized the picturesque terms of black hole, wormhole, and gravitational radiation, etc. in modern physics (Narlikar, 2013, pp. 23–24), proposed that "things—matter and radiation—should be viewed as secondary, as carriers of a more abstract and fundamental entity: information" (Greene, 2011, p. 239). Greene (2011) explained that what Wheeler argued is that matter and radiation "should be viewed as the material manifestations of something more basic. He believed that information... forms an irreducible kernel at the heart of reality" (p. 239). Greene (2011) continued that, for Wheeler, "such information is instantiated in real particles..., is something like an architect's drawings being realized as a skyscraper" (p. 239). Wheeler called his theory *It from Bit* and elucidated that the universe sprang into being because it was observed (Kaku, 2005, pp. 171–172). "This means that 'it' (matter in the universe) sprang into existence when information ('bit') of the universe was observed," and Wheeler called this universe the "participatory universe" (Kaku, 2005, p. 172). In this participatory universe, "the universe adapts to us in the same way that we adapt to the universe... [and] our very presence makes the universe possible" (Kaku, 2005, p. 172).

Influenced by John Wheeler's writings regarding "law without law," QBism is one of the interpretations of quantum mechanics developed by Christopher Fuchs and some others since 1993 (Fuchs, 2016, p. 1). The theory of QBism suggests that "a quantum state does not represent an element of physical reality but an agent's personal probability assignments, reflecting his subjective degrees of belief about the future content of his experience" (Fuchs & Schack, 2014, p. 1). Coined in 2009, the term

QBism initially stood for Quantum Bayesianism, but now also associates the "B" with the idea of "bettabilitarianism"—the idea that "the world is loose at the joints, that indeterminism plays a real role in the world" (Fuchs, 2016, p. 10). In an interview, Fuchs emphasized that "quantum mechanics is not about how the world is without us; instead it's precisely about us in the world. The subject matter of the theory is not the world or us but us-within-the-world, the interface between the two" (Gefter, 2015, para. 14). As Fuchs and Schack (2014) explicated,

> in QBism, there are no agent-independent elements of physical reality that determine either measurement outcomes or probabilities of measurement outcomes. Rather, every quantum measurement is an action on the world by an agent that results in the creation of something entirely new. QBism holds this to be true not only for laboratory measurements on microscopic systems, but for any action an agent takes on the world to elicit a new experience. It is in this sense that agents have a fundamental creative role in the world. (pp. 9–10)

QBism and other voices in physics, such as "the 'Copenhagen' views of Bohr, Heisenberg, and Pauli, the observer-participator view of John Wheeler, the informational interpretation of Anton Zeilinger and Caslav Brukner, the relational interpretation of Carlo Rovelli" (Fuchs, 2016, p. 1) that seeks "to insert a first-person perspective into the heart of physics" (Fuchs, 2016, p. 1) have been termed as "participatory realism" (Fuchs, 2016, p. 1). Yet, "rather than relinquishing the idea of reality..., they are saying that reality is more than any third-person perspective can capture (Fuchs, 2016, p. 1). The question we would ask following the theory of QBism is: What, then, are the underlying rules that govern "an agent's personal probability assignments... [that reflect] his subjective degrees of belief about the future content of his experience" (Fuchs & Schack, 2014, p. 1)?

In the Buddhist doctrine of karma, akin to Wheeler's theory of It from Bit, each of our virtuous or non-virtuous actions of body, speech, and mind simultaneously deposits a corresponding karmic seed into the storehouse consciousness (*Alaya*) which carries the potential to ripen into corresponding pleasant or suffering type of results that is never inconsistent with the type of its seed (Sopa, 2005, pp. 20–22). Similar to the way a tiny seed can grow into an enormous tree, a small inner karmic seed can possibly produce great results (Sopa, 2005, pp. 22–23). In Buddha's teaching, the order in which various virtuous and non-virtuous karmic seeds ripen is as follows:

1. Whichever karma is weightiest will ripen first.
2. If weights are equal, whatever karma is manifest at the time of death will ripen first.
3. If this also is the same, whatever karma you have predominantly become habituated to will ripen first.
4. If this also is the same, whatever karma you have done first will ripen earliest. (Tsong-kha-pa, 1402/2000, p. 242)

The order of the ripening of karmic seeds provides us with a glance at the mechanics underlying the law of cause and effect of karma. Since Buddha's doctrine of karma is profound and complicated, the details of the rules will not be discussed here. These rules, however, suggest the possibility of understanding the karmic seeds as the "Bit" (i.e., information) in Wheeler's It from Bit theory that, like an architect's drawings, hold the potential to be realized as a skyscraper. This understanding, combined with Wheeler's theory of participatory universe and particles as carriers of information, QBism and participatory realism, Bostrom's computer-simulated universe, quantum entanglement, the holographic principle, and Bohm's implicate order, allows us to conceptualize an expanded holographic computer-simulation model of participatory universe that will always, in a sense, reflect the "Bit" or the information or the karmic seeds in our consciousness by virtue of following its own rules. This model is conducive to the speculation regarding the likelihood of the law of cause and effect of karma and the possible answer to Greene's question regarding how one potential outcome embodied in a wave-function wins and is realized in the material realm.

In this model, despite the fact that we do not always experience the immediate results of karma in our everyday lives, each of our actions of body, speech, and mind would simultaneously deposit corresponding information or karmic seeds into our database or storehouse consciousness. The probabilities of various potential future happenings inspired by accumulated information are therefore constantly altered by our actions, and, in this sense, the potential happenings vie for realization as certain type of life experience. Although it is extremely difficult to verify the law of cause and effect of karma by means of methods other than deep meditation (particularly when it involves multiple lives), the above conjecture serves as a basis for developing confidence in the certainty of the law of cause and effect of karma for those who are willing to cultivate this belief.

In summation, the phenomena, theories, and philosophies of quantum physics greatly extend our understanding of the concepts of truth in Buddhism, including emptiness, dependent origination, the law of cause and effect of karma, and the Consciousness-Only doctrine. In the following section, the implications of this dialogue between Buddhism and quantum physics for education and educational purposes are investigated.

3.4 THE IMPLICATIONS OF THIS DIALOGUE FOR EDUCATION

In the preceding section, the dialogue between Buddhism and quantum physics demystifies the religious language of Buddhist concepts of truth, including the meaning of emptiness, dependent origination, the law of cause and effect of karma, and the Consciousness-Only doctrine. Rather than contradicting each other, to our surprise, these two branches of thought exhibit common threads of continuity and a startling tendency toward convergence. Echoing Heidegger's interpretation of Plato's cave allegory, both Buddhism and quantum physics reveal that the phenomenal world we experience in everyday life is indeed a "deft master of disguise" (Greene, 2004, p. 22) and is in fact merely "*a meager slice of reality*" (Greene, 2004, p. 18) empty of any absolute, essential, and independent nature. Both branches of thought suggest the inseparability of consciousness, the inner self, and external reality. Both refute absolutism and objectivism, signify infinite possibilities, and uncover the profound dependently arising nature and the oneness of all phenomena. This convergence not only renews our comprehension of both branches of thought and deepens our understanding of the concepts of the transcendent and the non-dualistic worldview found in educational literature, but also increases our confidence in the truthfulness of both Plato's doctrine of truth and the concepts of truth in Buddhism.

As discussed earlier, the holographic principle makes manifest the fact that this phenomenal world we experience in everyday life is but "a reflection of laws and processes acting themselves out on the boundary" (Greene, 2011, p. 263) in much the same way "as what we see in a holographic projection is determined by information encoded on a bounding piece of plastic" (Greene, 2004, p. 482) and is therefore "but a faint inkling of a far richer reality that flickers beyond reach" (Greene, 2011, p. 238). Given the consistency between Plato's allegory of the cave and the holographic principle, Greene (2011) opened his book chapter on the holographic principle by introducing this allegory, remarking that "two millennia later, it seems that Plato's cave may be more than a metaphor" (p. 238). This increased confidence in the truthfulness of Plato's doctrine of truth and the concepts of truth in Buddhism provides us with a deepened and broadened conceptual ground for reconsidering the significance of spiritual truth and the relationship between truth and education found in Chap. 2. As Greene (2004) stressed, only when our understanding of the true nature of physical reality is deepened does a profound reconfiguration of our sense of ourselves and our experience of the universe emerge (p. 5). This reconfiguration inevitably propels us into a reconsideration of the essence and purpose of education.

Attesting the value of understanding the true nature of the universe to the appraisal of life's meaning and significance, Greene (2004) reasoned by the analogy that if evolution had proceeded differently and we had only the sense of touch, then everything we knew would come only from tactile impressions, or, if human development halted during early childhood and our emotional and intellectual skills never progressed beyond those of a five-year-old, then our assessment of life would be thoroughly compromised (p. 4). In such a case, if we suddenly gained the senses to see, hear, smell, and taste, or the freedom to develop mental faculties beyond those of a five-year-old, our collective view of the meaning and significance of life would, of necessity, change profoundly (Greene, 2004, p. 4). Following this analogy, in comparison with the true nature of consciousness, self, and reality unveiled in the above dialogue between Buddhism and quantum physics, what we know from our rudimentary perceptions of everyday life would be parallel to the mere tactile impressions, or a five-year-old's conception of the world. From this perspective, the espousal of positivism and its associated concepts of absolutism and objectivism, as well as the exclusion of spirituality from education, could be tantamount to confining human sensory perception to mere touch or restraining the human development of mental faculties from progressing beyond those of a five-year-old.

Greene's analogies, as well as the dialogue between quantum physics and Buddhism, reveal the significance of the realization of the true nature of human existence for the recognition of the essence and purpose of education.

As revealed in the dialogue between Buddhism and quantum physics—as well as in the perennial philosophy and Plato's allegory of the cave—for thousands of years, what the spiritual and religious traditions endeavor to achieve is to emancipate human beings from the imprisonment of a shadowy and deceptive phenomenal reality and to guide us to the unhidden or the Highest Idea of the upper world outside of the cave (Heidegger, 1942/1962, p. 260) by means of exposing the generally unrecognized truth that there is something beyond the facade of our everyday experience. From this perspective, the essence of spirituality could be understood as the unveiling of the ultimate truth of human existence that brings about ultimate liberation. However, over the past 300 years, since the introduction of classical physics, the gradual neglect and exclusion of spirituality from curriculum and education has further confined human beings to the prison of shadowy phenomenal reality. By means of deterring generations of human beings from turning around and accessing their true nature, this exclusion hinders the transition of humankind toward the ultimate truth of the most extremely unhidden, and consequently prevents genuine education from occurring. The resulting thoroughly compromised appraisal of human nature and the value and purpose of life not only prevents us from leading a fulfilled and meaningful life, but also becomes the root of various global crises. From this viewpoint, the revival of spirituality in education is never dispensable or optional, but rather imperative.

As discussed in Chap. 2, the deliberation of the essence of education as fundamental concerns of "our Being as men" (Heidegger, 1942/1962, p. 257) can be traced back to Plato. By virtue of apprehending Plato's allegory of the cave as not only a metaphor for education but also as an explication of the four-stage transition of the essence of truth as presumed or realized by an individual, Heidegger (1942/1962) illuminated the essential relationship between education and the truth that underpins the significance of spiritual truth for education found in educational literature. The preceding exploration of the concepts of truth in Buddhism and the dialogue between Buddhism and quantum physics resolves our questions regarding the extent of the truthfulness of Plato's doctrine of truth and the significance of the four-stage transition of the essence of truth for human beings; it also points to the fundamental role played by consciousness in dominating the possibilities of transplanting human beings into the region of their essence in pure education, wherein "everything commonly known to man up to this time and the way it was known become different" (Heidegger, 1942/1962, p. 257).

According to Heidegger (1942/1962), in Plato's own interpretation of this allegory, the things that are lying in the sunlight outside of the cave are "the image for what the real reality of beings consists in" (p. 254), and are that "through which beings display themselves in their 'outward appearance'" (p. 254). Yet this "outward appearance" (from the Greek word ἰδέα or *idea*) does not mean a mere "aspect," but rather "something of an extrusion through which each thing 'present' itself" (Heidegger, 1942/1962, p. 254). For Plato, if a person

> did not have these ideas before his gaze as the respective "outward appearance" of things, living creatures, men, numbers, and the gods, then he would never be able to perceive this or that particular thing as a house, as a tree, or as a god. (Heidegger, 1942/1962, p. 254)

Nevertheless, Heidegger (1942/1962) pointed out that a person usually believes what he or she sees is exactly this house, that tree, and everything that is, and seldom suspects that "everything holding value for him in all its familiarity as the 'real' is always seen only in the light of 'ideas'" (p. 254). From Plato's perspective, what "is supposed to be alone and really real, the immediately visible, audible, comprehensible, and calculable, still steadily remains… only the silhouette projected by the ideas, and consequently a shadow," and it is this "reality" that "keeps man in its grasp day in and day out. He lives in a prison and leaves all 'ideas' behind him" (Heidegger, 1942/1962, p. 254).

Heidegger's restatement of Plato's own interpretation of cave allegory echoes with Wheeler's theory of It from Bit, which contends that things should be viewed as carriers and manifestations of something more basic—information—that forms the irreducible kernel at the heart of reality (Greene, 2011, p. 239). The "outward appearance" or "ideas" in Plato's interpretation of this allegory can thus be understood as playing the role of the "Bit" or the information carried by particles and radiation akin to an architect's drawings waiting for being realized as a skyscraper, or the karmic seeds which have the potential of ripening into future life experiences. Heidegger (1942/1962) further argued:

> Consciousness, properly speaking, has to do with the way outward appearance manifests itself and is preserved in the brightness of its steady appearance. Through this one can view whatever each being is present as. Consciousness, properly speaking, applies to the ἰδέα. The "idea" is the outward appearance which gives a perspective upon what is present. The ἰδέα is

pure shining in the sense of the phrase "the sun shines." The "idea" does not just let something else (behind it) "make an appearance," it itself is what appears, and it depends upon itself alone for its appearing. The ἰδέα is the apparent. The essence of the idea lies in the qualities of being apparent and visible. The idea achieves presence, namely the presence of every being as what it is. Each being is continuously present in the What of beings. Presence however is really the essence of Being. Being, then for Plato, has its real essence in its What. (pp. 261–262)

Heidegger's clarification of the concepts of and relationship between consciousness and idea resonates with not only Wheeler's theory of It from Bit, but also Bohm's contention of the oneness of the thinking process and its content (Bohm, 1980, pp. 23–24), and the two truths and Consciousness-Only doctrine in Buddhism. It also reaffirms the existential significance of the "What" that resides in consciousness, particularly the essence of truth presumed or realized by an individual. From this perspective, the concern of our Being as humans is in essence the concern of human consciousness, and the essence and purpose of education as the four-stage transition of the essence of truth is in essence the transformation of consciousness—from the grasping of deceptive phenomenal everyday experiences to the conceptual understanding of the true nature of self and reality, the direct non-dualistic realization of the ultimate truth of emptiness, ultimate personal liberation, and the highest spiritual goal of the liberation of all sentient beings from the cyclic forms of existence in the suffering-laden shadowy phenomenal world.

Following the realization of the essence and purpose of education as consciousness transformation (a realization informed and supported by Huebner's and other curriculum theorists' work as well as Heidegger's interpretation of Plato's cave allegory, Buddhism, and quantum physics), in the next chapter, I investigate into the Buddhist spiritual practices of consciousness transformation for educational use and explore how we might begin to understand curriculum as an experience of consciousness transformation.

NOTES

1. "Right view" or "right-view" is the translation of *sammā-diṭṭhi* or *samyag-dṛṣṭi* and refers to the "right seeing." The rendering of right view as "right views" is not accepted, "since it is not a matter of holding 'views' (opinions) but of 'seeing things as they really are'" (Walshe, 2007, para. 5).

According to Fuller (2005), "the notion of 'view' or 'opinion' (*diṭṭhi*) as an obstacle to 'seeing things as they are' (*yathābhūtadassana*) is a central concept in Buddhist thought" (p. 1). While Buddhist literature talks about right-view (*sammā-diṭṭhi*) and wrong-views (*micchā-diṭṭhi*), right-view does not stand in opposition to or correct wrong-views, neither does it mean the relinquishment of all views (Fuller, 2005, p. 1). Rather, right-view is:

> A detached order of seeing, completely different from the attitude of holding to any view, wrong or right. Right-view is not a doctrine, a correct proposition... Right-view is practiced, not adopted or believed in... A correct knowledge of doctrine should not involve attachment. A true statement, if it is an object of attachment, is *micchā-diṭṭhi* [wrong-views], even though it is still true. Wrong-view is a form of greed and attachment, right-view the cessation of greed and attachment. Right-view signifies the cessation of craving, not the rejection of all views. (Fuller, 2005, p. 1)

Usually, our attachment to views or opinions originates from our inclination to hypostatize, reify, or "thingify" concepts, and then take what is only a useful form of speech to refer to some absolute and real entity. For a more detailed discussion on hypostatization and the Middle Way approach to attaining the right view of both the ultimate truth and phenomenal truth, please refer to Chap. 4.

2. *Yogacara* (*Yogācāra*, in Sanskrit) is composed of *yoga*, which means discipline, and *cara*, meaning practice. *Yogacara* Buddhism, then, is in essence a Buddhist practice of discipline (Butler, 2010, pp. 33–34). According to Wei (1973), centered at the doctrine of *vijñapti-mātra* or *cittmata* (usually translated as consciousness-only or mind-only), which means "all is mind only" (p. 39) or "nothing exists except in the consciousness" (p. 1), *Yogacara* is called *Wei-shih* (mere-consciousness) school of Buddhism by the Chinese (p. 1). However, some modern researchers object to the translation of *vijñapti-mātra* or *cittmata* as consciousness-only or mind-only and their accompanying labels of absolute idealism or idealistic monism, and suggest *representation-only* is a better translation (Kochumuttom, 1989, p. 5). In the context of western academia, *Yogacara* texts have been available for 50 years or so, and since then, "there has been a debate as to how *Yogacara* Buddhism should be interpreted" (Butler, 2010, p. 33). For example, while Lusthaus (2002) interpreted *Yogacara* as Buddhist phenomenology and indicated that "idealism is too vague to be meaningful" (p. 4) and that the commonly used idealistic positions are inappropriate for *Yogacara* (p. 5), Butler (2010) argued that while Lusthaus is correct in recognizing the phenomenological aspect of *Yogacara*, he incorrectly

believed in that *Yogacara* is phenomenology alone (p. 39). For Butler (2010), the idealistic and phenomenological claims of *Yogacara* are not mutually exclusive, and one cannot deny that *Yogacara* constitute idealism. He emphasized, however, that "Yogacara, though similar in many regards with idealisms in the West, must be viewed as its own form of idealism" (Butler, 2010, p. 42).

3. As a Buddhist philosopher, Vasubandhu (fourth to fifth century C.E.) was a great light at the peak of India's resplendent Gupta empire (Gold, 2015). He set a new standard for *Yogacara* philosophy in three concise works, and, thereafter, *Yogacara* became the mainstream Buddhist metaphysics in India for half a millennium (Gold, 2015).

4. The Sanskrit *Śūnyatā* most often translated as emptiness; other translations includes non-substantiality, void, latency, or relativity.

5. In Buddhist understanding and some Western schools of scientific thought, "only something that doesn't change, that can't be affected by time and circumstance, or broken down into smaller, connected parts, can be said to be absolutely real" (Mingyur, 2007, p. 63).

6. Nagarjuna "is a Buddhist philosopher of the second century and a key figure in the development of Mahayana Buddhism in ancient India. Few figure in the history of Buddhism stand out more prominently than Nagarjuna" (Walser, 2005, p. 1). He "is prominently represented in the transmission lineages for both the Zen tradition and the various Tantric traditions. He has been cited as a source of authority by personages as diverse as Tsongkhapa in Tibet and Dogen and Shinran in Japan" (p. 1).

7. Also translated as Tsongkhapa, the founder of the Gelug school of Tibetan Buddhism.

8. The Sanskrit *samsara* literally means "wheel" or "circle", and "refers to the wheel or circle of unhappiness, a habit of running around in circle, chasing after the same experiences again and again, each time expecting a different result" (Mingyur, 2007, p. 117).

9. *Yogacara* philosophy defines consciousness as eightfold. According to Wei (1973), the first six consciousnesses include the five senses consciousnesses—the sight, hearing, smell, taste, and touch consciousnesses—and the sixth consciousness, also known as sense-center consciousness or *Manovijnana* (p. lviii). These are consciousnesses that perceive and discriminate between spheres of objects (Wei, 1973, p. lviii). The seventh consciousness, also known as thought-center consciousness or *Manas* consciousness, is consciousness that cogitates or deliberates (Wei, 1973, p. lvii). The eighth consciousness, also known as *Alaya* consciousness or storehouse consciousness or *Alayavijnana*, is consciousness whose fruits (retribution) mature at varying times (Wei, 1973, p. lvii). The *Alaya* consciousness can be understood as the synthesis of the Subconscious Mind

and the Supermind (Wei, 1973, p. lx). It is the most important among the eight kinds of consciousness. It actively stores up the potential or "seeds" (*Bijas*) for the development or activities of the other seven consciousnesses, and is also passively habituated or "perfumed" by defiling dharmas of the other seven consciousnesses, thus creating more "seeds" in it (Wei, 1973, p. lxi). The *Manas* consciousness "has the nature and character of cogitation or intellection" (Wei, 1973, p. lxxii). This consciousness takes the eighth consciousness as its object and its supporting basis for manifesting itself. It "perpetually thinks about the ego (Atman), to which it clings" and has a "close relationship with the four fundamental *Klesas* or vexing passions (source of affliction and delusion)" (Wei, 1973, p. lxxii).

10. The two levels of attachment—craving and grasping—are "the critical factors in actualizing and ripening karmic seeds, and thereby bringing about rebirth and all the experience of cyclic existence" (Sopa, 2005, p. 335).
11. According to Tibetan exposition of *Madhyamaka*, dependent arising happens at three levels: causal dependence, whole/part dependence, and conceptual dependence (Thompson, 2015, p. 330).
12. A *bodhisattva* is a spiritual practitioner of Mahayana Buddhism with spontaneous motivation of *bodhicitta*, meaning "the desire to attain complete enlightenment in order to be able to benefit all sentient beings" (Sopa, 2008, p. 6).
13. In Sanskrit, *paramita* literally means crossing over to the other shore. In Mahayana Buddhism, the *six paramitas* are the six spiritual practices that ferry one across the sea of suffering and mortality to the other shore of *nirvana* (Hsuan-Tsang, 659/1973, p. 675).
14. According to bodhisattva Maitreya, the six perfections or six *paramitas* can also be categorized into two groups: the first three perfections are the basis for helping other sentient beings, while the last two result in one's own goal of emancipation. The fourth perfection, joyous perseverance, is included in both groups (Sopa, 2008, p. 238).
15. In 2002, Young's double-slit experiment with single electrons was voted by readers of *Physics World* as "the most beautiful experiment [of all time] in physics" (Rosa, 2012). Rosa (2012) quotes historian-philosopher Robert Crease's observation that "the double-slit experiment with electrons possesses all of the aspects of beauty most frequently mentioned by readers… [and] is transformative, being able to convince even the most die-hard sceptics of the truth of quantum mechanics" (p. 180).
16. According to the *Avatamsaka Sutra*, *Indra*'s net is brought into existence by the Hindu god *Indra* and is used to describe the interconnectedness and interpenetration of the universe (Mingyur, 2007, p. 174). At every connection of *Indra*'s infinite net "hangs a magnificently polished and infinitely faceted jewel, which reflects in each of its facets all the facets of every

other jewel in the net" (Mingyur, 2007, p. 174). Given that the net, the number of jewels, and the facets of every jewel are all infinite, the number of reflections in each jewel is also infinite (Mingyur, 2007, pp. 174–175). Additionally, "when any jewel in this infinite net is altered in any way, all of the other jewels in the net change too" (Mingyur, 2007, pp. 174–175).

REFERENCES

Bohm, D. (1980). *Wholeness and the Implicate Order*. New York, NY: Routledge.
Bohm, D. (1990). A New Theory of the Relationship of Mind and Matter. *Philosophical Psychology*, 3(2), 271–286.
Butler, S. (2010). Idealism in Yogācāra Buddhism. *The Hilltop Review*, 4(1), 6.
Chang, G. C. C. (1983). *A Treasury of Mahāyāna Sūtras: Selections from the Mahāratnakāta Sūtra*. Pennsylvania, PA: The Pennsylvania State University Press.
Cho, A. (2010). The First Quantum Machine. *Science*, 330(6011), 1604.
Choi, D. (2011). *Mechanism of Consciousness During Life, Dream and After-Death*. Bloomington, IN: AuthorHouse.
Fuchs, C. A. (2016). On Participatory Realism. *Information and Interaction: Eddington, Wheeler, and the Limits of Knowledge*, 113.
Fuchs, C. A., & Schack, R. (2014). QBism and the Greeks: Why a Quantum State Does Not Represent an Element of Physical Reality. *Physica Scripta*, 90(1), 015104.
Fuller, P. (2005). *The Notion of Diṭṭhi in Theravāda Buddhism*. New York, NY: RoutledgeCurzon.
Gefter, A. (2015, June 4). A Private View of Quantum Reality. *QuantaMagazine*. Retrieved from https://www.quantamagazine.org/quantum-bayesianism-explained-by-its-founder-20150604/
Gold, J. C. (2015). Vasubandhu. In E. N. Zalta (Ed.), *The Stanford Encyclopedia of Philosophy*. Retrieved from http://plato.stanford.edu/archives/sum2015/entries/vasubandhu/
Greene, B. (2004). *The Fabric of the Cosmos: Space, Time, and the Texture of Reality*. New York, NY: Alfred A. Knopf.
Greene, B. (2011). *The Hidden Reality*. New York, NY: Alfred A. Knopf.
Heidegger, M. (1962). Plato's Doctrine of Truth (J. Barlow, trans.). In B. William & D. A. Henry (Eds.), *Philosophy in the Twentieth Century* (Vol. 3, pp. 251–270). New York, NY: Random House. (Original work published 1942).
Hsuan-Tsang (1973). *Ch'eng Wei-Shi Lun: The Doctrine of Mere-Consciousness* (T. Wei, trans.). Hong Kong, China: The Ch'eng Wei-shih Lun Publication Committee. (Original work published 659). Retrieved from http://www.dhalbi.org/dhalbi/html_t/authors/author_main.php?p_id=8
Kaku, M. (1994). *Hyperspace: A Scientific Odyssey Through Parallel Universes, Time Warps, and the Tenth Dimension*. Oxford: Oxford University Press.

Kaku, M. (2005). *Parallel Worlds: A Journey Through Creation, Higher Dimensions, and the Future of the Cosmos.* New York, NY: Random House.

Kochumuttom, T. A. (1989). *A Buddhist Doctrine of Experience: A New Translation and Interpretation of the Works of Vasubandhu, the Yogacarin.* Delhi: Motilal Banarsidass.

Lee, K. C., Sprague, M. R., Sussman, B. J., Nunn, J., Langford, N. K., Jin, X. M., ... Jaksch, D. (2011). Entangling Macroscopic Diamonds at Room Temperature. *Science, 334*(6060), 1253–1256.

Lusthaus, D. (2002). *Buddhist Phenomenology: A Philosophical Investigation of Yogacara Buddhism and the Ch'eng Wei-shih Lun.* New York, NY: RoutledgeCurzon.

Miller, J. P. (2007). *The Holistic Curriculum* (2nd ed.). Toronto, ON: University of Toronto Press.

Mingyur, Y. (2007). *The Joy of Living: Unlocking the Secret and Science of Happiness.* New York, NY: Harmony Books.

Narlikar, J. V. (2013). John Archibald Wheeler: Man with Picturesque Imagination. *Resonance, 18*(1), 22–28.

Newland, G. (2009). *Introduction to Emptiness: As Taught in Tsong-kha-pa's Great Treatise on the Stages of the Path* (2nd ed.). Ithaca, NY: Snow Lion Publications.

Rosa, R. (2012). The Merli–Missiroli–Pozzi Two-Slit Electron-Interference Experiment. *Physics in Perspective, 14*, 178–195.

Siderits, M. (2007). *Buddhism as Philosophy: An Introduction.* Aldershot: Ashgate Pub.

Sopa, L. (2005). *Steps on the Path to Enlightenment: A Commentary on Tsongkhapa's Lamrim Chenmo. Volume II: Karma.* Somerville, MA: Wisdom Publications.

Sopa, L. (2008). *Steps on the Path to Enlightenment: A Commentary on Tsongkhapa's Lamrim Chenmo. Volume III: The Way of the Bodhisattva.* Somerville, MA: Wisdom Publications.

Talbot, M. (2011). *The Holographic Universe* (2nd ed.). New York, NY: Harper Perennial.

Theckedath, K. K. (1997). David Bohm and the Holomovement. *Social Scientist, 25*(7/8), 57–67.

Thompson, E. (2015). *Waking, Dreaming, Being: Self and Consciousness in Neuroscience, Meditation, and Philosophy.* New York, NY: Columbia University Press.

Tsong-kha-pa. (2000). *The Great Treatise on the Stages of the Path to Enlightenment* (Vol. 1, The Lamrim Chenmo Translation Committee, trans.). Ithaca, NY: Snow Lion Publications. (Original work published 1402).

Vedral, V. (2011). Living in a Quantum World. *Scientific American, 304*, 38–43.

Vienna University of Technology. (2015, April 27). Is the Universe a Hologram? *ScienceDaily.* Retrieved from www.sciencedaily.com/releases/2015/04/150427101633.htm

Walser, J. (2005). *Nāgārjuna in Context: Mahāyāna Buddhism and Early Indian Culture*. New York, NY: Columbia University Press.

Walshe, M. O. (Trans.). (2007). *Kaccaayanagotto Sutta: Kaccaayana [On Right View]*. Retrieved from http://www.accesstoinsight.org/tipitaka/sn/sn12/sn12.015.wlsh.html

Wei, T. (1973). Introduction. In Hsuan-Tsang, *Ch'eng Wei-shi Lun: The Doctrine of Mere-Consciousness* (T. Wei, trans.). Hong Kong, China: The Ch'eng Wei-shih Lun Publication Committee. (Original work published 659). Retrieved from http://www.dhalbi.org/dhalbi/html_t/authors/author_main.php?p_id=8

Yin-shun. (1998). *The Way to Buddhahood* (W. H. Yeung, trans.). Somerville, MA: Wisdom Publications. (Original work published 1960).

PART III

Consciousness Transformation

CHAPTER 4

The Concepts and Process of Consciousness Transformation

4.1 Introduction

In the preceding chapter, the dialogue between Buddhism and quantum physics expanded our understanding of the nature of consciousness, self, and reality, and increased our confidence in the truthfulness of Plato's doctrine of truth and the doctrine of truth in Buddhism which is in accordance with the core wisdom common to various spiritual and religious traditions (as exhibited in the perennial philosophy). This expanded understanding and increased confidence provide us deepened insights into the essence and purpose of education as the transformation of consciousness toward the conceptual and direct non-dualistic realization of the ultimate truth of emptiness, ultimate personal liberation, and the highest spiritual goal of the liberation of all sentient beings from the cyclic forms of existence in the suffering-laden shadowy phenomenal world. Following this realization, I ask: How might we further understand the concepts and process of consciousness transformation? What are the main barriers to be overcome in that process? What are the characteristics of various stages of progress? What disciplines and practices are necessary in various stages? What are the features of these disciplines and practices? How might we facilitate the transformation of consciousness in educational contexts?

To seek answers to these questions, keeping the idea of a spiritual path with educational intent foremost in my mind, in this chapter, I draw on the doctrine of *Yogacara* (the Consciousness-Only school of Buddhism) and *Madhyamaka* (the Middle Way school of Buddhism) and explore the main concepts and process of the Buddhist spiritual path of consciousness transformation to gain a panoramic view of a spiritual path for educational use. These concepts and process of consciousness transformation include the main barriers to be overcome, the characteristics of various stages, the main spiritual disciplines and practices at each stage, and the core approach for attaining the goal of consciousness transformation.

4.2 The Two Barriers to Consciousness Transformation

As discussed in Chap. 3, from the Buddhist perspective, the right view (*sammā-diṭṭhi* or *samyag-dṛṣṭi*) of both the ultimate and conventional truths—meaning the correct seeing of emptiness and a proper understanding of the law of cause and effect of karma—is the basis for various spiritual goals and all positive, happy, and blissful experiences. Nonetheless, owing to our ignorance of both truths and the habitual wrong view that clings firmly to the dichotomy of a subjective self (who takes or grasps) and an objective universe (that is taken or grasped) as absolute, essential and independent existence, we constantly deposit contaminated karmic seeds of afflictive and noetic barriers that carry the potential to ripen into various cyclic forms of existence and trap us in the imprisonment of *samsara* (Hsuan-Tsang, 659/1973, p. 671). In *Yogacara* doctrine, the karmic seeds of afflictive barriers and noetic barriers that originate respectively from the attachment to a subjective self and an objective universe as absolute, essential, and independent existence are identified as the underlying causes of worldliness (Hsuan-Tsang, 659/1973, p. 703). The attachment to a sharp subject–object dichotomy[1] that posits the subject and object as absolute, essential, and mutual independent existence, therefore, is the main characteristic of the shackled prisoners described in the first stage of Plato's cave allegory, and the afflictive and noetic barriers that originate from this dualistic worldview are recognized as the main barriers to be overcome in the process of consciousness transformation. While these two barriers are not different in nature, their functions are distinct, and although afflictive barriers necessarily associate with noetic barriers as their basis, the reverse is not true. According to Hsuan-Tsang (659/1973), an afflictive barrier perturbs and torments the bodies and minds of sentient beings and acts as a barrier to *nirvana*, and a noetic barrier offers a false view of the external reality which, along with doubt, ignorance, desire, hate, and conceit obscures the true nature of the known world and acts as a barrier to perfect transcendental wisdom (*Bodhi*) (p. 671). Yet, according to Hsuan-Tsang (659/1973), through the process of persistent cultivation and transformation of consciousness, the karmic seeds of these two barriers can be suppressed and then totally cut off and cleared away, and when this is attained, two fruits of Buddhahood will be experienced (p. 705). One of the two fruits is *Mahaparinirvana*, also known as Buddha Nature, meaning the original state of consciousness not contaminated by the wrong views rooted in the ignorance of the ultimate and conventional truths (Hsuan-Tsang, 659/1973, p. 759). The other is *Mahabodhi*, which describes the totality of the mental attributes associated with the perfection of four transcendental wisdoms, which are the uncontaminated functioning of Buddha Nature (Hsuan-Tsang, 659/1973, p. 767) and will be explored in the following section. The whole doctrine of Consciousness-Only "is established in order to enable sentient beings to experience these two fruits resulting from this process of 'revolution' or 'inner transformation'" (Hsuan-Tsang, 659/1973, p. 705).

4.3 The Transformation of Consciousness into Four Transcendental Wisdoms

In the doctrine of *Yogacara*, human consciousness is classified into eight consciousnesses: sight, sound, smell, taste, touch feeling, mind, thinking (*Manas*), and storage (*Alaya*) (Choi, 2011, p. vii). The process of the suppression and eradication of karmic seeds of afflictive and noetic barriers is prescribed as a five-stage gradual path of consciousness transformation that transforms the mental attributes of the first five, the sixth, the *Manas*, and the *Alaya* consciousnesses respectively into the perfection of four transcendental wisdoms, including the perfect achievement wisdom, the profound contemplation wisdom, the universal equality wisdom, and the great mirror wisdom (Hsuan-Tsang, 659/1973, pp. 665, 759, 767, 769). The perfect achievement wisdom "manifests itself through the desire to promote the welfare and happiness of all sentient beings in a diversity of fictitious actions of the body, of the voice, and of the mind" (Choi, 2011, p. 90). This wisdom is regarded as important in this material world, for although this world is not the ultimate reality and there is no true and essential self within it, it cannot be ignored (Choi, 2011, p. 90). The profound contemplation wisdom "discerns in excellent ways the peculiar and common characteristics of all dharmas" (Choi, 2011, pp. 90–91). It strips away all doubts and can manifest itself in infinite activities without any hindrance and enable sentient beings to obtain blessings and joys (Choi, 2011, p. 91). The universal equality wisdom bears on both the ultimate and phenomenal aspects of reality (Hsuan-Tsang, 659/1973, p. 777) and perceives the identity of all phenomena and "the complete equality between its own self and other sentient beings" (Choi, 2011, p. 91). The great mirror wisdom is "entirely dissociated from all mental discrimination. Like a mirror, such wisdom reflects the absolute reality of all things as they are" (Choi, 2011, p. 91).

The perfection of the four transcendental wisdoms not only signifies the fulfillment of *bodhicitta* (Sopa, 2008, pp. 6, 17, 99, 189)—which, as explained previously, is the aspiration to attain the highest spiritual goal of Buddhahood for the liberation all sentient beings—but also represents the recovery of various spiritual qualities intrinsic to our Buddha Nature. By means of providing us with an overview of the spiritual qualities and achievement of a Buddha, these four wisdoms illuminate the transcendental human potentialities beyond our current forms of existence. The recognition of such transcendental possibilities is conducive to both the deliberation and improvisation of curriculum as an experience of consciousness transformation. However, in contemplating the four transcendental wisdoms, it is important to bear in mind Lama Anagarika Govinda's reminder that wisdom should not be comprehended as "merely intellectually formulated doctrine, proclaimed at a certain point in human history, but a movement which reveals its deepest nature in contact with different conditions and circumstances of human life and on every new level of human consciousness" (Lemkow, 1990, p. 17). Additionally, as exhibited in the four transcendental wisdoms, "buddhahood is not just a blank mind; it is a combination of many perfect things" (Sopa, 2008, p. 201). With a proper understanding of the dependently arising nature of all phenomena, including Buddhahood, we can be certain that such a complex constellation of perfect spiritual qualities requires multiple causes and multiple lifetimes' cultivation.

4.4 THE FIVE-STAGE GRADUAL PATH OF CONSCIOUSNESS TRANSFORMATION IN BUDDHISM

Akin to the four-stage transition of the essence of truth in Plato's allegory of the cave, in the doctrine of *Yogacara*, the gradual[2] spiritual path of consciousness transformation toward the perfection of four transcendental wisdoms is composed of five stages, including the stage of moral provisioning (the path of preparation), the stage of intensified efforts (the path of application), the stage of unimpeded penetrating understanding (the path of seeing), the stage of exercising cultivation (the path of meditation), and the stage of ultimate realization (the path of no more learning) (Choi, 2011, p. 91; Hsuan-Tsang, 659/1973, p. 665). While the last three stages are identified as supramundane paths, the first two are usually referred to as worldly paths (Choi, 2011, p. 92), and are therefore of particular educational significance.

In the first stage, the stage of moral provisioning (also known as the path of preparation), the spiritual practitioner develops a profound conceptual understanding of the whole doctrine of Consciousness-Only, including the two truths doctrine and the four noble truths explored earlier, a panoramic view of the whole spiritual path, the significance of the cultivation of *bodhicitta*, the nature of the spiritual approach and practices, the obstacles eliminated by these spiritual practices, and the positive results brought about by these practices. On one hand, with a view to attaining enlightenment for oneself, the spiritual practitioner "accumulates diverse and excellent 'moral provisions'" (Hsuan-Tsang, 659/1973, p. 669). On the other hand, for the benefit of others, the practitioner "makes constant efforts to seek the deliverance of sentient beings" (Hsuan-Tsang, 659/1973, p. 669). The significance of the accumulation of moral provisions is profound. In his kindness and skillfulness to make the accumulation of merit and moral provisions easier, Buddha condensed all negative actions of body, mind, and speech into ten non-virtues (Sopa, 2005, p. 45). The ten non-virtues are covetousness, malice, wrong view, lying, slander, harsh speech, senseless speech, killing, stealing, and sexual misconduct (Sopa, 2005, pp. 45–46). The ten virtues are actions taken to oppose and prevent the ten non-virtues (Sopa, 2005, p. 45). As shown in previous exploration of the two truths and the truth of the path embodied in the practices of the three trainings and six perfections, rather than imposing meaningless restraints or control, the goal of Buddha "is to protect sentient beings, to free them from the cycle of misery, to lead them to the highest bliss" (Sopa, 2005, p. 43). According to the Buddha, "just as the earth is the foundation of all things that exist upon the earth, practicing the ten virtuous actions is the foundation of all worldly and supramundane goals" (Sopa, 2005, p. 41). Relying on a profound conceptual understanding of, and deep faith in, the whole Consciousness-Only doctrine, the main practices in this stage are the six perfections (*paramitas*) (Hsuan-Tsang, 659/1973, p. 675). As discussed earlier, the six perfections are generosity, ethical discipline, patience, joyous perseverance, meditative stabilization, and wisdom (Sopa, 2008, p. 8).

Although the practices of the six perfections are emphasized as the main practices in only the first stage of the five-stage gradual spiritual path of consciousness transformation, in the treatise *Lamrim Chenmo* (The Great Treatise on the Stages of the Path to Enlightenment), finished in 1402 following Buddha's teachings in the Perfection of the Wisdom and other sutras and the great bodhisattva Maitreya's sixfold exposition in the Ornament for the Mahayana Sutras, Tsong-kha-pa elucidated the sufficiency[3] of the six perfections for fulfilling all of individual sentient beings' temporary and ultimate spiritual goals (Sopa, 2008, p. 233; Tsong-kha-pa, 1402/2000, p. 17).

After the spiritual practitioner has well equipped him or herself with the spiritual provisions of merits/virtues and transcendental wisdoms, he or she proceeds into the second stage—the stage of intensified efforts (the path of application) (Hsuan-Tsang, 659/1973, p. 679). In this stage, aiming to embark on the path of spiritual discernment, the practitioner learns to suppress and eradicate the conception of subject–object duality by making preparatory efforts conducive to decisive distinction (Hsuan-Tsang, 659/1973, p. 679). These efforts are grounded on *four reflections* on the names, essences, self-nature, and differences of things and ideas, as well as the *four exact realizations* that these four concepts do not exist apart from our consciousness and that the process of consciousness that knows them does not have absolute and independent existence either (Hsuan-Tsang, 659/1973, pp. 679, 681). The practices of this stage also include meditation on the four noble truths (Choi, 2011, p. 92). The perfection of this stage comes when the dualistic subject–object distinction vanishes and non-discriminating transcendental wisdom is attained. In this state, the practitioner no longer clings to the objective world, because "both the object to be apprehended and the act of apprehending by consciousness are absent" (Hsuan-Tsang, 659/1973, p. 687). This means the practitioner experiences the ultimate reality of emptiness and oneness directly and enters into the third stage (Hsuan-Tsang, 659/1973, p. 687). Given the worldly nature of the stage of moral provisioning (the path of preparation) and the stage of intensified efforts (the path of application), the main practices in these two stages are of great educational significance and will be revisited later.

In the third stage, the stage of unimpeded penetrating understanding (or the path of seeing), by developing the five spiritual faculties of faith, effort, mindfulness, concentration, and wisdom to the utmost, the practitioner cures his or her doubt, laziness, heedlessness, distraction, and ignorance, and perfects true insights into ultimate reality (Choi, 2011, p. 93).

After attaining the perfection of true insights into ultimate reality, the practitioner moves into the fourth stage, exercising cultivation (also known as the path of meditation), and constantly cultivates the non-discriminating wisdom (Choi, 2011, p. 93). Although the practitioner practices meditation from the first stage onward, in this stage, the practitioner begins to "gain certain experiences and realizations that were not present previously" (Choi, 2011, p. 93). The perfection of this stage comes when the aforementioned four transcendental wisdoms are all achieved. Thereafter, the practitioner enters into the fifth stage of ultimate realization (also known as the path of no more learning) equated with the full enlightenment of Buddhahood (Choi, 2011, pp. 93–94).

4.5 The Union of Wisdom and Method

The above exploration of the five-stage gradual path of consciousness transformation makes clear that a profound conceptual understanding of and deep faith in spiritual truths are crucial for the unshackling of the chains that confine the prisoners depicted in Plato's allegory of the cave and for the liberation of their sights from the captivity of mere shadows. Nevertheless, this is not yet real liberation. As shown in the second stage of Plato's allegory of the cave, the newly unchained prisoner in the cave would be perplexed and believe the shadows he formerly saw to be more real and more unhidden than the objects now shown to him, and would try to turn back if he were forced to look at the firelight itself (Heidegger, 1942/1962, pp. 252–253). Similarly, the mere conceptual understanding of spiritual truths cannot genuinely emancipate us from the imprisonment in shadowy cyclic forms of existence. Genuine transformation and liberation—overcoming habitual ways of thinking and doing that are entrenched in an absolutistic and objectivistic dualistic subject–object worldview—requires the union of wisdom and compassion. Wisdom is mainly attained through meditative insights (the accumulation of wisdom, or the wisdom-side practices) and compassion is embodied in the everyday spiritual practices motivated by *bodhicitta* (the accumulation of merit, or the method-side practices). Without this union, even for one who has attained a profound conceptual understanding of the whole Consciousness-Only doctrine, or has had profound experiences in meditation, the components of deeds and view could potentially remain mutually exclusive and one might "never develop a long-lasting and very forceful certainty about both the view and deeds" (Tsong-kha-pa, 1402/2004, p. 96). In a process of profound self-inquiry, Sean Park (2014) recalled the difficulties he once encountered in his spiritual practice and shared his reflection that "unconsciously, I had reified my meditation practice into something that took me out of the world and away from deeper parts of myself... I thought I could meditate the pain away" (p. 29). In a 1959 unpublished manuscript titled *The Inner Experience*, Thomas Merton asserted that "contemplation is man's highest and most essential spiritual activity. It is his most creative and dynamic affirmation of his divine sonship... Solitude is necessary for spiritual freedom" (Miller, 2007, p. 28). According to Miller (2007), however, Merton maintained that the spiritual freedom needs to be put back "to work in the service of a love in which there is no longer subjection or slavery. Mere withdrawal, without the return to freedom in action, would lead to a static and death-like inertia of the spirit" (p. 28) rather than to awakening. Huebner (1987/1999b) also indicated that for the majority of people nowadays, the practice of the presence of God is limited to moments of prayer and worship (p. 388); yet for Brother Lawrence, a barefoot lay brother in the 1600s, "times set aside for prayer were not different from the other times... because his greatest business did not divert him from God" (as cited in Huebner, 1987/1999b, p. 388).

The requirement of the union of wisdom-side practices (the accumulation of wisdom) and method-side practices (the accumulation of merit) for consciousness transformation was emphasized by Buddha and numerous bodhisattvas, and was well summarized by Tsong-kha-pa (Tsong-kha-pa, 1402/2004, pp. 85–99). In his refutation of such discourses as "everything to do with method is not an actual path to buddhahood" (Tsong-kha-pa, 1402/2004, p. 96), Tsong-kha-pa clarified that, in Mahayana scriptures, Buddhahood, also known as non-abiding *nirvana*, is the highest spiritual goal that does not abide in the two extremes—*samsara* (the attachment to the phenomenal aspect of reality) or the peace of *nirvana* (the attachment to the empty aspect of reality) (Sopa, 2008, p. 202). To avoid abiding in the extreme of *samsara*, one requires the practice of the accumulation of wisdom; to avoid abiding in *nirvana*, one needs the practice of the accumulation of merit (Sopa, 2008, p. 202). The accumulation of wisdom is aimed at cutting the root of *samsara*—the primary ignorance originating from an egotistic and dualistic view that grasps at an absolute and essential self as being independent of the universe—by means of meditating on the deep realization of the ultimate truth of emptiness with no dual perception (Sopa, 2008, p. 203). However, "by itself this deep meditation on ultimate truth of emptiness does not lead to buddhahood; mere cessation of one's own ignorance cannot help others" (Sopa, 2008, p. 202). Without concern for other sentient beings, not only would the multiple causes for a complex of spiritual qualities of Buddhahood be missing, but after attaining *nirvana*, one might simply remain in the enjoyment of that state for eons and eons rather than progressing toward Buddhahood (Sopa, 2008, p. 202). Therefore, as revealed in the four transcendental wisdoms, the highest spiritual goal of Buddhahood for the liberation of all sentient beings "is not just a mere negation or perfect cessation; it is also a combination of various positive qualities" (Sopa, 2008, p. 202) and requires also the accumulation of merit, or method-side practices—the practices based on love and compassion and motivated by *bodhicitta*, such as the six perfections—as "the causes for one to become a basis of enjoyment for all sentient beings" (Sopa, 2008, p. 203). This means if we want to take responsibility for other sentient beings' liberation in addition to our own liberation, we must train ourselves in the practices of *bodhicitta* along with wisdom (Sopa, 2008, p. 24).

As Buddha said, "wisdom not held by the method is bondage. Wisdom held by the method is liberation. Methods not held by wisdom are bondage. Methods held by wisdom are liberation" (Sopa, 2008, p. 204). However, this "does not mean that wisdom becomes compassion or that compassion becomes wisdom. *Held* means that, within the mental continuum, the two assist each other all the time" (Sopa, 2008, p. 204). For example, if one contemplates *bodhicitta* before practicing a meditation on emptiness, although no *bodhicitta* would be present in a meditating state of mind during the meditation session, the whole meditation is imbued with, and empowered by, the wish to attain enlightenment for the benefit of all sentient beings (Sopa, 2008, p. 215). This instantiates the meaning of wisdom "held" by method (Sopa, 2008, p. 215). In turn, the openness, clarity, and power brought about by the direct realization of emptiness attained in meditation can be carried over to infuse the method-side practices of generosity, ethical discipline, and so on (Sopa, 2008, p. 215). In this way, method is held by wisdom. The question, therefore, is not whether anything to do with method is an actual path to Buddhahood, but rather how wisdom and method should be applied in a way that will lead to genuine liberation rather than more bondage, and what is really meant by the union of the wisdom-side and method-side practices.

In the educational context, owing to the rejection of spiritual wisdom and the taken-for-granted attachment to the shadowy phenomenal aspect of reality, the existential significance of the accumulation of wisdom is largely neglected and the means and ends of the accumulation of merit, in the absence of spiritual wisdom, are usually misconstrued. For instance, the moral and ethical doctrine, rather than being comprehended as pointing to a pathway for approaching and living the ultimate truth of human existence, is usually dogmatized and degraded, and risks being easily dismissed as merely a means of social control or the building of personal reputation. More often than not, people either observe moral and ethical doctrine passively, by virtue of blindly following such belief systems, or practice it actively—yet in a way that nurtures only a dualistic and absolute sense of self and reality. In other words, in the absence of spiritual wisdom that knows emptiness and the oneness of self and reality, the promotion of moral and ethical doctrine can be futile, and the method-side practices or the accumulation of merit alone can possibly create only increased paranoia and fragmentation and result in more bondage rather than in genuine transformation toward ultimate truth and genuine liberation. As Kumar (2013) argued, the nature of existential problems, such as fear, is that "they are always in the present; and when they are approached with a method [that is not held by wisdom], which employs the past, they are never comprehended in their totality" (p. 88). Without comprehending both the phenomenal and ultimate aspects of an existential situation of a specific individual in their totality in the present, a method—be it moral doctrine, psychological analysis, strategies informed by behavioral science, rational analysis, or even the six perfections—which misconceives the three spheres of agent, object, and recipient as having certain absolute, independent, and essential attributes and existence (rather than as being dependently arising and signifying infinite possibilities), in Kumar's (2013) words, can at most "bring about a 'modification' in the existing psychological state, which does not qualify as real change" (p. 88). This is why Buddha would admonish us in the *Three Heaps Sutra* to "confess each of these: descending to the level of objective existence and giving gifts, observing ethical discipline because of a belief in the supremacy of ethics, etc." (Tsong-kha-pa, 1402/2004, p. 95). In this passage, Buddha cautioned us against "falling into objectifying" (Sopa, 2008, p. 217), and hinted that "it is evil to practice any perfection motivated by a perverted view that holds the self to exist absolutely" (Sopa, 2008, p. 217); "any action, even the perfections [*paramitas*], is evil if it is done with this kind of misunderstanding" (Sopa, 2008, p. 217). Such an action is "evil" in the sense that such objectifying practices only hinder us from penetrating and experiencing the ultimate nature of self and reality and, as a result, perpetuate the relentless cycle of suffering-laden *samsaric* experiences. After all, even the six perfections themselves "are empty of inherent existence; they are relatively or nominally existence. The deed itself, the object, and the doer of the deed do not absolutely exist as they appear to our sense or thoughts; they exist phenomenally or dependently" (Sopa, 2008, p. 220).

Nonetheless, acting without falling into objectifying—for example, generosity with no object, or non-perceptual generosity—"does not mean not having a thought to give" (Sopa, 2008, p. 216). Rather, "the correct meaning of objectless or nonperceptual generosity is giving gifts without hypostasizing or superimposing the idea that something or someone exists in an ultimate real way" (Sopa, 2008, p. 216). In such objectless or nonperceptual generosity, the sharp subject–object distinction and preconceived notions give way, truthful knowing occurs, and the three spheres of agent, object, and recipient are equally perceived as dependently arising and carrying infinite possibilities—each is part of the whole and each encompasses the magnificent whole. The concept of "non-perceptual" can also be understood from the perspective of what Krishnamurti referred to as "observe without observer or Ego" (Kumar, 2013, p. 86). In such pure observation, "we meet life directly with each moment rather than through the screen of our past experiences... which inhibits a clear perception of things as they are" (Kumar, 2013, pp. 86–87).

The conception of "objectless"—meaning with no object, nonperceptual—seems easy to understand, yet in practice, given our habitual ways of thinking and speaking which are prone to hypostatization—meaning "the process of reification or 'thing-ifying': taking what is actually just a useful form of speech to refer to some real entity" (Siderits & Katsura, 2013, p. 15)—it can be easy for us to fall prey to the other extreme opposing the subject–object duality and hold that "there are no subjects and objects at all" (Sopa, 2008, p. 213). However, cultivating a non-absolutistic and non-dualistic worldview is a matter not of holding views or opinions, but rather of "seeing things as they really are" (Walshe, 2007). For the purpose of preventing us from falling into the conceptual proliferation that hypostatizes the two aforementioned extreme aspects of reality, Nagarjuna extracted Buddha's central teaching of dependent origination, which represents the correct middle path between the two extremes, into the famous eight negations: "There is neither cessation nor origination, neither annihilation nor the eternal, neither singularity nor plurality, neither the coming nor the going [of any dharma or phenomena]" (Siderits & Katsura, 2013, p. 13). This approach of negation points not only to the most significant feature of the union of wisdom and method but also to the correct mindset for practicing the accumulation of wisdom and merit. The educational significance of this approach of negation is discussed in the next section.

4.6 The Approach of Negation

As revealed in the preceding sections, by means of pointing out explicitly that the origin of the karmic seeds of afflictive and noetic barriers that trap us in the endless cyclic forms of existence is the absolutistic and objectivistic dualistic subject–object worldview which attaches to a subjective self and an objective world as absolute, essential, and independent existence, the Yogacarian doctrine of consciousness transformation provides us with profound empirical insights into the nature of the spiritual path and spiritual practices, and their potential for educational use.

In the preceding dialogue between Buddhism and quantum physics, we have seen how the world that we experience in our everyday life is a "deft master of disguise" (Greene, 2004, p. 22), and we have also realized why the "overarching lesson that has emerged from scientific inquiry over the last century is that human experience is often a misleading guide to the true nature of reality" (Greene, 2004, p. 5) and why "assessing existence while failing to embrace the insights of modern physics would be like wrestling in the dark with an unknown opponent" (Greene, 2004, p. 5). By virtue of unmasking this "unknown opponent" as the absolutistic and objectivistic dualistic subject–object worldview, the dialogue between Buddhism and quantum physics not only deepens and broadens our understanding of the concepts of truth and the relationship between truth and education, but also makes the spiritual practices of the five-stage gradual path of consciousness transformation sensible, graspable, meaningful, practicable, and achievable.

The spiritual practices prescribed in the five-stage gradual path of consciousness transformation can be understood as efforts toward the suppression and then the eradication of karmic seeds of afflictive and noetic barriers that originate from an absolutistic and objectivistic dualistic subject–object worldview. As indicated in Chap. 3, even emptiness is itself empty; therefore, rather than advocating for the positive pursuit of a hypostasized ideal of emptiness, the pedagogical foundation of this Yogacarian gradual path of consciousness transformation is grounded on the negation of the dualistic subject–object worldview that attach to a subjective self and an objective world as absolute, essential, and independent existence. It is also a negation of the conception that *"things having their own way of existing without being posited through the force of consciousness"* (Newland, 2009, p. 70). However, as emphasized earlier, the negation of this dualistic subject–object worldview does not mean assuming the other extreme worldview which holds that there are no subjects or objects at all. Rather, it means seeing things as they really are by means of following the Middle Way approach of negation that grasps simultaneously the ultimate and phenomenal aspects of self and reality, and features the conception of objectlessness in the union of wisdom-side and method-side practices.

Grasping simultaneously the ultimate and phenomenal aspects of self and reality, this negative approach recognizes the ineffable and unfathomable nature of the original state of human consciousness which is sometimes referred to as the Buddha Nature, the Emptiness, the God, the Divine, the Otherness, the Atman, the Tao, the divine Reality, the Kingdom of God within, the Idea of the Good, the Idea of all ideas, or the Highest Idea by various religious and spiritual traditions. This state cannot possibly be fully grasped with the sensorial tools of the body or the analytical mind—which is fragmentary both in nature and in effect—but only manifests itself when the attachment to the sharp subject–object dichotomy dissolves and the contaminated karmic seeds of afflictive and noetic barriers are suppressed or cleared away. By means of orienting the focus of practices on the suppression and then eradication of the contaminated karmic seeds that originate from the attachment to the dualistic subject–object worldview and on the union of wisdom-side and method-side practices, the negative approach prescribed in *Yogacara* and informed by the Middle Way doctrine safeguards practitioners from the deviation of conceptual proliferation and the pursuing of something ideally hypostatized by the ego as spiritual, and therefore prevents further inner fragmentation in consciousness from the very beginning of the path onward.

The essence of the approach of negation is well illustrated in Nagarjuna's famous eight negations. As discussed in the previous section, the eight negations offer strong protection against the practitioners falling prey to the two extremes of nihilism and reificationism. As Kumar (2013) explained, "the positive—be it love or non-violence—is not born through following [hypostatized] ideals [of love or non-violence], which are opposite to the present state, but through negatively thinking and observing the present state of the mind" (p. 89). In other words, the positive manifests only through the negation of the afflictions originating from the dualistic subject–object perception that has caused the present unwanted state. Kumar (2013) underscored that "the negative approach is not reactionary in nature. It is not a mere replacement of one approach for another" (p. 89). As Krishnamurti argued, if the negative approach is a mere reaction to the positive, then it would be merely the same thing in a different form (Kumar, 2013, p. 90). Kumar elucidated the approach by drawing on Krishnamurti's discussion on love:

> Is thought love? Does thought cultivate love? It is not pleasure, it is not desire, it is not remembrance, although they all have their places. Then what is love? Is love jealousy? Is love a sense of possession, my wife, my husband, my girl—possession? Has love within it fear? It is none of these things, entirely wipe them all away, end them, putting them all in their right place—then love is. (as cited in Kumar, 2013, p. 89)

In other words, love as a given that is intrinsic in everything can never be genuinely attained through positive pursuits of hypostatized ideals, but only manifests itself when all of the contaminated clouds are dispelled. This elucidation deepens our understanding of not only the essence of the approach of negation but also the relationship between spirituality and truthful knowing and the dialectic between knowing and loving as explicated by Huebner and Palmer. As discussed in Chap. 2, both Huebner and Palmer criticized the dualistic subject–object worldview and the sharp distinction between the knower and the known. On the one hand, Huebner (1985/1999a) indicated that the distortion of love occurs "when caring is for the self and knowing becomes an act of control, often an act of violence" (p. 349). Both Huebner's and Krishnamurti's insights instantiate how falling into objectifying, or the subject–object dichotomy, becomes the origin of the afflictive and noetic barriers that not only contaminate and distort pure love, which is intrinsic in the original state of human consciousness, but also hinder truthful knowing. On the other hand, Palmer (1983/2003) maintained that "truthful knowing weds knower and the known… We find truth by pledging our troth, and knowing becomes a reunion of separated beings whose primary bond is not of logic but of love" (p. 67). This dissolving of the distinction between the knower and the known, or the observer and the observed, echoes with the conception of objectlessness that unites wisdom and method, and is one of the most significant features of the approach of negation. Given its epistemological and empirical significance for the genuine transformation of consciousness, this approach of negation is identified as the core approach for curriculum as an experience of consciousness transformation.

4.7 THE IMPLICATIONS

Aiming for the eradication of the karmic seeds of the afflictive and noetic barriers that originate from a dualistic subject–object worldview, the Yogacarian five-stage gradual spiritual path provides us with a panoramic view of the whole process of consciousness transformation culminating in the perfection of the four transcendental wisdoms of the full enlightenment of Buddhahood. This panoramic view not only reveals the existential significance of the spiritual path of consciousness transformation for human beings, but also provides answers to our questions regarding the main barriers to be overcome along a spiritual path, the characteristics of various stages of progress, the main disciplines and practices and their interrelationships in various stages, and the core approach to consciousness transformation. In contrast to the misunderstanding that the spiritual path entails only the accumulation of wisdom by means of cultivating meditative stability and serenity, and to the misconception that moral suasion and ethical doctrine per se can bring about a genuine uplift of ethics and morality and the resolution of various global crises, this gradual spiritual path illustrates the significance of following Buddha's teaching of the Middle Way which emphasizes the simultaneous grasping of the ultimate and phenomenal aspects of self and reality and features the approach of negation and the union of wisdom and method in practice.

On the basis of the realization of the essence and purpose of education as the transformation of consciousness attained in previous chapters, the educational significance of this five-stage gradual spiritual path of consciousness transformation is threefold. Firstly, based on a profound conceptual understanding of the whole Consciousness-Only doctrine, including the concepts of truth, a panoramic view of the whole spiritual path, the cultivation of *bodhicitta*, the nature of the spiritual approach and practices, the obstacles eliminated by these practices, and the positive results brought about by them, this gradual path establishes from the very first a doctrine of the true nature of human existence, a vision of various spiritual goals, a selfless motivation, the recognition of the significance of the negative approach and the union of wisdom and method. In this way, this gradual path effectively protects practitioners from potential dangers and deviations from the outset of their pursuit of various spiritual goals. In deliberating how we might facilitate the transformation of consciousness in an educational context, such protection is of extreme significance.

Secondly, by virtue of uniting wisdom-side and method-side practices and including everyday experiences and phenomena as the entry points for developing spiritual discernments and overcoming the two barriers that originate from the dualistic subject–object worldview, the spiritual practices prescribed in this gradual path open up infinite possibilities in every moment and turn even trivial everyday experiences into transcendental opportunities. Moreover, the requirement of consistency between the view (wisdom-side) and deeds (method-side) components of spiritual practices empowers practitioners to experience along the path a long-lasting and profound consciousness transformation that, as discussed earlier, connotes the real occurrence of education.

Finally, the panoramic view of this five-stage gradual path—which refers to both the phenomenal and ultimate aspects of reality and includes both the worldly and supramundane paths—provides us with deepened hermeneutic insights into the essence, language, and pedagogical genius and expediency of various spiritual and religious traditions, and how they resonate with each other. Veins of language within various religious traditions "contain centuries of experience and experiencing of the supra-sensory, the qualitative, the transcendent-experiences that are stored in histories, stories, myths, and poems" (Huebner, 1985/1999a, p. 344), the interpretation of them, as Huebner (1985/1999a) emphasized, requires more hermeneutical skills than merely reading texts based upon more tangible traces (e.g., existing textbooks and historical accounts, scientific reports, behavioral science descriptions) (p. 344). Referring to both the phenomenal and ultimate aspects of reality, this gradual path offers us an expanded conceptual framework for interpreting experiences of the supra-sensory, the qualitative, and the transcendent in various religious traditions. Including both the worldly and supramundane paths, this gradual path provides us with insights into diverse hidden pedagogical genius and expediency in the doctrines of various religious traditions for accommodating special needs of practitioners in certain stages of progress, or in specific historical-political contexts. Such hermeneutical insights prevent not only potential misinterpretations of spiritual doctrines but also unnecessary debates—debates among people who sometimes speak at cross-purposes as a result of referring implicitly to different aspects of reality or different stages of spiritual practices. The hermeneutical skills provided by the panoramic view of the five-stage gradual path are therefore of crucial significance in cross-religious conversation and in conversation between spirituality and education. Truly, as Huebner (1985/1999a) indicated, if we hope the veins of language regarding the spiritual within various religious and spiritual traditions can well be mined for educational use, hermeneutical skills are indispensable.

On the basis of the above exploration of the concept and process of consciousness transformation in Buddhism and the deliberation of its educational significance, along with the relationship between truth and education and the dialogue between Buddhism and quantum physics set forth in the preceding two chapters, in the following chapters in Part IV, I proceed to investigate how we might understand curriculum as an experience of consciousness transformation through an examination of six key elements.

николаеNOTES

1. In this book, the terms "subject–object dichotomy," "subject–object duality," and "dualistic subject–object worldview" refer to the conception that posits the subject and object as absolute, essential, and mutual independent existence.
2. The gradual and sudden paradigms in Buddhism have long been a source of debates in history (Faure, 1994, p. 41). In contrast to the five-stage gradual path in *Yogacara*, Zen Buddhism features the "sudden" teaching (Faure, 1994, p. 32). According to Lusthaus (2002), while in the Pali texts Buddha repeated that "awakening is consequent upon uncovering and removing the deep, underlying psycho-cognitive roots of avidya [ignorance or delusion]" (p. 108), some Theravadins argued that "if disentangling one's karmic condition involved the gradual activity of discovering and overcoming, piece by piece, one's karmic legacy, the task would be interminable, since each counter-karmic action is itself an action, and thus productive of further karma" (p. 108). The controversies of gradual vs. sudden and modificatory vs. disruptive re-emerged in China, Japan, and Tibet (Lusthaus, 2002, p. 108; Sopa, 2008, pp. 195–199). The main cause of the debate in 8th-century Tibet was that, while the whole doctrine of Zen Buddhism is much more profound than the mere "sudden" aspect of teaching, there developed an attractive Zen-like misconception that practicing the thought-free meditation *alone* is enough to attain enlightenment, and that all other practices, such as meritorious practices and rigorous analysis, etc., are not worth doing (Sopa, 2008, pp. 198–200). According to Sopa (2008), King Trisong Detsen saw the danger of this view and resorted to a debate held at Samye Monastery (p. 198); he subsequently decided to follow the Indian *Madhyamaka* (the Middle Way) system, which formed the basis of *Yogacara*

and maintained that "the method to come to a direct realization of the truth is to first learn about it. Next one examines and analyzes what one has studied. Through inferential reasoning one gains an understanding that becomes more vivid through meditation" (p. 200).

In regards to debate referenced above, Faure (1994) indicated that "the protagonists of the debate were in fact speaking at cross-purposes" (p. 41), and emphasized that, as Paul Demieville once suggested, "the 'sudden' and 'gradual' were universal categories" (p. 32) and "this antinomy is not only a psychological and methodological order, it applies to two conceptions of truth itself and actually spreads to all planes of thought" (as cited in Faure, 1994, p. 32). Faure (1994) elucidated that "the philosophical framework of the controversy was provided by the Two Truths theory: sudden and gradual refer to whether awakening is regarded from the point of view of ultimate truth or of conventional truth" (pp. 32–33). Nevertheless, in practice, the positions of the protagonists were not so different: "both were 'sudden'... and both were to some degree 'gradual'" (Faure, 1994, p. 36). For example, while the founding patriarch of Japanese RinZai school Linji "himself came to Awakening in part by abandoning the modificatory model in favor of the disruptive model" (Lusthaus, 2002, p. 108), he also stressed that, "you must first fathom things yourself, purify yourself, polish yourself; then one day you will awaken" (Faure, 1994, p. 36). The significance of the need of both the gradual and sudden models (referring to conventional truth and ultimate truth respectively) was illustrated by Buddha in *The Diamond Sutra* by means of employing the metaphor of a raft; Buddha emphasized that his doctrine of the dharma, like a raft—"having fulfilled its function in bearing you to the other shore (Nirvana)—with its coincident qualities and ideas must inevitably be abandoned" (Gemmell, 1912, pp. 22–23, 97). This metaphor points to the concept of the Middle Way taught by Buddha and later restored by Nagarjuna. Rather than being a neutral or neutralized position, the Middle Way is achieved by simultaneously grasping the two truths and by the "refusal to reduce one level to the other or to reconcile them in a convenient hierarchy" (Faure, 1994, p. 37).

While the sudden and gradual paradigms are, in essence, not so different, and for the more advanced practitioners, the sudden teaching serves as a remedy for the overreliance upon gradual and analytical activities, given the fact that this five-stage gradual path includes both the worldly path (with an emphasis on the method-side practices contingent on the conventional truth) and the supramundane path (with an emphasis on the wisdom-side practices contingent on the ultimate truth), I consider this gradual path to be of profound significance for the revival of spirituality in educational context. The details of the educational significance of this gradual path are explored in Sect. 4.7.

3. Given that the teachings of Buddha are so vast and diverse, "Tsongkhapa's purpose in composing *Lamrim Chenmo* was to draw out the essence of all the Buddha's teachings and arrange them in a practical manual" (Sopa, 2004, p. 2). Tsong-kha-pa (Tsongkhapa) had received much personal instruction and guidance from Manjusri bodhisattva in visionary experiences (Culter, 2000, p. 10; Thurman, 1984, pp. 4–5).

References

Choi, D. (2011). *Mechanism of Consciousness During Life, Dream and After-Death*. Bloomington, IN: AuthorHouse.
Culter, J. W. C. (2000). Editor's Preface. In *Tsong-kha-pa, The Great Treatise on the Stages of the Path to Enlightenment* (Vol. 2, pp. 9–11) (The Lamrim Chenmo Translation Committee, trans.). Ithaca, NY: Snow Lion Publications.
Faure, B. (1994). *The Rhetoric of Immediacy: A Cultural Critique of Chan/Zen Buddhism*. Princeton, NJ: Princeton University Press.
Gemmell, W. (1912). *The Diamond Sutra (Chin-Kang-Ching): Or Prajna-Paramita, Translated from the Chinese with an Introduction and Notes*. London: Kegan Paul, Trench, Trübner & Co.
Greene, B. (2004). *The Fabric of the Cosmos: Space, Time, and the Texture of Reality*. New York, NY: Alfred A. Knopf.
Heidegger, M. (1962). Plato's Doctrine of Truth (J. Barlow, trans.). In B. William & D. A. Henry (Eds.), *Philosophy in the Twentieth Century* (Vol. 3, pp. 251–270). New York, NY: Random House. (Original work published 1942).
Hsuan-Tsang (1973). *Ch'eng Wei-Shi Lun: The Doctrine of Mere-Consciousness* (T. Wei, trans.). Hong Kong, China: The Ch'eng Wei-shih Lun Publication Committee. (Original work published 659). Retrieved from http://www.dhalbi.org/dhalbi/html_t/authors/author_main.php?p_id=8
Huebner, D. E. (1999a). Spirituality and Knowing. In V. Hillis (Ed.), *The Lure of the Transcendent: Collected Essays by Dwayne E. Huebner* (pp. 340–352). New York, NY: Routledge. (Original work published 1985).
Huebner, D. E. (1999b). Practicing the Presence of God. In V. Hillis (Ed.), *The Lure of the Transcendent: Collected Essays by Dwayne E. Huebner* (pp. 388–395). New York, NY: Routledge. (Original work published 1987).
Kumar, A. (2013). *Curriculum as Meditative Inquiry*. New York, NY: Palgrave Macmillan.
Lemkow, A. F. (1990). *The Wholeness Principle: Dynamics of Unity Within Science, Religion, and Society*. Wheaton, IL: Quest Books.
Lusthaus, D. (2002). *Buddhist Phenomenology: A Philosophical Investigation of Yogacara Buddhism and the Ch'eng Wei-shih Lun*. New York, NY: RoutledgeCurzon.

Miller, J. P. (2007). *The Holistic Curriculum* (2nd ed.). Toronto, ON: University of Toronto Press.
Newland, G. (2009). *Introduction to Emptiness: As Taught in Tsong-kha-pa's Great Treatise on the Stages of the Path* (2nd ed.). Ithaca, NY: Snow Lion Publications.
Palmer, P. J. (2003). Education as Spiritual Formation. *Educational Horizons,* 82(1), 55–67. (Reprinted from *To Know as We Are Known: Education as a Spiritual Journey,* pp. 17–32, 1983, New York, NY: HarperCollins).
Park, S. R. (2014). *Embodied Inner Work: An Educator's Journey of Body-Mind-Heart Integration.* Unpublished doctoral dissertation, Simon Fraser University, Burnaby, Canada.
Siderits, M., & Katsura, S. (2013). *Nāgārjuna's Middle Way.* Somerville, MA: Wisdom Publications.
Sopa, L. (2004). *Steps on the Path to Enlightenment: A Commentary on Tsongkhapa's Lamrim Chenmo. Volume I: The Foundation Practices.* Somerville, MA: Wisdom Publications.
Sopa, L. (2005). *Steps on the Path to Enlightenment: A Commentary on Tsongkhapa's Lamrim Chenmo. Volume II: Karma.* Somerville, MA: Wisdom Publications.
Sopa, L. (2008). *Steps on the Path to Enlightenment: A Commentary on Tsongkhapa's Lamrim Chenmo. Volume III: The Way of the Bodhisattva.* Somerville, MA: Wisdom Publications.
Thurman, R. A. F. (1984). *The Central Philosophy of Tibet: A Study and Translation of Jey Tsong Khapa's Essence of True Eloquence.* Princeton, NJ: Princeton University Press.
Tsong-kha-pa (2000). *The Great Treatise on the Stages of the Path to Enlightenment* (Vol. 1, The Lamrim Chenmo Translation Committee, trans.). Ithaca, NY: Snow Lion Publications. (Original work published 1402).
Tsong-kha-pa (2004). *The Great Treatise on the Stages of the Path to Enlightenment* (Vol. 2, The Lamrim Chenmo Translation Committee, trans.). Ithaca, NY: Snow Lion Publications. (Original work published 1402).
Walshe, M. O. (Trans.). (2007). *Kaccaayanagotto Sutta: Kaccaayana [On Right View].* Retrieved from http://www.accesstoinsight.org/tipitaka/sn/sn12/sn12.015.wlsh.html

PART IV

Curriculum as an Experience of Consciousness Transformation

CHAPTER 5

Understanding the Nature of Consciousness, Self, and Reality

5.1 Introduction

In earlier exploration of the review of educational literature and the dialogue between Buddhism and quantum physics, we have seen how the essence and purpose of education revealed in Plato's allegory of the cave can be understood as in essence the transformation of consciousness toward the conceptual and direct non-dualistic realization of the ultimate truth, personal liberation, and the highest spiritual goal of the liberation of all sentient beings from cyclic forms of existence in the shadowy phenomenal world. Propelled by this realization, in the previous chapter, I explored Buddhist spiritual practices of consciousness transformation to gain deeper insights into how we might facilitate the transformation of consciousness in educational contexts. In Part IV, I investigate how we might understand curriculum as an experience of consciousness transformation by means of examining six key elements (Chaps. 5, 6, 7, 8, 9, and 10). These elements are: understanding the nature of consciousness, self, and reality; learning to appreciate human temporality; cultivating impartiality and *bodhicitta*; becoming responsibly responsive; cultivating selflessness; and learning to embody a non-dualistic worldview.

Among the six key elements of curriculum for consciousness transformation, understanding the nature of consciousness, self, and reality is of primary importance and is fundamental to the other elements. On the five-stage gradual path of consciousness transformation, developing a profound conceptual

© The Author(s) 2019
E. L. Chu, *Exploring Curriculum as an Experience of Consciousness Transformation*, Curriculum Studies Worldwide,
https://doi.org/10.1007/978-3-030-17701-0_5

understanding of the whole doctrine of Consciousness-Only is the first and foremost step. In the dialogue between Buddhism and quantum physics, we attained the realization that the doctrines of various spiritual and religious traditions are in essence all about the true nature of self and reality, we have also discussed how we might attain the direct realization of it by virtue of both everyday and meditative spiritual practices. Without being informed about the ultimate nature of self and reality that is contradictory to our everyday experiences, we can hardly penetrate the disguise of the shadowy phenomenal world and recognize the profound significance of spiritual wisdom and existential knowledge for human beings and for education. As Sopa (2008) explained, we need to know "what we are doing and why we are doing it" (p. 17); "if one lacks knowledge or strong interest before beginning, one's practice will be shallow" (p. 232) and "if one's practice is weak the results will be feeble as well" (p. 232).

In his concern for human temporality, Huebner (1967/1999b) also underscored the significance of "probing the very nature of what it means to be a human being" (p. 135) for addressing the problems caused by the "dependency upon 'learning' as the major concept in curriculum thought" (p. 135) that were reflected in such expressions as "learning how to learn" or "how a person learns to be creative" (p. 134). Speaking from a theological perspective that sees humans as transcendent beings, Huebner (1967/1999b) considered the inquiry about "learning how to learn" as a misleading question that stems from an inadequate explanation of human characteristics, and asked, "Could it be that creativity is not learned, but an aspect of man's nature?" (p. 134). He maintained that the adequate questions are what *prevents* creativity and how to explain fixation, rather than how to be creative or how to learn (Huebner, 1967/1999b, p. 134). He was also concerned that by considering learning as implying the process of abstraction and generalization, "it yanks man out of his world and freezes him at a stage in his own biographic evolution" (Huebner, 1967/1999b, p. 136). He indicated that, owing to a misapprehension of the nature of human existence,

> learning is assumed to be something that happens within the individual. Education is consequently conceived as doing something to an individual. This leads to the proposition that there is the individual and there is the world, and that the individual develops in such a way that he has power over the world or to act upon the world. Such thinking leads to consideration of the individual as something distinct. Obviously, this is not the case. The individual is not separated from the world, or apart from it—he is a part of

it. The unit of study, as Heidegger, among others, points out, is a "being-in-the-world." Any system of thought dealing with human change as something that happens within the individual is likely to lead the educator astray. However, if a curricular language can be developed so that the educator looks at the individual or the situation together, not separately, then his powers of curricular design and educational responsibility might be increased. (Huebner, 1967/1999b, pp. 135–136)

Huebner's insights illuminate how objectivism, despite no longer being convincing, is institutionalized in our educational language and practices and in the ways we teach and learn through the power of hidden curriculum rooted in a lack of awareness regarding the ultimate nature of human existence. The lack of existential knowledge and spiritual wisdom regarding the nature of consciousness, self, and reality not only prevents the genuine transformation of consciousness and real education from occurring, but, I believe, is also the root cause of various current moral issues, the depreciation of human existence, and various global crises. However, despite the fact that modern physics and other branches of science have penetrated the disguise of the shadowy phenomenal world and indicated that it is far from the ultimate reality, decision-makers are hesitant to integrate a comprehensive interdisciplinary exploration of various human existential inquiries regarding the ultimate nature of consciousness, self, and reality into school and university curricula. While the underlying causes of this hesitation are complicated, one of the main obstacles might be the overreliance on science and rational analysis in addressing existential inquiries and issues.

5.2 THE LIMITATIONS OF SCIENTIFIC METHOD AND RATIONAL ANALYSIS

Concerned over the tendency toward the overreliance on scientific knowledge about human beings in education, Huebner (1959/1999a) reminded us that "psychological or behavioral science is not the only channel of information about human beings available to educators" (p. 2) and "behavioral scientists are not the only ones who speculate about and know men, women, and children" (p. 2). He pointed out our curious position in education that we must run the schools and educate both the younger generations and ourselves anyhow and "to do this job we need to use all available knowledge and more. We cannot postpone the educational task until we have the results of the 'scientific' knowledge" (Huebner, 1959/1999a, p. 2). Moreover, "scientific validity is not the only kind of validity. In the existential situation in which we must plan for and act with boys and girls, we must bring all of our knowledge and creative powers to bear" (Huebner, 1959/1999a, p. 2). Taking behavioral science as an example, Huebner (1959/1999a) reminded us of our strange positions and stated that although "the information coming through [behavioral science] is incomplete, charged with static, we nevertheless accept the picture we receive as the real representation. Yet during the next ten—twenty—or one hundred years that picture may change considerably" (p. 2). Moreover, such overreliance on science and rationalism could also possibly develop into an attachment to scientific knowledge and lead to what David Smith (2000) called frozen futurism, "in which what are expected to be revealed *has* been revealed" (p. 17). As a result,

> teaching is understood primarily as an act of implementation, with the curriculum as a settled commodity emerging from a settled anterior logic headed for a settled posterior conclusion. Teaching itself is reduced in the process to being nothing but a form of procedural manipulation in which the being of the teacher requires no true encounter with the being of the student, nor with curriculum. (Smith, 2000, p. 19)

In the absence of interest in genuine conversation and truthful knowing between teachers, parents and, students for finding out the sources of a given problem in a present situation, "a unilateral importation of externally derived behavior modification strategies... according to predetermined criteria for future results" (Smith, 2000, p. 20) might be implemented mechanically or with love and care. Yet, even if it is implemented with love and care, "the future is frozen in an anticipatory set through which nothing ever really seems to change, although all of the language perpetually gives assurance that things are always changing" (Smith, 2000, p. 17); in actuality, there is "no change in the sense that it actually seems to make a difference in the way one lives" (Smith, 2000, p. 17). This kind of frozen futurism demonstrates how, in the absence of spiritual wisdom, such as the wisdom of emptiness or the transcendent that signifies infinite possibilities and the oneness of everything, the overreliance on scientific knowledge can close up true conversation and form noetic barriers that inhibit truthful ways of knowing, being, and living here and now, and hinder the "intricacies, the complexities and the living quality of clarity" (Krishnamurti & Smith, 1996, p. 202) from the students, parents, and educators.

Such a technical ethos developed from the language of scientific method and curriculum implementation becomes "a cultural version of instrumentalism—a way of life that is not fully bodily lived" (Aoki, 1991a/2004a, p. 369). Aoki (1991a/2004a) cautioned us that "the danger in speaking this language is that we become the language we speak" (p. 369) and "in so becoming, we might become forgetful of how instrumental language disengages us from our bodies, making of us disembodied, dehumanized beings, indifferent to the nihilistic drying out of inspiritedness" (p. 369). As Huebner (1959/1999a) indicated, the approach to the world through intellectual analysis "makes us more powerful by providing more control and prediction. But it may also lead to new enslavements—enslavement to the known, the abstract, and consequently to the past" (p. 8). Such enslavement to disembodied instrumentalism is also a concern to Aoki. Drawing on the wisdom of jazz trumpeter Bobby Shew, Aoki (1991a/2004a) suggested, "instead of 'curriculum implementation', how about 'curriculum improvisation'?" (p. 369). Curriculum improvisation "provokes in us a vitalizing possibility that causes our whole body to beat a new and different rhythm" (Aoki, 1991a/2004a, p. 369). As Bobby Shew indicated, for an instrument to cease to be an instrument, "the trumpet, music, and body must become as one in a living wholeness" (Aoki, 1991a/2004a, p. 368). In such moments, the subject–object dichotomy is no longer present, and nothing is reduced to an object. Aoki (1991b/2004b) cited Heidegger that "objective meanings hide lived meanings. The later become silent and man becomes heedless of this silence" (p. 381). In this way, the oblivion of Being occurs, and this oblivion of Being "applies not only to the people objectified but also to the subject that objectifies. Usually unconsciously, the subject diminished itself to a half-life. An oppressor becomes oppressed by the half-lives he or she produces" (Aoki, 1991b/2004b, p. 381). From this perspective, scientific methods that objectify and fragment can at most give a half-answer to human existential inquires and issues.

Drawing on Krishnamurti, Kumar (2013) also pointed out that "analysis and thinking—central features of intellectual pursuits—alone cannot solve human problems" (p. 77). However, given its extraordinary capacity for addressing scientific inquiries regarding the phenomenal world and for the accumulation and expansion of knowledge, consciously or unconsciously, rational analysis has gradually become supposed to be an omnipotent force that will, sooner or later, provide answers to various human existential questions. Nevertheless, as discussed earlier, the dissolving of the sharp subject–object distinction in either a meditative state or an everyday existential situation cannot possibly be achieved by rational analysis alone, for analysis by itself, if not coupled with spiritual wisdom that knows emptiness, has the potential to cause further fragmentation rather than the dissolving of the self–world dichotomy. As Kumar (2013) inferred, in the process of analysis and thinking, *"is not 'the analyzer/ observer/thinker/controller' also 'the analyzed/observed/thought/controlled'?* If the very structure of thought is deeply conditioned, fragmented [by the sharp subject–object dichotomy], and ridden with fear how can it understand and transform itself?" (pp. 77–78).

Theoretical physicist Michio Kaku (2005) also highlights the limitations of science and rational analysis in addressing existential issues. He illustrated that "if string theory is eventually experimentally confirmed as the theory of everything, then we must ask where the equations themselves came from. If the unified field theory is truly unique,… then we must ask where this uniqueness came from" (p. 358). Since science can never answer such a question as "Why it is this?" in the very end of a series of the whys and wherefores, Kaku (2005) claimed, from a pure scientific viewpoint, he personally believes that the strongest argument for the existence of the God of Einstein or Spinoza might be teleology (p. 358). He reasoned that "physicists who believe in this God believe that the universe is so beautiful and simple that its ultimate laws could not have been an accident" (Kaku, 2005, p. 358). Nevertheless, Kaku further argued that, should physicists one day succeed in discovering one ultimate equation from which all physical laws can be derived from, he would believe that this simply implies some sort of design, but not "that this design gives personal meanings[1] to humanity" (p. 358). He quoted theoretical physicist Alan Guth's assertion that

> it's okay to ask those questions [regarding the purpose of the universe or the meaning of life], but one should not expect to get a wiser answer from a physicist. My own emotional feeling is that life has a purpose—ultimately, I'd guess that the purpose it has is the purpose that we've given it and not a purpose that came out of any cosmic design. (as cited in Kaku, 2005, p. 359)

Kaku's illustration revealed the limitations of rational analysis and science per se in answering the existential inquiries regarding value and end. Such insights shed light on the existential issues caused by the exclusion of existential knowledge and spiritual wisdom from education.

5.3 THE IMPERATIVE OF INTEGRATING EXISTENTIAL KNOWLEDGE AND SPIRITUAL WISDOM INTO CURRICULUM

As revealed earlier, in aiming for the suppression and then the eradication of karmic seeds of the afflictive and noetic barriers that originate from an absolutistic and objectivistic subject–object worldview, the approach of negation that grasps simultaneously the phenomenal and ultimate aspects of self and reality and features the conception of objectlessness in the union of wisdom-side and method-side practices is identified as the core approach to consciousness transformation. In contrast, the dominant scientific approach that has been developed for ages is based on a dualistic subject–object worldview (Bohm, 1980, p. 19). Apparently, there exist fundamental differences between the approach of negation and the approach of science in terms of their modes of looking at the world and their methodologies of exploring reality. In scientific research, the dualistic way of looking, thinking, and acting "tends very strongly to re-enforce the general fragmentary approach" already present in our society (Bohm, 1980, p. 19). Bohm (1980) indicated that "in this way, people are led to feel that fragmentation is nothing but an expression of 'the way everything really is' and that anything else is impossible. So there is very little disposition to look for evidence to the contrary" (p. 19). In other words, like the prisoners in the cave in Plato's allegory, we are led to reaffirm fragmentary shadows as what reality really is, rather than merely "a form of insight, i.e. a way of looking at the world" (Bohm, 1980, p. 4). In this manner, the prevailing scientific way of looking at the world becomes a fortified shackle that further prevents the transitions from one stage to another as described in Plato's cave allegory, and therefore hinders the real occurrence of education which, according to Heidegger (1942/1962), is "a shift in the definition of the essence of truth" (p. 251).

From this perspective, the hesitation to integrate a comprehensive interdisciplinary exploration of human existential inquiries and the ultimate nature of consciousness, self, and reality into school and university curricula with the excuse that spiritual truths and wisdom have not yet been fully scientifically proven could be a meaningless and ultimately detrimental procrastination. The following is a parable taught by Buddha, which illustrates how this hesitation could be harmful.

There was a bhiksu who was frustrated by fourteen difficult questions and went to Buddha to seek answers. The fourteen difficult questions were: Is the world eternal, or not, or both, or neither? Is the world finite, or not, or both, or neither? Is the self identical with the body, or not? Does the Buddha exist after death, or not, or both, or neither (Lamotte, 1949/2001, p. 711)? The bhiksu thought to himself: "If the Buddha will explain these fourteen difficult questions for me and satisfy my mind, I will remain his disciple; if he does not succeed in explaining them to me, I will seek another path" (Lamotte, 1949/2001, p. 711). Buddha knew what the bhiksu was thinking, and told him, "If I answered, you would not understand; at the time of death, you would have understood nothing and you would not be liberated from birth, old age, sickness and death" (Lamotte, 1949/2001, p. 711). Buddha continued that an ignorant person who is struck by a poisoned arrow, rather than allowing a physician to remove the arrow and apply an antidote immediately, might insist that he will not let the physician take out the arrow and apply the antidote until he knows the physician's name, family, and, age, as well as which mountain the arrow came from, what the arrow is made of, and where the antidote comes from and what its name is (Lamotte, 1949/2001, p. 711). Buddha said to this bhiksu:

> You are like him: the arrow of wrong views... dipped in the poison of thirst... has pierced your mind; I want to remove this arrow from you, my disciple; but you are unwilling to let me take it out, and you want to know if the world is eternal or non-eternal, finite or infinite... You will not find what you are looking for, but you will lose the life of wisdom...; you will die like an animal and fall into the shadows. (Lamotte, 1949/2001, p. 711)

In an educational context, the flat rejection of spiritual truth and wisdom—which have been prudently preserved and handed down by various religious and spiritual traditions—with the excuse that these spiritual doctrines have not yet been fully scientifically proven is, in a way, following the same logic as this bhiksu, and risks similarly grave consequences.

Huebner (1959/1999a) also reminded us that "in our concern to make the study of education scientific we have ignored other channels" (p. 2). He indicated that the study of the nature of being in the works of certain existentialists is one of the channels of "information about human being to which we as professional educators have not been attuned by the producers and users of educational knowledge. As university people we do an injustice by not making these notions available to the educator" (Huebner, 1959/1999a, p. 3). From my perspective, the injustice we have done is much grosser than we might so far have thought. Taking into consideration the foregoing deliberation over the limitations of science, rational analysis, and moral systems, as well as the renewed understanding of the spiritual truth and the essence and purpose of education attained in previous chapters, I am concerned that by means of excluding existential knowledge and spiritual wisdom from curriculum, we have done a very great injustice to numerous students. By suggesting the incredibility and dispensability of the spiritual wisdom and the irreconcilability of various religious traditions with various forms of hidden curriculum, we have perpetuated both inner and external fragmentation and conflict, and hindered the genuine education from occurring.

As discussed in Chap. 4, in the absence of spiritual wisdom that knows emptiness, moral suasion, and ethical doctrine per se—working under the model of objectification—cannot possibly bring about any real change in human consciousness, let alone provide the solution to current moral issues or the resolution of various global crises. Moreover, given the permeation of the market logic of contemporary globalization and the falling of public education into this logic, Smith (2000) was concerned that it has brought about new levels of paranoia "along with an almost complete collapse of any older virtue of learning being valued for its own sake" (p. 13). Given the fact that genuine consciousness transformation crucial to our shared future requires the union of wisdom and method in practices, human beings need to be informed about, and engage with, existential knowledge and spiritual wisdom regarding the true nature of consciousness, self, and reality from various perspectives so that wisdom and method can possibly be held and imbued by each other. As Sri Nisargadatta Maharaj (1973) said,

> your love towards others is the result of self-knowledge, not its cause. No virtue is genuine without knowledge of oneself. When you have certain knowledge that life itself flows through all that is, and that you are such life, you will love everything naturally and spontaneously… But, when you see anything as something separate from yourself, you cannot love it, because you are afraid of it. Alienation produces fear, and fear intensifies alienation. It is a vicious circle. Only self-knowledge can break that cycle. (p. 244)

Maharaj's insights illuminate why the shortage of existential knowledge and spiritual wisdom regarding the ultimate nature of consciousness, self, and reality is the root cause of various moral issues, the depreciation of human existence, and various global crises. Maharaj also made explicit the vicious circle wherein the attachment to the alienating subject–object worldview becomes a source of fear that in turn reinforces alienation. His emphasis that this vicious circle cannot possibly be broken down unless certain self-knowledge is attained also points to the futility of the sort of moral education with its existential roots removed. It is clear that, for Maharaj, self-knowledge does not refer to the psychologistic conceptions of knowledge of self established upon an objectifying mode of worldview. The method of psychological analysis, if not imbued with wisdom that knows emptiness and non-duality, might result in more bondage rather than in genuine transformation and liberation. Drawing on Boler's (1999) assertion that "the Socratic admonition to 'know thyself' may not led to self-transformation" (p. 177), Pinar (2012) also indicated that self-reflection, by itself, particularly as a narrow psychological process, might not result in any measurable change to oneself or others (p. 47). Rather, "self-reflection can easily be reduced to a form of solipsism" (Boler, 1999, p. 177). This is true especially when the concept of the self is narrowly defined and remains entrenched in an absolutistic and objectivistic subject–object duality.

In the above, I demonstrate that the integration of spiritual wisdom and existential knowledge regarding the ultimate nature of consciousness, self, and reality into school and university curricula is imperative rather than optional. Integrating existential knowledge and spiritual wisdom into curriculum in a way that encompasses the vast diversity of religious, spiritual, philosophical, scientific, and intellectual traditions surely involves formidable challenges and enormous efforts. Yet in the face of various global crises, spiritual tensions, and the dominance of the market logic of contemporary globalization, I see no better and securer option for ensuring a bright shared future—a future that is grounded on mutual care and love, is open to infinite transcendental possibilities, and is genuinely sustainable in a noble and dignified way—than recovering the place of existential knowledge and spiritual wisdom in education. With the belief in the truth force demonstrated by Gandhi and explicated by Gore (explored in Chap. 1), I am convinced that "in every land, the truth—once known—has the power to set us free" (Gore, 2008, p. 57) and that "truth also has the power to unite us and bridge the distance between 'me' and 'we,' creating the basis for common effort and shared responsibility" (Gore, 2008, p. 57), no matter how formidable this task might be.

Yet, very significantly, the integration of existential knowledge and spiritual wisdom into curriculum for the transformation of consciousness is not just a matter of enlarging the stock of knowledge in the form of curricular materials and attaining a mere conceptual understanding of these materials. As discussed in Chap. 4, while a profound conceptual understanding of a comprehensive existential and spiritual doctrine is crucial for progress on a spiritual path, genuine transformation of consciousness and the attainment of self-knowledge also entail the union of the wisdom-side practices of meditative stabilization and serenity (the accumulation of wisdom) and the method-side practices based on love, compassion, and *bodhicitta* in everyday existential conditions (the accumulation of merit). Only when wisdom is held by method, and method by wisdom, can genuine transformation of consciousness and real education possibly occur. This point is well explicated by Sopa (2008):

> At first wisdom comes from extensive study—we learn from a teacher and from books. After we have learned about the goal and method to attain it, we analyze what we have studied. We establish our understanding by independent examination. Once we understand things through the first two techniques, we meditate on these topics. (p. 16)

As discussed in Chap. 4, the wisdom and insights attained in meditation can then be carried over to infuse everyday method-side practices based on love, compassion, and *bodhicitta*, and vice versa.

The crucial role of meditation in bringing about the genuine transformation of consciousness and the direct realization of the nature of consciousness, self, and reality has been found in various experimental studies in neuroscience. For example, the results of the studies of brain scans conducted by Lutz, Greischar, Rawlings, Ricard, and Davidson (2004) have shown that "meditation on nonreferential compassion—a meditation practice based on the union of emptiness and compassion—produced a profound increase in what are often referred to as *gamma waves*" (Mingyur, 2007, p. 228). A gamma wave is a very high-frequency brain wave that reflects "an integration of information among a wide variety of brain regions" (Mingyur, 2007, p. 228). For neuroscientists, gamma waves represent "activity that occurs when various neurons communicate in a spontaneously synchronous manner across large areas of the brain" (Mingyur, 2007, p. 228). As one of the subjects of various empirical studies on meditation, including the aforementioned one, Tibetan Buddhist meditation master Yongey Mingyur Rinpoche exhibited a staggering result: "During a meditation on compassion, [his] neural activity in a key center in the brain's system for happiness jumped by 700 to 800 percent," while for ordinary subjects "who had just begun to meditate, the same area increased its activity by a mere 10 to 15 percent" (Goleman, 2007, p. viii). Speaking from his personal experience, combined with strong experimental evidence, Mingyur (2007) asserted that

> meditation on compassion fosters a broadening of insight into the nature of experience that stems from unchaining the habitual tendency of mind to distinguish between self and other, subject and object—a unification of the analytical and intuitive aspects of consciousness that is both extremely pleasurable and tremendously liberating. (p. 227)

The personal experiences of Yongey Mingyur Rinpoche and the related experimental evidence convincingly demonstrate the mighty transformative power of meditation based on the union of wisdom and compassion for attaining the direct realization of the true nature of consciousness, self, and reality that features the dissolving of the sharp distinction between self and other, subject and object. It is clear that the exclusion of existential knowledge and spiritual wisdom and the unilateral emphasis on rational analysis and scientific reasoning in educational contexts have impeded both the conceptual understanding and the direct meditative realization of the true nature of consciousness, self, and reality and, as a result, have hindered the full development of human potential and the occurrence of real education. The existential and educational significance of meditation and the union of wisdom-side and method-side practices will be revisited later in the exploration of the other elements of curriculum for consciousness transformation. In the meantime, given that human temporality is one of the most significant features of human existence and experience, I will delve in the following chapter into the significance of learning to appreciate human temporality for consciousness transformation.

Note

1. According to Kaku (2005), "Einstein once confessed that he was powerless to give comfort to the hundreds of well-meaning individuals who wrote stacks of letters pleading with him to reveal the meaning of life" (pp. 358–359).

REFERENCES

Aoki, T. T. (2004a). Sonare and Videre: A Story, Three Echoes and a Lingering Note. In W. F. Pinar & R. L. Irwin (Eds.), *Curriculum in a New Key: The Collected Works of Ted T. Aoki* (pp. 367–376). New York, NY: Routledge. (Original work published 1991a).
Aoki, T. T. (2004b). Taiko Drums and Sushi, Perogies and Sauerkraut: Mirroring a Half-Life in Multicultural Curriculum. In W. F. Pinar & R. L. Irwin (Eds.), *Curriculum in a New Key: The Collected Works of Ted T. Aoki* (pp. 377–388). New York, NY: Routledge. (Original work published 1991b).
Bohm, D. (1980). *Wholeness and the Implicate Order*. New York, NY: Routledge.
Boler, M. (1999). *Feeling Power: Emotions and Education*. New York, NY: Routledge.
Goleman, D. (2007). Foreword. In Y. Mingyur (Ed.), *The Joy of Living: Unlocking the Secret and Science of Happiness* (pp. vii–vix). New York, NY: Harmony Books.
Gore, A. (2008). Finding the Moral Resolve to Solve the Crisis of Global Climate Change. *Vital Speeches of the Day, 74*(2), 55–58.
Heidegger, M. (1962). Plato's Doctrine of Truth (J. Barlow, trans.). In B. William & D. A. Henry (Eds.), *Philosophy in the Twentieth Century* (Vol. 3, pp. 251–270). New York, NY: Random House. (Original work published 1942).
Huebner, D. E. (1999a). The Capacity for Wonder and Education. In V. Hillis (Ed.), *The Lure of the Transcendent: Collected Essays by Dwayne E. Huebner* (pp. 1–9). New York, NY: Routledge. (Original work published 1959).
Huebner, D. E. (1999b). Curriculum as Concern for Man's Temporality. In V. Hillis (Ed.), *The Lure of the Transcendent: Collected Essays by Dwayne E. Huebner* (pp. 131–142). New York, NY: Routledge. (Original work published 1967).
Kaku, M. (2005). *Parallel Worlds: A Journey Through Creation, Higher Dimensions, and the Future of the Cosmos*. New York, NY: Random House.
Krishnamurti, J., & Smith, H. (1996). Can One Have Lucidity in This Confused World? In D. Skitt (Ed.), *Questioning Krishnamurti: J. Krishnamurti in Dialogue with Leading Twentieth Century Thinkers* (pp. 200–214). Bramdean, Hampshire: Krishnamurti Foundation Trust Ltd.
Kumar, A. (2013). *Curriculum as Meditative Inquiry*. New York, NY: Palgrave Macmillan.
Lamotte, É. (2001). *The Treatise on the Great Virtue of Wisdom of Nagarjuna (Mahāprajñāpāramitā)* (G. K. M. Chodron, trans.). (Original work published 1949). Retrived from http://read.84000.co/resources/Indian%20 Buddhist%20Classics/Lamotte,%20%20Vol%202.%20Maha-prajnaparamita-sastra-%20by%20Nagarjuna%20(english%20translation).pdf
Lutz, A., Greischar, L. L., Rawlings, N. B., Ricard, M., & Davidson, R. J. (2004). Long-Term Meditators Self-Induce High-Amplitude Gamma Synchrony During Mental Practice. *Proceedings of the National Academy of Sciences of the United States of America, 101*(46), 16369–16373.

Maharaj, S. N. (1973). *I Am That: Conversations with Sri Nisargadatta Maharaj* (M. Friedman, trans.). Bombay: Chetana.
Mingyur, Y. (2007). *The Joy of Living: Unlocking the Secret and Science of Happiness.* New York, NY: Harmony Books.
Pinar, W. F. (2012). *What Is Curriculum Theory?* (2nd ed.). New York, NY: Routledge.
Smith, D. G. (2000). The Specific Challenges of Globalization for Teaching and Vice Versa. *The Alberta Journal of Education Research, XLVI*(1), 7–26.
Sopa, L. (2008). *Steps on the Path to Enlightenment: A Commentary on Tsongkhapa's Lamrim Chenmo. Volume III: The Way of the Bodhisattva.* Somerville, MA: Wisdom Publications.

CHAPTER 6

Learning to Appreciate Human Temporality

6.1 Time and Human Existence

Human temporality is one of the most significant features of human existence. Yet, as Greene (2004) indicated, "time is among the most familiar yet least understood concepts that humanity has ever encountered" (p. 127). It is so elusive that St. Augustine (397/1876) himself confessed: "What, then, is time? If no one ask of me, I know; if I wish to explain to him who asks, I know not" (p. 244). Even today, the subtle subject of time is far from fully grasped by science (Greene, 2004, p. 141). What is sure is that current scientific studies of time have exhibited various mind-boggling discrepancies between what is revealed in deep physical laws (e.g. Einstein's theory of relativity) and how we experience our everyday lives (Greene, 2004, pp. 127–142). This fact again demonstrates how human experience is often a misleading guide to the true nature of reality.

Considered within the two truths framework, while conventionally the objective concept of time provides us with a very handy tool and a very useful form of speech, ultimately speaking, time in itself is empty of any absolute, essential, and independent nature—it is dependently arising. As Huebner (1967/1999b) indicated, "the very notion of time arises out of man's existence, which is an emergent" (p. 137). The dependently arising nature of time in relation to human existence or human consciousness is made clear through Huebner's insights into the nature of future, past, and present. Drawing on Heidegger, Huebner (1967/1999b) indicated that

© The Author(s) 2019
E. L. Chu, *Exploring Curriculum as an Experience of Consciousness Transformation*, Curriculum Studies Worldwide, https://doi.org/10.1007/978-3-030-17701-0_6

115

the future is man facing himself in anticipation of his own potentiality for being. The past is finding himself already thrown into a world. It is the having-been which makes possible the projection of his potentiality. The present is the moment of vision when Dasein,[1] finding itself thrown into a situation (the past), projects its own potentiality for being. (p. 137)

Human existence, thus, "is not simply given by his being in a given place, but by a present determined by a past and a future; thus offering possibilities for new ways of being in the anticipated future" (Huebner, 1967/1999b, p. 135). For Huebner (1967/1999b), "there is no such 'thing' as a past or a future" (p. 137); rather, past and future "exist only through man's existence as a temporal being. This means that human life is never fixed, but is always emergent as the past and future become horizons of a present" (Huebner, 1967/1999b, p. 137). This elucidation of the relationship between humans and time not only increases our awareness of the dynamic and emerging nature of human existence and deepens our appreciation of the present which signifies infinite transcendental possibilities, but also makes clear the inseparability of human being and the world in which one already finds oneself. As Huebner (1967/1999b) stressed, human "temporality, or historicity, is not a characteristic of isolated man, but a characteristic of being-in-the-world" (p. 137). Given its resonances with the ultimate truth of emptiness, Huebner's concern for human temporality is in essence the concern for the ultimate nature of human existence that connotes infinite transcendental possibilities in the present and features the non-duality of being and world.

In Buddhism, based on Buddha's profound transcendental perception of human nature, human temporality is considered within an indefinitely prolonged framework of time that expands beyond both birth and death in the current life. The dispelling of the wrong views about the past, the future, and the present is fundamental to various spiritual progresses on the path of consciousness transformation. As Buddha states in the *Rice Seedling Sutra*:

> When you properly understand dependent origination, it clears away wrong views about the past, the future, and the present... "Wrong views about the past" refers to denying that existence has a cause, or imputing an incompatible cause...; "Wrong views about the future" refers to thinking that there is no future life after this life ends, that the causes you create in this life will have no results in the future. This is a kind of nihilism that leads to "wrong views about the present." This is the belief that your present behavior does

not matter because virtue and nonvirtue have no effect on future experience; you can do whatever you please because you will not suffer any consequences. (as cited in Sopa, 2005, p. 353)

A proper understanding of dependent origination also deepens our understanding of the theological description of human nature, which states that a human

> participates in both the conditioned and unconditioned, or in necessity and freedom. Man is conditioned to the world; he participates in the world's structures of necessity. But given this patterning, fixation, and conditioning, he also participates in the unconditioned—in freedom, or (if you wish) in the continual creation of the world. (Huebner, 1967/1999b, p. 135)

On one hand, the twelve links of dependent origination discussed in Chap. 3 reveal how our current *samsaric* form of existence is conditioned by the ripening of past karmic seeds or information deposited in our consciousness. On the other hand, the dependently arising nature of all phenomena and the ultimate truth of emptiness reveal how we are unconditioned in respect to how we respond to current experiences. From the perspectives of both Buddhism and theology, the opportunities to transcend our current forms of existence are always in the present, which is determined by both a conditioned past and an unconditioned future.

Learning to appreciate human temporality is thus, in essence, learning to appreciate the present, which is "the foundation of reverence" (Huebner, 1985a/1999c, p. 360). Drawing on Whitehead, who proposed "reverence as the other dimension of education that makes it religious" (Huebner, 1985a/1999c, p. 360), Huebner (1985a/1999c) asserted:

> The foundation of reverence "is the perception that the present holds within itself... eternity." In the present is the past *and* the future. In the present is the sum of all existence... In the traditions of Jewish and Christian faith communities, in the present dwells God—beyond comprehension, beyond knowing except for the glimmerings and the hints that shine forth in the acts of love, dwell in the awesome appearance of beauty and overwhelm us at the gift of life in birth and the loss of life in death. (p. 360)

The perception that the present holds within itself eternity and that in the present dwells God or the grand source that overwhelms us at the gift of life in birth and the loss of life in death suggests the significance of living in the present with humility for approaching the direct non-dualistic realization of emptiness. This perception also reminds us of our mortality, and human mortality, if revered and faced up to, is able to nurture the appreciation of the present and open the door to the grand, ultimate nature of human existence.

6.2 Death and Authenticity

In contemplating the question of how one should live, Heidegger addressed the concept of authenticity and its relationship with death. For Heidegger, "anxiety in the face of death... if faced up to, can open the door to an authentic existence" (Dreyfus & Wrathall, 2005, p. 8) because anxiety "liberates one from possibilities which 'count for nothing', and lets one become free-for those which are authentic" (as cited in Dreyfus & Wrathall, 2005, p. 8). Death, for Heidegger, is "the possibility of the impossibility of every way of comporting oneself toward anything, of every way of existing" (Dreyfus & Wrathall, 2005, p. 8). According to Dreyfus and Wrathall (2005), from Heidegger's perspective, "the way we relate to death is a fundamental kind of dealing in the world, one that affects the character of the way things show up at a very basic level" (p. 8). The certainty of death, thus, is not an empirical one, "but instead certain because it is the basis for disclosing ourselves to us. That is, our experience of every-thing is an experience in the light of the fact that we are mortal and temporal beings" (Dreyfus & Wrathall, 2005, p. 8). While there are, of course, various ways of trying to deal with death,

> an authentic being towards death means taking death as a possibility—that means, not thinking about it or dwelling on it, but rather taking it up in the way it shapes all our particular actions and relations... That is, we are ready for the world in light of the fact that each decision has consequences, and will someday culminate in our not being able to get by any longer. This, in turn, makes it possible for me to live my life as my own. (Dreyfus & Wrathall, 2005, p. 8)

However, Dreyfus and Wrathall (2005) indicate that, according to Heidegger, Dasein (the term Heidegger uses to refer to the peculiar human way of being whereby one is always already existing in a world) often "disguises from itself—primarily by taking up societal norms as if they somehow revealed the ultimate truth about how one should live"

(p. 7), to the extent that it becomes "all too easy never to take a stand for oneself" (p. 7); this aspect of conformism is called inauthenticity by Heidegger. According to Heidegger, "in [Dasein's] very being, that being is an issue for it" (as cited in Dreyfus & Wrathall, 2005, p. 8). As stated in Dreyfus and Wrathall's (2005) reading of Heidegger, this issue can be understood in terms of moods, which "are often dismissed as merely subjective colorings of our experience of the world" (p. 5); however, Heidegger insisted that "moods actually reveal something important about the fundamental structure of the world and our way of being in it" (p. 5). In other words, moods reflect one's realization of the nature of self and reality. According to Dreyfus and Wrathall (2005), Heidegger also maintained that

> while it is clear that moods are not objective properties of entities within the world, it is also clear that moods in fact are not merely subjective either. A boring lecture really is boring, a violent person really is frightening. This shows that the subjective–objective distinction fails to capture the interdependence of our being with the world and the entities around us. In addition, moods in fact make it possible for us to encounter entities within the world by determining how those entities will matter to us. (p. 5)

Echoing Buddha's teaching of dependent origination, Heidegger made clear how the subject–object dichotomy hinders us from realizing the dependent arising nature of self and reality, from living in light of our true nature as an authentic being-in-the-world, and from seeing new meanings and new possibilities in everyday encounters with the world. Moods, therefore reflect one's worldview and the presumed or realized "truth" grasped by an individual that influences one's relationship to the world, and reveal the ways one might take up death as a possibility for reshaping one's actions and relations. For Heidegger, authentic Dasein does not surrender itself to the public interpretation of the self, although it depends on it (Dreyfus & Wrathall, 2005, pp. 7–8). Furthermore, authentic Dasein "is open to the particular needs of the situation. Having recognized the fact that its being is at issue, it responds appropriately to the particular situation before it" (Dreyfus & Wrathall, 2005, p. 8). Therefore, in its authenticity, Dasein recognizes its being-in-the-world, challenges the public interpretation of the self, and takes up the public understanding of its world and makes it its own by projecting its own possibilities (Dreyfus & Wrathall, 2005, p. 8); such possibilities, in Heidegger's sense, constitute "a way of dealing with things that shows them as the things they are" (Dreyfus & Wrathall, 2005, p. 6). In other words, in authenticity, Dasein knows the ultimate nature of consciousness, self, and reality. Keeping in sight both the shadows and the source—its own consciousness, authentic Dasein recognizes the existence of infinite transcendental possibilities at each singular present and responds appropriately with the awareness that each action of body, mind, or speech has consequences.

6.3 Learning to Appreciate Human Temporality

Given its resonance with the ultimate nature of human existence explored in earlier discussion, Heidegger's insight into death and the authentic Dasein provides educators with a new perspective for contemplating how one might learn to appreciate human temporality and mortality, and how one might live and educate in light of the true nature of human existence. In the educational context, there have been numerous obstacles that have hindered Dasein from facing its temporality and mortality, from realizing its authentic existence as a being-in-the-world, and from living in a way that deals with things that shows them as they really are. Such obstacles originate partly from the disadvantages intrinsic in knowledge. As Huebner (1962/1999a) indicated, "the negative aspects of knowledge arise from the imposition of a symbolic curtain or screen between the person and reality" (p. 38). While this symbolic curtain does empower a person in his or her encounter with, and exploration of, reality, the very same curtain may also blind a person to what really is (Huebner, 1962/1999a, p. 38). Huebner (1962/1999a) quoted Cassirer's observation that "no longer can man confront reality immediately; he cannot see it, as it were, face to face" (p. 38). Given this screening quality of knowledge, a human "is apt to forget that reality is not seen 'as it is,' but through a man-made screen which filters out certain information and organizes the rest into patterns which exist not necessarily in the world" (Huebner, 1962/1999a, p. 38). In other words, in the absence of spiritual wisdom that knows emptiness, we are apt to forget that knowledge and various methods it serves are empty of any absolute, essential, and independent nature. Yet this disadvantage of knowledge can be overcome, Huebner (1962/1999a) suggested, when the human "uses knowledge with humility and tempers it with doubt, willing and eager to entertain other ways of knowing that which is beheld" (p. 39).

In educational contexts, as a result of the upholding of objective knowledge that serves various scientific methods as well as the neglect of spiritual wisdom, this screening and objectifying quality of knowledge also hinders human beings from seeing death as it is and, in turn, hinders humankind from living with authenticity. Thompson (2015) indicated that all of us will die, and that this is a fact like no other: "It's not just that every one of us will die; it's that I, myself, am going to die" (p. 274). Yet, despite this certainty, we don't believe that death will happen to us (Thompson, 2015, p. 274). Thompson (2015) also pointed out that "modern Western society, like no other society in human history, reinforces our blindness to the inevitability of our own death" (p. 274) in countless ways. One peculiar and powerful way is that biomedicine usually "talks about death as if it were essentially an objective and impersonal event instead of a subjective and personal one" (Thompson, 2015, p. 274). A purely biomedical perspective of death "consists in the breakdown of the functions of the living body along with the disappearance of all outer signs of consciousness" (Thompson, 2015, p. 274). Missing from this biomedical perspective, Thompson (2015) emphasized, "is the subjective experience of this breakdown and the significance of the inevitable fact of one's own death. Biomedicine hides the inner experience of dying and the existential meaning of death" (Thompson, 2015, p. 274). In sharp contrast, according to Thompson (2015), "the Indian and Tibetan yogic traditions claim to provide detailed accounts of the transformations of consciousness during the dying process" (p. 275), and Tibetan Buddhism also "offers a rich contemplative perspective on death, including meditations to prepare for death and to practice as one dies. This kind of experiential view of dying and death is missing from the biomedical perspective" (p. 275). Various experiential views of dying and death can also be found in the records of different religious and spiritual traditions (e.g., the records of successful practitioners in the Pure Land school[2] of Buddhism, and guidance on dying and *bardo* experiences,[3] meaning the intermediate state between death and the next rebirth, in Tibetan Buddhism) and in the burgeoning research into near death experiences (e.g., the works of Raymond Moody and Bruce Greyson) and reincarnation in the last few decades. In Buddhism, such experiential views of death are categorized as extremely remote or extremely obscure phenomena that cannot be known through direct perception nor through inference, but are known only through the testimony of a third person (Thompson, 2015, p. 288). Yet such experiential accounts as "the records of those who have been transformed, or have experienced transcending moments" (Huebner, 1985b/1999d, p. 346) are of great educational significance. In Huebner's (1985b/1999d) words, these moments constitute "ways to know others, and consequently also ways to know one's self" (p. 347) and "provide ways to think and talk about one's self, with others, from birth to death. They provide possibilities, to be chosen or rejected" (p. 347). For the purposes of educating toward the truth and of facilitating the transformation of consciousness, such experiential views of death should be mined by educators.

Learning to appreciate human temporality, therefore, is learning to appreciate the ultimate nature of human existence as unveiled in the dialogue between Buddhism and quantum physics, and learning to appreciate the present that connotes infinite transcendental possibilities of attaining authentic existence. This requires one to liberate oneself from those possibilities that count for nothing, based on the reverence for human mortality and on the right view that allows one to see death as it is. When we appreciate human temporality, we recognize the significance of learning to take responsibility for our decisions and respond appropriately to the world.

As suggested in the stage of intensified efforts—the second stage of the five-stage gradual path of consciousness transformation—learning to take responsibility for one's decisions and respond appropriately to the world requires a vision to enter the path of spiritual discernment by making efforts to cultivate the non-dualistic worldview conducive to decisive distinction. The vision to enter the path of spiritual discernment necessitates the cultivation of a righteous mindset and motivation to guide and support us through the path. Therefore, before investigating how we might learn to take responsibility for our decisions and respond appropriately to the world, in the next chapter, I explore the cultivation of impartiality and *bodhicitta* that is crucial to developing significant spiritual discernment.

NOTES

1. Dasein is a term used by Heidegger (1927/2010) to refer to the peculiar human way of being—with the fundamental structure being-in-the-world—whereby one is always already existing in a world.
2. Successful practitioners of Pure Land Buddhism usually know (mostly being informed by Amitabha Buddha or Guanyin bodhisattva) the exact time of their death and prepare for it in advance. At the moment of death, the dying

practitioner would inform those people who are on the scene of the advent of the Three Saints of the West (Amitabha Buddha, and bodhisattvas Avalokiteśvara (Guanyin) and Mahāsthāmaprāpta) who are going to escort this dying person to Amitabha Buddha's Pure Land. After passing away, the facial expression of the dead practitioner is usually very peaceful, and their body remains extremely soft and flexible.

3. Compiled and edited by Evans-Wentz (1927/2000), *The Tibetan Book of the Dead: Or the After-Death Experiences on the Bardo Plane, According to Lama Kazi Dawa-Samdup's English Rendering* is one of the best-known English translations of the experiential teaching on death in Tibetan Buddhist literature.

References

Augustine, S. (1876). *The Confessions of St. Augustine* (J. G. Pilkington, trans.). Garden City, NY: International Collectors Library, American Headquarters. (Original work published 397). Retrieved from https://en.wikisource.org/wiki/The_Confessions_of_Saint_Augustine_(Pilkington)

Dreyfus, H., & Wrathall, M. (2005). Martin Heidegger: An Introduction to His Thought, Work, and Life. In H. Dreyfus & M. Wrathall (Eds.), *A Companion to Heidegger* (pp. 1–15). Malden, MA: Wiley-Blackwell.

Evans-Wentz, W. Y. (2000). *The Tibetan Book of the Dead: Or the After-Death Experiences on the Bardo Plane, According to Lama Kazi Dawa-Samdup's English Rendering*. New York, NY: Oxford University Press. (Original work published 1927).

Greene, B. (2004). *The Fabric of the Cosmos: Space, Time, and the Texture of Reality*. New York, NY: Alfred A. Knopf.

Heidegger, M. (2010). *Being and Time* (J. Stambaugh, trans.). Albany, NY: State University of New York Press. (Original work published 1927).

Huebner, D. E. (1999a). Knowledge: An Instrument of Man. In V. Hillis (Ed.), *The Lure of the Transcendent: Collected Essays by Dwayne E. Huebner* (pp. 36–43). New York, NY: Routledge. (Reprinted from an unpublished manuscript 1962).

Huebner, D. E. (1999b). Curriculum as Concern for Man's Temporality. In V. Hillis (Ed.), *The Lure of the Transcendent: Collected Essays by Dwayne E. Huebner* (pp. 131–142). New York, NY: Routledge. (Original work published 1967).

Huebner, D. E. (1999c). Religious Metaphors in the Language of Education. In V. Hillis (Ed.), *The Lure of the Transcendent: Collected Essays by Dwayne E. Huebner* (pp. 358–368). New York, NY: Routledge. (Original work published 1985a).

Huebner, D. E. (1999d). Spirituality and Knowing. In V. Hillis (Ed.), *The Lure of the Transcendent: Collected Essays by Dwayne E. Huebner* (pp. 340–352). New York, NY: Routledge. (Original work published 1985b).

Sopa, L. (2005). *Steps on the Path to Enlightenment: A Commentary on Tsongkhapa's Lamrim Chenmo. Volume II: Karma*. Somerville, MA: Wisdom Publications.

Thompson, E. (2015). *Waking, Dreaming, Being: Self and Consciousness in Neuroscience, Meditation, and Philosophy*. New York, NY: Columbia University Press.

CHAPTER 7

Cultivating Impartiality and *Bodhicitta*

7.1 Introduction to Impartiality and *Bodhicitta*

Among the four transcendental wisdoms explored in Chap. 4, the perfection of universal equality wisdom—which bears on both the ultimate and phenomenal aspects of reality and sees the identity of all phenomena and the equality between its own self and other sentient beings—is one of the four mental attributes of Buddhahood that represent the fulfillment of *bodhicitta* (the aspiration to attain the highest spiritual goal of the omniscience of enlightenment for the liberation of all sentient beings in the same miserable situation). Such non-discriminating transcendental wisdom is "equally divorced from the aspects of subject and object… Both aspects constitute discrimination, being the sophistic manifestation of the mind which clings to something as its object" (Hsuan-Tsang, 659/1973, p. 687). While the dissolution of the subject–object dichotomy is crucial for the transformation of consciousness toward the ultimate spiritual truth, given that "our dualistic perspective of 'self' and 'other' didn't develop overnight, we can't expect to overcome it all at once" (Mingyur, 2007, pp. 176–177). As Sopa (2008) indicated, "our minds are like wild elephants drunk with self-centered egoism. If anything looks like it might harm us we try to destroy it" (p. 42). In the long run, such attempts at self-protection that originate from the ignorance of the ultimate truth of emptiness create only more problems and suffering rather than positive, happy, and blissful experiences. However, the elephant can be tamed gradually, and one day "we can reverse our habitual selfish inclinations and develop universal compassion free from partiality" (Sopa, 2008, p. 12) by means of the unwavering cultivation of *bodhicitta*.

As the principal motivation for attaining the highest enlightenment, *bodhicitta* arises from superior thought, which is a special kind of love and compassion. As Sopa (2008) indicated,

> superior love is taking responsibility for the happiness of all others. Superior compassion is thinking "I will take responsibility for eliminating the suffering of other beings." This is far greater than kindly thinking, "How nice it would be if others were happy and free from misery." Once we decide to take the responsibility to free others from misery and lead them to bliss, we see that attaining enlightenment is the only way to do it.[1] (p. 43)

At first glance, the aspiration of *bodhicitta* may seem daunting or even impossible, but if we begin with the cultivation of superior love (devoting to bringing others positive things such as happiness) and superior compassion (focusing on freeing others from negative circumstances by the means of applying the antidote to partiality), it becomes more practicable. The significance of recognizing the equality of all sentient beings lies in the fact that "if we do not take the antidote to partiality—being attached to some, hating others and ignoring the rest—our compassion and love will be discriminatory" (Sopa, 2008, p. 63) and "if we try to generate compassion before mastering equanimity [or impartiality] the result will not be the great universal compassion" (Sopa, 2008, p. 63). In other words, without recognizing the equality of all sentient beings and cultivating impartiality, we can never develop proper spiritual discernment conducive to the attainment of various spiritual goals. Nevertheless, the cultivation of impartial love and compassion does not mean that we do not counteract oppression. Rather, with sympathy for the oppressors' ignorance of the true nature of human existence and concern regarding the grave consequences of their perpetration of the non-virtues, we learn to undertake ethical counteractions (uniting both method and wisdom), inspired by compassion rather than by anger or hatred.

One basic way to get rid of partiality is to consider "why sentient beings are equal from *their* side and why there is no reason for us to discriminate from *our* side" (Sopa, 2008, p. 64). From *their* side, all sentient beings, whether they are our friends or our enemies, just like ourselves, "equally want to have happiness. None of them want any problems, disagreement, or suffering; on this basis there is no difference between them. If we think about it deeply we will realize that they are equal" (Sopa, 2008, pp. 64–65). From *our* side, within the broad framework of time, we have been born innumerable times high or low in the six realms,[2] and have had various relationships with each sentient being (Sopa, 2008, p. 65). Each of them has once been our best friend and our worst enemy, "so to which ones should we be attached? Which of them should we hate? There is no way to make this distinction objectively" (Sopa, 2008, p. 65). Another way of getting rid of partiality is to contemplate the ultimate truth of emptiness and the dependently arising nature of all phenomena. Although there always exist phenomenal differences between sentient beings, ultimately speaking, all sentient beings, no matter who or what they are at a given time, are temporal and impermanent manifestations based on various causes and conditions; therefore, all are equally empty of any absolute, essential, fixed, and independent nature, and are equally participating in the unconditioned, in the present that signifies infinite transcendental possibilities.

After developing the superior thoughts of love and compassion toward all sentient beings without partiality, one can then train the mind to develop *bodhicitta*—the aspiration to attain the highest spiritual goal of the omniscience of enlightenment for the liberation of all sentient beings. *Bodhicitta* can be understood from various perspectives. Usually, it is understood as having two aspects: *absolute bodhicitta* and *relative bodhicitta*. Absolute *bodhicitta* refers to the "spontaneous recognition[3] that all sentient beings, regardless of how they act or appear, are already completely enlightened" (Mingyur, 2007, p. 177). When the state of absolute *bodhicitta* is achieved, "there is no distinction between sentient beings; every living creature is understood as a perfect manifestation of Buddha nature" (Mingyur, 2007, p. 190). However, as Mingyur (2007) indicated, since very few people are capable of attaining this state immediately and most of us are still caught up in regarding other sentient beings from a dualistic perspective, we need to begin by developing relative *bodhicitta*, which itself has two aspects—aspiration and application (pp. 188–189). According to Mingyur (2007), with impartial love and compassion as its basis, "aspiration bodhicitta involves cultivating the heartfelt desire to raise all sentient beings to the level at which they recognize their Buddha nature" (p. 190), and thinking that "*I wish to attain complete awakening in order to help all sentient beings attain the same state*" (p. 190); application *bodhicitta* is actually taking actions to accomplish this aspiration

(p. 190). The practices of relative *bodhicitta*, such as the six perfections, cultivate within us an open mindset that allows the dualistic perspective of self and other to dissolve, and thereby allow the wisdom and power to help others and ourselves to grow (Mingyur, 2007, p. 190). In spite of the fact that the cultivation of relative *bodhicitta* is working within the framework of duality, it is grounded on the approach of negation that features the simultaneous perception of both the ultimate and phenomenal aspects of reality. This double vision is the realization that every sentient being is already a perfect manifestation of the Buddha Nature, God, or the Divine intrinsic in everyone, and that all sentient beings and phenomena are impermanent and dependently arising in accordance with the underlying law of cause and effect of karma, and therefore are empty of any absolute, independent, and fixed nature. Such Middle Way perception provides us with a substantial philosophical ground for deliberating the significance of the axiom of equality for education.

7.2 The Axioms of Equality and Inequality

In a talk on *ignorant* schoolmasters, Jacques Rancière (2010) indicated that "the most important quality of a schoolmaster is the virtue of ignorance" (p. 1). Yet, by ignorance, Rancière (2010) meant being ignorant of the "explanatory logic that presents inequality axiomatically" (p. 5). According to Rancière (2010), in this explanatory logic, "one must start from inequality in order to reduce it" (p. 4) and "the way to reduce inequality is to conform to it by making it an object of knowledge" (p. 4). In his reading of Joseph Jacotot, Rancière (2010) indicated that, with inequality as the presupposition, the goal of an equality-to-come that consists simply of the unequal equality, "will, in turn, only drive a system that produces and reproduces inequality" (p. 5). The explanatory logic of the axiom of inequality, for Rancière (2010), "is a social logic in which the social order is presented and reproduced" (p. 6) and thus merits the name of *stultification* (Rancière, 2010, p. 5).

Rather than being an ignorant person who is thrilled by playing teacher, an ignorant schoolmaster is a teacher "who shows us that the so-called 'transmission of knowledge' consists in fact of two intertwined relations that are important to dissociate: a relation of will to will and a relation of intelligence to intelligence" (Rancière, 2010, p. 2). However, Rancière (2010) emphasized that it is not "the desire to undermine the relation of educational authority in order that one intelligence might enlighten another more effectively" (p. 2) that "is the principle of numerous anti-authoritarian pedagogies whose model is the maieutic[4] of the Socratic pedagogue" (p. 2). Rather, he underscored that the ignorant schoolmaster

> indeed knows the double gambit of the maieutic. Under the disguise of creating a capacity, the maieutic aims, in fact, to demonstrate an incapacity... The "liberalist" maieutic is just a sophisticated variation of ordinary pedagogical practice, which entrusts to the teacher's intelligence the ability to bridge the gap separating the ignorant person from knowledge. (Rancière, 2010, p. 2)

By contrast, an ignorant schoolmaster exercises an authority—"a will that sets the ignorant person down a path, that is to say to instigate a capacity already possessed" (Rancière, 2010, pp. 2–3). For ignorant schoolmasters, equality is "an axiom to be verified. It relates the states of inequality in the teacher–student relation not to the promise of an equality-to-come that will never come, but to the reality of a basic equality" (Rancière, 2010, p. 5). Rancière (2010) argued that "equality, in general, is not an end to be attained. It is a point of departure, a presupposition to be verified by sequences of specific acts" (p. 9). Significantly, for Rancière, equality and inequality are not two states, but two opinions, meaning two distinct axioms by which education can operate (pp. 4–5). An ignorant schoolmaster who refuses the knowledge of inequality "addresses him or herself to the ignorant person not from the point of view of the person's ignorance but of the person's knowledge" (Rancière, 2010, p. 5). For Rancière (2010), "the obstacle stopping the abilities of the ignorant one is not his or her ignorance, but the consent to inequality" (p. 5), and what can suspend this submission to inequality is not the teacher's knowledge, "but the teacher's will" (p. 6). The emancipatory teacher's call, asserted Rancière (2010), "forbids the supposed ignorant one the satisfaction of what is known, the satisfaction of admitting that one is incapable of knowing more" (p. 6). The emancipatory teacher "forces the student to prove his or her capacity, to continue the intellectual journey the same way it began" (Rancière, 2010, p. 6). In other words, emancipatory teachers recognize the Buddha Nature (or the dwelling God, or the transcendent) intrinsic equally in everyone despite the phenomenal and temporal differences in their manifestations at a given time. With the heartfelt desire to raise all their students to the level at which they recognize their Buddha Nature or God within, emancipatory teachers embody spiritual wisdom and impartial love and compassion in their will and authority that open new possibilities, instigate the transcendent of the current forms of existence, and give assurances that life will be enhanced and can be whole again in the face of the lure of the transcendent that might look threatening. With an open mindset that knows the ultimate equality of all sentient beings and allows dualistic and discriminating perspectives to dissolve, emancipatory teachers also make possible genuine conversation and truthful knowing. As Rancière (2010) explained, an emancipatory teacher "is first of all a person who speaks to another, who tell stories and returns the authority of knowledge to the poetic condition of all spoken interaction" (p. 6). For Rancière (2010), the logic that operates under the presupposition of equality deserves the name of *intellectual emancipation* (p. 6).

The distinction between stultification and intellectual emancipation (i.e., the logics that presume inequality and equality, respectively), however, is not a distinction between methods of instruction but one of philosophy (Rancière, 2010, p. 6). From the perspective of the two truths doctrine, the major philosophical distinction between the two logics is that the logic that presumes inequality refers to the mere phenomenal aspect of self and reality, while the logic that presumes equality as a point of departure follows the Middle Way approach and grasps simultaneously both the ultimate and phenomenal aspects of self and reality. For Rancière (2010), this distinction "concerns an idea of intelligence that guides the very conception of intellectual training" (p. 6). Rather than affirming any specific virtue for those who do not know, Rancière (2010) maintained that the axiom of equality of intelligences "simply affirms that there is only one sort of intelligence at work in all intellectual training" (p. 6) and "concerns the very conception of the relation between equality and inequality" (p. 6) that is in question. What is questioned is the logic of the equalization of inequality in a society that puts "into harmony its productive forces, its institutions, and its beliefs, making them act according to a singular regime of rationality" (Rancière, 2010, p. 7). The problem lies in the fact that such explanatory logic of rationality, akin to our earlier discussion on the limitation of rational analysis, is "characterized by infinite regress... [in that] an explanation is usually accompanied by an explanation of that explanation" (Rancière, 2010, p. 3). Referring to Jacotot's summation, Rancière observed that "if explanation [of inequality] is in principle infinite, it is because its primary function is to infinitize the very distance it proposes to reduce" (p. 3). People's education, thus, becomes "an 'explanation' of society; it is a working allegory of the way that inequality is reproduced by 'making visible' equality" (Rancière, 2010, p. 8).

By means of embracing such knowledge of inequality—"knowledge about why those who are left behind are left behind" (Rancière, 2010, p. 13)—accumulated from the explanatory logic of rationality, both educators and students risk falling prey to a hidden social bond. This hidden bond features the overreliance on rational analysis and scientific knowledge based on the subject–object dichotomy which, as discussed earlier, can hinder us from confronting reality directly and from seeing reality as it is, and can hardly enable genuine conversation and true comprehension of a specific existential situation in its totality in the present which connotes infinite transcendental possibilities.

In contrast, emancipatory teachers refuse to blindly take up the knowledge of inequality and the explanatory logic of societal norms which presumes inequality as a point of departure. As Huebner (1985/1999a) underscored, all knowing requires openness, meaning that

> present forms of knowledge, which relate the person to the vast otherness in the world and which hold together past, present, and future, must be acknowledged as limited, fallible, insufficient. To have new forms emerge, old forms must give way to relationship: love takes priority over knowledge. (p. 350)

However, without taking the antidote to partiality, our love will be discriminatory. One of the subtlest forms of partiality is revealed in the act of taking the axiom of inequality for granted and accepting without hesitation the knowledge and explanatory logic of inequality. What distinguishes emancipatory teachers from others, therefore, is that by means of recognizing the ultimate equality of all sentient beings, they prioritize impartial love rather than the explanatory knowledge of inequality. From Buddhist perspectives, emancipatory teachers are emancipatory because they respect both the ultimate and phenomenal aspects of self and reality, are open to new possibilities, and act based on truthful knowing from a non-objectifying perspective and proper spiritual discernment informed by the ultimate truth, rather than on the mere explanatory knowledge of societal norms. Imbued with spiritual wisdom that knows emptiness and the ultimate equality of all sentient beings, emancipatory teachers' methods and intelligence thus become emancipatory—not only do they themselves live in accordance with the true nature of human existence, but their impartial love and their will to activate the capacity already possessed by their students also become a call for their students to recognize their full potential and live with authenticity.

The above discussion explored how the universal equality wisdom as well as absolute and relative *bodhicitta* might provide us with deepened insights for contemplating the impact of the subtle philosophical differences between the axioms of equality and inequality held by teachers. This exploration not only demonstrates the significance of impartiality and *bodhicitta* for education but also suggests the crucial role teachers play in facilitating the transformation of consciousness. Importantly, as Huebner's (1993/1999b) observed, "it is futile to hope that teachers can be aware of the spiritual in education unless they maintain some form of spiritual discipline" (p. 415). In the following, we turn our attention to another aspect of the educational significance of *bodhicitta* as the motivation of teaching, learning, and knowing, in contrast with market logic.

As the essence of the Mahayana spiritual path, *bodhicitta* is the most powerful virtue since it dispels our great enemy—selfishness (Sopa, 2008, pp. 25–29)—and guides us directly to the highest spiritual goal of the omniscience of enlightenment for the liberation of all sentient beings. As the core motivation of the method-side practices, such as the six perfections, *bodhicitta* not only prevents practitioners from falling into the habitual tendency of objectifying, but also transforms ordinary everyday routine into meaningful practices and transcendental opportunities. As Sopa (2008) observed, like an alchemical elixir that turns iron into gold, *bodhicitta* "transforms every activity so that it is for the benefit of other sentient beings" (p. 32). "When bodhisattvas eat or sleep," explained Sopa (2008), "their motivation is to keep up their strength so they can attain their goal of helping other sentient beings," thus "with bodhicitta, everything we do—even eating or sleeping—becomes a virtue" (p. 32).

7.3 BODHICITTA AS AN ALTERNATIVE TO THE MARKET LOGIC AND GLOBAL COMPETITIVENESS

In educational contexts, *bodhicitta*—akin to what Einstein (1930/1954) called "the cosmic religious feeling" (p. 39)—when accompanied with spiritual wisdom that knows emptiness, can be the strongest and noblest motive for engaging in various modes of teaching, learning and knowing, and can transform every activity into the cause of blissful experiences and spiritual progress for oneself and others. In contrast to the formulaic logic of the market and the language of global competitiveness that instigate social and educational planning inspired by the sheer desire to win, the motivation of *bodhicitta* restores knowledge to the eternal cycle of openness, love, and hope, and returns dignity, value, meaning, and purpose to human beings. It is worthwhile at this point to revisit Huebner's (1985/1999a) observation, explored in Chap. 2, that "every mode of knowing is also a mode of being in relationship. It is a relationship of mutual care and love" (p. 349), yet the distortion of this relationship of mutual care and love occurs when "caring is for the self and knowing becomes an act of control, often an act of violence" (p. 349). The sheer desire to win, as a prevailing form of the distortion of the relationship of mutual care and love entrenched in the sharp subject–object dichotomy, has, according to Smith (2000), led to "hypercompetitiveness in the social realm" (p. 18) and "heightened social paranoia and the turning of friends into enemies" (p. 18) that can hardly bring about true conversation and truthful knowing. Being ignorant of the true nature of human existence, and being blinded by the rhetoric that posits global competitiveness as necessary for securing one's own happiness, we fall prey to the deviation of conceptual proliferation and reification, and begin to pursue something ideally hypostatized by the ego as "happiness." Yet, as shown in earlier exploration of the approach of negation, positive states and outcomes such as happiness can never be attained through the pursuit of ideally hypostatized objects (e.g., people, fame, wealth, etc.) in a dualistic mode and through a sheer desire to win, but rather manifest themselves only through the negation of the afflictions originating from the dualistic subject–object perception, and through living in accordance with our true nature as an authentic being-in-the-world. In the words of Adam Smith in *The Theory of Moral Sentiments*:

> If we placed our happiness in winning the stake, we placed it in what depended upon causes beyond our power and out of our direction. We necessarily exposed ourselves to perpetual fear and uneasiness, and frequently to grievous and mortifying disappointments. If we placed it in playing well, in playing fairly, in playing wisely and skillfully, in the propriety of our own conduct, in short, we placed it in what, by proper discipline, education, and attention, might altogether be in our own power, and under our own direction. Our happiness was perfectly secure and beyond the reach of fortune. (Smith, as cited in Ahmed, 2010, p. 208)

Smith's words make clear that the formulaic logic of the market and the language of global competitiveness that instigate social and educational planning motivated solely by the desire to win expose human beings to perpetual fear and uneasiness rather than happiness. While Smith's argument addressed only personal happiness, it is obvious that if we place our happiness "in playing well, in playing fairly, in playing wisely and skillfully, in the propriety of our own conduct" (as cited in Ahmed, 2010, p. 208) motivated by *bodhicitta* imbued with the wisdom that knows emptiness, we secure not only our own happiness and ultimate liberation but also the happiness and liberation of all sentient beings.

As discussed earlier, while objectivism is no longer upheld in today's educational landscape, Palmer (1983/2003) reminds us that it is institutionalized in our educational practices, in our ways of teaching and learning (p. 65), and in our motivations for teaching and learning. Huebner (1993/1999b) also drew our attention to the problem that "the schools are not places where the moral and spiritual life is lived with any kind of intentionality" (p. 415). It seems to me that the motivation instigated by the sheer desire to win at least partly explains "how the spiritual and moral is being denied in everything" (Huebner, 1993/1999b, p. 414) and how objectivism is institutionalized. Smith (2000) cautioned us that, as the central logic of contemporary globalization, market logic "is not adequate for ensuring a future that is truly open and capable of sustaining human fellowship in any decent sense. It is a logic that requires a profound deconstruction" (p. 25). In the face of various global crises, I am convinced that with its alchemical-elixir-like transformative power, the altruistic motivation of *bodhicitta* provides us an alternative logic for educational planning, teaching, learning, and studying, and for sustaining human life in a noble and dignified way.

In this chapter, for the purpose of cultivating a righteous mindset and motivation for entering the path of spiritual discernment that is conducive to decisive distinction and to learning to take responsibility for one's decisions and respond appropriately to the world, I have explored the educational significance of cultivating impartiality and *bodhicitta*. On the basis of the understanding of the nature of consciousness, self, and reality, as well as the appreciation of human temporality and the impartial and altruistic motivation of *bodhicitta*, in the next chapter, I explore how we might cultivate the spiritual discernment conducive to decisive distinction and become responsibly responsive.

NOTES

1. According to Sopa (2008),

    the accumulation of wisdom is meditation on the deep realization of the truth with no dual perception... When one arises from meditation on emptiness, one keeps in mind the understanding that the nature of things is illusory and empty of substantive existence, and engages in various activities to accumulate merit. Practiced together in this way, wisdom and method will result in buddhahood. (p. 203)

Usually, bodhisattvas engage in both practices over many lifetimes, sometimes for eons (Sopa, 2008, p. 203). Only when one attains Buddhahood can one practice the accumulation of wisdom and the accumulation of merit simultaneously (Sopa, 2008, p. 64) and achieve the perfection of the four transcendental wisdoms.
2. "Six realms" refers to six directions of reincarnation or six states of existence, including hell, hungry ghost, animal, asura (malevolent nature spirits), human existence, and deva (heavenly existence).
3. From a Buddhist perspective, sentient beings' spontaneous cognition of things differs according to their karma. One radical example is that, while a cup of liquid appears to a human to be cool clean water, it appears to a hungry ghost to be pus and blood, and appears to a god to be nectar (Cabezón, 1992, p. 335). With the liquid substance as the material cause and the hungry ghost's evil karma as the dominant cause, the cup of liquid arises as pus and blood; similarly, with a god's own karma as the dominant cause, the cup of liquid arises as nectar for the god (Cabezón, 1992, p. 336).
4. The maieutic method, also known as the Socratic method, "is that of eliciting ideas by questioning; the image is that the ideas are already there in the pregnant subject's mind, but require midwifery to be made manifest" (Blackburn, 2016).

References

Ahmed, S. (2010). *The Promise of Happiness*. Durham: Duke University Press.
Blackburn, S. (2016). Maieutic Method. In *The Oxford Dictionary of Philosophy*. Oxford University Press. Retrieved April 9, 2018, from http://www.oxfordreference.com/view/10.1093/acref/9780198735304.001.0001/acref-9780198735304-e-1914
Cabezón, J. I. (1992). *A Dose of Emptiness: An Annotated Translation of the sTong thun chen mo of mKhas grub dGe legs dpal bzang*. Albany, NY: State University of New York Press.
Einstein, A. (1954). Religion and Science. In A. Einstein (Ed.), *Ideas and Opinions* (pp. 36–54, S. Bargmann, trans.). New York: Crown. (Reprinted from *The New York Times Magazine*, pp. 1–4, November 9, 1930).
Hsuan-Tsang (1973). *Ch'eng Wei-shi Lun: The Doctrine of Mere-Consciousness* (T. Wei, trans.). Hong Kong, China: The Ch'eng Wei-shih Lun Publication Committee. (Original work published 659). Retrieved from http://www.dhalbi.org/dhalbi/html_t/authors/author_main.php?p_id=8
Huebner, D. E. (1999a). Spirituality and Knowing. In V. Hillis (Ed.), *The Lure of the Transcendent: Collected Essays by Dwayne E. Huebner* (pp. 340–352). New York, NY: Routledge. (Original work published 1985).

Huebner, D. E. (1999b). Education and Spirituality. In V. Hillis (Ed.), *The Lure of the Transcendent: Collected Essays by Dwayne E. Huebner* (pp. 401–416). New York, NY: Routledge. (Original work published 1993).

Mingyur, Y. (2007). *The Joy of Living: Unlocking the Secret and Science of Happiness.* New York, NY: Harmony Books.

Palmer, P. J. (2003). Education as Spiritual Formation. *Educational Horizons,* 82(1), 55–67. (Reprinted from *To Know as We Are Known: Education as a Spiritual Journey,* pp. 17–32, 1983, New York, NY: HarperCollins).

Rancière, J. (2010). On Ignorant Schoolmasters. In C. Bingham & G. Biesta (Eds.), *Jacques Rancière: Education, Truth, Emancipation* (pp. 1–24). London: Continuum Publishing Group.

Smith, D. G. (2000). The Specific Challenges of Globalization for Teaching and Vice Versa. *The Alberta Journal of Education Research, XLVI*(1), 7–26.

Sopa, L. (2008). *Steps on the Path to Enlightenment: A Commentary on Tsongkhapa's Lamrim Chenmo. Volume III: The Way of the Bodhisattva.* Somerville, MA: Wisdom Publications.

CHAPTER 8

Becoming Responsibly Responsive

8.1 Introduction

In this chapter, I explore the concept of being responsibly responsive and its relationship with the dilemma of change or non-change, and then examine how we might become responsibly responsive from three different perspectives. Firstly, drawing on the practices of the four reflections and four exact realizations, I examine the role of language in dominating our worldview; I discuss how the habitual force of hypostatization and reification might cause us to forget the symbolic function of language and mistake what is just a useful way of speech for reality as it really is, and might thus hinder us from seeing things as they really are—which is the moral basis for becoming responsibly responsive. Secondly, I explore the educational significance of the injunctions of the four noble truths for overcoming the stultifying effects of passivity brought about by pain and for awakening us to our responsibility as temporal beings-in-the-world. Thirdly, drawing on Lusthaus's (2002) analysis of the quandary of human change and changelessness and its relationship with identities and the appropriational circuit between the grasper and the grasped, as well as Pinar's (1974) analysis of dehumanization (or estrangement) and movie consciousness, I show that becoming responsibly responsive is first and foremost an inner process which we undertake by means of exploring how the sharp self–world dichotomy may nurture our attachment to the outward pursuit of hypostatized happiness and, as a result, blind us to infinite possibilities and hinder us from becoming truly responsibly responsive.

In Chap. 3, through the dialogue between Buddhism and quantum physics, we came to the realization that the concern of our being as humans is in essence the concern of human consciousness, and that the essence and purpose of education is the transformation of consciousness from the grasping of deceptive phenomenal everyday experiences toward the conceptual and direct non-dualistic realization of the ultimate truth of emptiness, personal liberation, and the highest spiritual goal of the liberation of all sentient beings. The real occurrence of education thus always entails the examination, overcoming, transformation, reformation, shifting, and transcendence of the presently assumed "truth" grasped by an individual. This suggests that change is essential for education. Yet the desired changes are not arbitrary ones. In Huebner's (1966/1999b) words, "it isn't simply change that is wanted, it's something else" (p. 118).

In his concern for human temporality, Huebner (1967/1999c) underscored that "man is a transcendent being, i.e., he has the capacity to transcend what he is to become something he is not. In religious languages this is his nature, for he is a creator" (pp. 134–135). He indicated that since the ability to transcend is intrinsic in human nature, as educators, the appropriate question we should ask is not how to explain change, but how to explain non-change (Huebner, 1967/1999c, p. 134), or "what gets in the way of the great journey—the journey of the self or soul" (Huebner, 1993/1999d, p. 405). Huebner (1966/1999b) also observed that perhaps, for the majority of educators, neither ideas of change nor ideas of non-change are desired; rather, educators are interested in something in between—a balance (p. 119). As Lusthaus (2002) indicated, "radical change disrupts what we are used to, while routine deadens our senses" (p. 3), both extremes harbor dangers (p. 3). Huebner (1966/1999b) also expressed his concerns regarding the terms "change" and "innovation" (p. 118). While he emphasized that "by all means schools should have innovations and a climate should be fostered in which innovations can come to the surface; for these are the sources of renewal" (p. 118), he expressed wariness regarding the notion of novelty and the meaning of innovation, which is somewhat distinct from evolution and history (pp. 118–119). He explained that

> evolution takes place not by simply introducing something new, but also through respect for the historicity of a given situation [or individual]... Newness can be introduced, or an old situation brought up to date, but the

new in a short time can become the old. It is the continuous process of keeping something alive and viable that should concern educators. (Huebner, 1966/1999b, p. 119)

Huebner (1966/1999b) thus proposed that perhaps "a more adequate term to describe that which is needed in schools today is neither 'change' nor 'innovation,' but 'responsiveness'" (p. 119), meaning a person's ability to respond. One important form of a person's response is "his understanding of himself in the moment of vision, as he projects his own possibility for being in terms of 'having been'" (p. 138). However, given that responsiveness can be anything at either side of, or at any point between, the change–permanence continuum, Huebner stressed that what is desirable is being responsibly responsive (p. 119).

Huebner's (1966/1999b) usage of the word "responsibly" is "in the sense of being aware of one's obligations as an historical and temporal being for the continual creation of the world and in the sense of being accountable for one's acts" (p. 120). He elucidated that, since each decision we make is in a particular time and place,

> those who share that time and place rightfully hold him responsible for the consequences of his decisions. However, his decision is a factor in the continual emergence or evolution of that situation as it exists through time, thus his accountability extends into the past and into the future. To be responsibly responsive, then, is to be aware of the history and destiny of the given situation and to be answerable for the consequences of any responses made. (Huebner, 1966/1999b, p. 120)

Huebner made clear that each of us is responsible for not only our own destiny but also our shared future on earth. On the basis of the renewed realization of the nature of human existence attained in the dialogue between Buddhism and quantum physics, we see that to be truly aware of the history and destiny of a given situation and to be answerable for the consequences of any responses made requires us to cultivate proper spiritual discernment grounded on the recognition of human nature as dependently arising and as signifying infinite transcendental possibilities in the present, the willingness to allow the self–world dichotomy to dissolve and to see things as they truly are, and a righteous mindset and an altruistic motivation of *bodhicitta*. Becoming responsibly responsive, therefore, involves cultivating spiritual discernment that allows one to make decisions grounded on the understanding of the true nature of consciousness, self, and reality, the appreciation of human temporality, and the impartial and altruistic motivation of *bodhicitta*.

8.2 Cultivating Spiritual Discernment in Language and Reality

Returning to the five-stage gradual path of consciousness transformation, learning to become responsibly responsive is parallel to the second stage—the stage of intensified efforts or the path of application. As discussed earlier, in this stage, with the aim of entering the path of spiritual discernment, the practitioner learns to suppress and eradicate the conception of subject–object or self–world dichotomy by making preparatory efforts conducive to decisive distinction (Hsuan-Tsang, 659/1973, p. 679). These preparatory efforts are based on *four reflections* on the names, essences, self-nature, and differences of things and ideas, as well as the *four exact realizations* that these four concepts do not exist apart from our consciousness and that the process of consciousness that knows them does not have absolute and independent existence either (Hsuan-Tsang, 659/1973, pp. 679, 681). In this stage, the practices also include meditating on the four noble truths (Choi, 2011, p. 92).

The practices of the four reflections and the four exact realizations for cultivating the non-dualistic worldview call our attention to the role of language in dominating our worldview and various aspects of life. In his analysis of the role of language structure in bringing about fragmentation in thought, Bohm (1980) noted that "though language is only one of the important factors involved in this tendency, it is clearly of key importance in thought, in communication and in the organization of human society in general" (p. 35). Similar to the contemplation of the four reflections and the four exact realizations regarding the names, essences, self-nature, and differences of things and ideas, in this inquiry, Bohm (1980) examined the pervasive structure of sentence—subject–verb–object—which tends "to divide things into separate entities, such entities being conceived of as essentially fixed and static in their nature" (p. 37). Being conditioned by force of habit, we generally fall unwittingly into the fragmentary mode, focusing exclusively on the content under discussion and neglecting the symbolic function of language, and thus mistaking the fragment implied in language as "actual breaks in 'what is'" (Bohm, 1980, p. 40). Yet, as revealed in the dialogue between Buddhism and quantum physics, this is far from the way everything really is. As explored earlier, from Bohm's perspective, the relationship between the content of thought and the process of thinking which produces this content is similar to the relationship between a turbulent mass of vortices and the flowing stream "which creates, maintains, and ultimately dissolves the totality of vortex structures" (p. 24). Thus, akin to the vortices in a flowing stream, the "apparently static and separately existent things [along with their names, essences, self-nature, and differences in our consciousness] are seen as [only] relatively invariant states of continuing movement" (Bohm, 1980, p. 38) and in actuality do not exist apart from our consciousness—and the process of consciousness that knows them does not have absolute and independent existence either.

In his attempts to end the aforementioned fragmentation, Bohm (1980) suggested that we should allow the verb rather than the noun to play a primary role in language, because "the verb describes actions and movements, which flow into each other and merge, without sharp separations or break" (p. 37). Bohm's concern is that, when people are guided by a fragmentary subject–object worldview, in the long run, they risk trying in their actions only "to break themselves and the world into pieces" (p. 20). Such "fragmentation is an attempt to extend the analysis of the world into separate parts beyond the domain in which to do this is appropriate, [and] it is in effect an attempt to divide what is really indivisible" (Bohm, 1980, p. 20). The logic of such an attempt, if reversed, leads us also to try to unite what is not in actuality unitable (e.g., forming a group, be it political, economic, or religious) (Bohm, 1980, p. 20). Bohm explained that, rather than uniting people, the very act of forming a group "tends to create a sense of separation of the members from the rest of the world" (p. 20). This is because unity or oneness is already the true nature of consciousness, self, and reality, and the positive pursuit of unity as a reaction to fragmentation is but the same fragmentation in a different form. Echoing the approach of negation, Bohm underscored that "true unity in the individual and between man and nature, as well as between man and man, can arise only in a form of action that does *not* [emphasis added] attempt to fragment the whole of reality" (p. 20). The problem of fragmentation, therefore, is that it "is in essence a confusion around the question of difference and sameness (or one-ness)" (Bohm, 1980, p. 21). Bohm expressed concern that since "the clear perception of these categories is necessary in every phase of life" (p. 21), "*to be confused about what is different and what is not, is to be confused about everything*" (p. 21). When the mind is caught up in such confusion, it will be futile "to try to impose some fixed kind of integrating or unifying 'holistic' principle on our self-world view" (Bohm, 1980, p. 21). From this perspective, positive and active advocacy for holistic education could be futile if people remain mired in the confusion about difference and oneness that usually leads to debating at cross-purposes without awareness of which aspect of reality—the phenomenal or the ultimate—is referred to. This points to the educational significance of the Middle Way doctrine that emphasizes the simultaneous grasping of the ultimate and phenomenal aspects of self and reality and features the approach of negation for clearing away the confusion around the question of difference and oneness—a clearing away that is crucial for cultivating proper spiritual discernment and becoming responsibly responsive.

For Bohm (1980), "any form of fixed self-world view implies that we are no longer treating our theories as insights or ways of looking, but, rather, as 'absolutely true knowledge of things as they really are'" (p. 21). Such misperception is well illustrated by the noted Zen metaphor of taking the finger pointing at the Moon for the Moon itself. The fact is that "our theories are not 'descriptions of reality as it is' but, rather, ever-changing forms of insight, which can point to or indicate a reality that is implicit and not describable or specifiable in its totality" (Bohm, 1980, pp. 21–22). As emphasized earlier, the cultivation of a non-dualistic worldview and spiritual discernment is not a matter of holding views or opinions, but of seeing things as they really are. Bohm's (1980) insights may remind us of our earlier discussion regarding our habitual ways of thinking and speaking that are prone to hypostatization, defined as "the process of reification or 'thing-ifying': taking what is actually just a useful form of speech to refer to some real entity" (Siderits & Katsura, 2013, p. 15). Huebner (1963/1999a) expressed concern over the blind acceptance and reification of language in an educational context, indicating that "if the user reifies the concepts, then language obscures the world rather than opens it" (p. 79). Kumar (2013) similarly asserted that "thought reduces existential things into words through 'verbalization' and 'naming' and thus stops their comprehension" (p. 78). For Kumar (2013), while "language and words are necessary to communicate things to others…, when verbalization happens mechanically, it acts as a barrier between awareness and feelings" (p. 78). For the purpose of preventing mechanical verbalization or naming, Krishnamurti suggests "pure observation that involves neither translating the state of being into words nor judging it with pre-determined ideals, but rather observing it with full attention" (Kumar, 2013, p. 79). Kumar (2013) underscores that although "intellect and language are very important, there is a level of our existence, which can only be experienced and understood in the state of 'pure observation'" (p. 79). In such pure observation, the symbolic curtain that divides the observer and the observed gives way, and it becomes clear that, in Krishnamurti's words, "the description is not the described" and "the word is not the thing" (as cited in Kumar, 2013, pp. 79–80). Only when things are perceived as they really are do we see "the specifics of human lives" (Phelan, 2001, p. 52) rather than the mere "general forms" (Phelan, 2001, p. 52) presented by objective knowledge, and this is the moral basis that enables us to respond to lived existential situations appropriately and responsibly.

The above exploration demonstrates how the four reflections on the names, essences, self-nature, and differences of things and ideas and the four exact realizations of their true nature might prevent us from falling unwittingly into the habit of hypostatization, verbalization, or naming that often mistakes what is only a useful form of speech or a structure of cognition for descriptions of reality as it truly is. Such contemplation is conducive to not only the suppression and eradication of our taken-for-granted dualistic subject–object worldview, but also the cultivation of spiritual discernment that is indispensable for becoming responsibly responsive.

8.3 The Injunctions of the Four Noble Truths and the Awakening to Responsibility

In addition to the four reflections and the four exact realizations, meditation on the four noble truths is also a vital practice in the stage of intensified efforts for entering the path of spiritual discernment. As mentioned in Chap. 3, the four noble truths consist of the truth of suffering, the truth of the cause of suffering, the truth of the cessation of suffering, and the truth of the path (Sopa, 2005). Rather than being intended as mere creeds or beliefs, these truths are taught as "active and performatively differentiated *injunctions*" (Sedgwick, 2003, p. 170). As bodhisattva Maitreya summed up metaphorically in the following stanza:

> The illness should be recognized, its cause removed,
> Health should be attained, the remedy should be applied.
> Like that, suffering, its cause, its cessation, and the path
> Should be recognized, eliminated, attained, and practiced. (Sopa, 2005, p. 196)

As discussed in Chap. 3, by situating the truth of suffering as the first of the four noble truths, Buddha pointed to the significance of recognizing the suffering nature of *samsara*. The significance of this recognition lies in the fact that even if we realize that we are trapped in cyclic forms of existence or experience, if we do not perceive this as a problem, we will not have any incentive to get out of the trap; instead, we will grow used to it and attached to it (Sopa, 2005, p. 192). However, the mere recognition of suffering is not enough. Sopa (2005) cautioned that "if you do not properly understand the causes of bondage in cyclic existence, you will miss the essential points of the path. You will head off the wrong direction, mistaking for the path to liberation activities that only lead to more suffering" (p. 197). In Buddha's teaching, *samsaric* suffering is caused by various forms of contaminated or unvirtuous karma produced by inner afflictions rooted in ignorance (meaning being ignorant of the emptiness of self and reality) that distorts the essentially open experience of awareness into dualistic distinctions between self and other (Mingyur, 2007, p. 117; Sopa, 2005, pp. 195, 296, 326). For the cessation of suffering, the truth of the path embodied in the three trainings and the six perfections provides us with a down-to-earth pathway that unites both the method-side and wisdom-side practices in everyday life to eliminate the causes of suffering and attain liberation from the cyclic forms of existence and experience. The meditation on the four noble truths reminds us of the significance of Heidegger's idea of authentic Dasein: "Having recognized the fact that its being is at issue, it responds appropriately to the particular situation before it" (Dreyfus & Wrathall, 2005, p. 8).

The educational significance of the injunctions of the four noble truths can be found in Ahmed's (2010) research. In her exploration of the concept of happiness, Ahmed (2010) quoted feminist Rosi Braidotti's observation that "taking suffering into account is the starting point; the real aim of the process, however, is the quest for ways of overcoming the stultifying effects of passivity, brought about by pain" (as cited in Ahmed, 2010, p. 215). Ahmed (2010) refused the idea that our access to the cause of pain is random. Using Audre Lorde's story as an example in which Lorde's mother "says to her that the woman who spits is spitting into the wind not spitting at her, a black child, as a way of protecting the child from the pain of racism" (p. 215), Ahmed (2010) commented that "it is a [mother's] desire for protection that is understandable—but it fails to protect" (p. 215). For Ahmed (2010), Lorde's story showed us that "the very idea that violence is random is what stops us from seeing what is at stake in an encounter" (p. 215), and she maintained that, as

Lorde argued, "we should not be protected from what hurts" (p. 215); rather, "we have to work and struggle not so much to feel hurt but to notice what causes hurt, which means unlearning what we have learned not to notice" (pp. 215–216). However, as Maxine Greene noted, "relatively few people are… courageous enough actually to 'see'" (as cited in Boler, 1999, p. 176), and unlearning what we have learned not to notice is not always easy, as "to recover can be to re-cover, to cover over the cause of pain and suffering" (Ahmed, 2010, p. 216). Ahmed (2010) thus argued that

> the desire to move beyond suffering in reconciliation, the very will to "be over it" by asking others to "get over it," means that those who persist in their unhappiness become causes of the unhappiness of many. Their suffering becomes transformed into our collective disappointment that we cannot simply put such histories behind us. (p. 216)

Paradoxically, as Braidotti puts it, it is also "those who have already cracked a bit, those who have suffered pain and injury, who are better placed to take the lead in the process of ethical transformation" (as cited in Ahmed, 2010, p. 216). Since each of us suffers in one way or another, Ahmed's argument awakens us to our responsibility as temporal and historical beings-in-the-world and makes clear why to be responsibly responsive "is to be aware of the history and destiny of the given situation and to be answerable for the consequences of any responses made" (Huebner, 1966/1999b, p. 120). By means of taking our own suffering as a starting point and unlearning what we have learned not to notice—that is, being courageous enough to actually see things as they really are—we learn to cultivate proper spiritual discernment that allows us to become aware of both the individual and collective history and destiny of a given situation, to recognize the root causes of sufferings, and to undertake decisions and actions that will truly lead to the cessation of suffering. This is how observing the injunctions of the four noble truths could help us become responsibly responsive and become answerable for the consequences of any responses made.

8.4 Identity, Appropriational Circuit, Movie Consciousness, and Responsibility

The quandary of "to recover or to re-cover" also harkens back to the dilemma of change or non-change. Exploring human change and changelessness from the perspective of identity, Lusthaus (2002) indicated that we project our theories onto our experience in the form of atman and dharmas [subjective self and objective world] in order to maintain an appropriational circuit. We appropriate because we desire, and desire stems from a sense of lack… According to Buddhism what we fundamentally lack is a "self," and our frantic search and grasping for "things" is at once a sign of our sense of this lack—a way of asking, suppressing or diverting the painful awareness of that lack—and a desperate attempt to fill the void with an acquirable "identity," a self which one owns—one's own self… One clings to those identities as an expression of a deep-seated desire for permanence, stability, as a shielding from death. These identities… are the theories each of us lives by, the grounding orientations through and by which we experience the world as we do. (p. 2)

Identities or theories about ourselves, however, as revealed in earlier discussion, are not so much descriptions of who or what we really are as they are ever-changing forms of insight that point to certain aspects of our whole existence—which is not describable or specifiable in its totality. These identities and theories, as discussed in Chap. 3, have arisen from causes and conditions and are in actuality empty of any absolute, essential, and independent nature, thus, "no matter how seamlessly we seem to project our desires and anxieties, eventually our experience itself challenges us. Everything is impermanent, and whatever is living must inevitably succumb to sickness, old age and/or death" (Lusthaus, 2002, p. 2). As a result, we are caught in the incoherence of two mutually exclusive drives: "we want to change, become otherwise, improve ourselves, and, on the other hand, we want to maintain our-selves as unalterable, immutable, immortal" (Lusthaus, 2002, p. 3)—in other words, "we want difference and identity to coincide" (Lusthaus, 2002, p. 3). Lusthaus (2002) further analyzed that the quandary between the extremes of change and changelessness do not, however,

reflect objective circumstances, but rather reveal our interpretive enterprise: To fail to cognize changes with acceptance due to our expectations and frustrations on the one hand, and to fail to see the uniqueness of each and every moment on the other. Caught between these extremes of our own devising (*parikalpita*), we suppress our dissatisfactions, only to reproject them into one set of circumstances after another (*samsara*). For Yogacara, the appropriational circuit running between grasper and grasped signifies that we are locked inside the narcissism of our own habits (*karma*). Rather than seeing, hearing, smelling, tasting, touching, and thinking our relation to the world in the manner it becomes [as it really is] (*yathabhutam, tathata*), we perpetually grasp at our own reflections, mistaking the images (*pratibimba*) in our self-constructed mirror for what is other than ourself. Ironically, in order that our projected images and ideas become graspable and appropriatable, we have to dispossess them, i.e., disown and disavow them as our own projections. If we recognized them as already ours, pursuing them further would be redundant. Only by pretending that they are not ours, can we appropriate them. (pp. 3–4)

Lusthaus's (2002) analysis of this quandary provides new insights into the questions regarding how to explain non-change, or "what gets in the way of the great journey—the journey of the self or soul" (Huebner, 19631999a, p. 405). Lusthaus's (2002) analysis also revealed how the quandary of change or non-change that hinders us from transcending our current form of existence and from becoming responsibly responsive is basically an interpretative enterprise that is deep-seated in the misleading dualistic subject–object worldview that attaches to the self as an absolute fixed subject independent of the world.

The appropriational circuit can also be understood from the concepts of estrangement or dehumanization. Dehumanization, according to Pinar (1974), is a description of man, particularly modern man, as "estranged and severed from his Self" (p. 3). Here, "Self is understood in the Jungian sense, as more than the ego or conscious 'I' of the personality" (Pinar, 1974, p. 3). Thus, "the conscious 'I' we identify as ego, is somewhat severed from his self, which is hidden from his ego; it is, in part, his unconscious" (Pinar, 1974, p. 3). In other words, "man is partially unaware of himself; he is not himself; he is dehumanized" (p. 3). This severance, Pinar (1974) continued, "appears to have the effect of forcing us to search for dignity and satisfaction outside ourselves. Ignoring the inner regions, intrigued by the elaborate labyrinthine exterior world, many of us spend our lives searching for meaning outside of ourselves" (p. 3). This symbolic search for satisfaction in the exterior world, or in Lusthaus's words, in the self-constructed mirror, while "at times achieve their aims, the achievement is usually short lived, as transient as feeling, or as thought, as transitory as prominence" (Pinar, 1974, p. 3). Pinar (1974) further indicated that this symbolic search "amounts to what Sartre terms one's project" (p. 3) and forces "a literary awareness and organization of one's life" (p. 3) that might be called *movie consciousness* (p. 4). Mistaking the projected for the source, in the movie consciousness, "one tells stories, and tells them as if they were ultimate reality" (Pinar, 1974, p. 4). Pinar elucidated by quoting Sartre's (1964) novel *Nausea*:

> This is what fools people: a man is always a teller of tales; he lives surrounded by his stories and the stories of others, he sees everything that happens to him through them; and tries to live his own life as if he were telling a story. But you have to choose: live or tell. (as cited in Pinar, 1974, p. 4)

The telling, according to Pinar (1974), "is a revealing manifestation of our absorption at the levels of personality, at the top of the iceberg. It indicates our absorption with the observable, with the external, and our comparative ignorance of what lies beneath the surface" (pp. 4–5). "Uprooted from our essence, we require securing of another sort, a stability derived from the steady gaze of others" (Pinar, 1974, p. 5). It is therefore "a sign of our uprootedness from our selves that we tell stories as if they were true, as if they portrayed an ultimate reality" (Pinar, 1974, p. 5), "as if there could possibly be true stories" (Sartre, 1964, as cited in Pinar, 1974, p. 4). In other words, being ignorant of the ultimate nature of consciousness, self, and reality, we grasp at the mere shadows or self-projected "movies" as absolute, essential, and, independent reality, interpret it through a dualistic lens ignoring the relationship between the inner and the outer and, instigated by fear, we react to it as if the world is not ours. This is how we dehumanize and fool ourselves. This is telling.

In telling, we shirk responsibilities, and by doing so, waste plenty of opportunities for transformation. Yet, as Sartre indicated, we have choices: to tell or to live. Pinar (1974) suggested that by means of developing a transcendent perspective, or the "third eye" or heightened consciousness,[1] it is possible to gain insights into how one's ego involves in the stories we tell, to understand the complex interplay of various forces, and to write or choose different scripts of stories (p. 5). This is living.

In living, we keep in sight both the conditioned and the unconditioned, both the phenomenal and ultimate aspects of reality. Recognizing the "movie" we now experience as a reverberation of our past actions of body, mind, and speech—the ripening of a mixture of pure and contaminated karmic seeds—we learn to develop equanimity toward the *eight worldly concerns* (happiness vs. suffering, fame vs. insignificance, praise vs. blame, gain vs. loss) and get rid of the worldly hope–fear cycle (Dorje, 2005,

p. 99; Lief, 2019); learn to identify the past–present and inner–outer correlations and open ourselves to new transcendental possibilities; learn to live mindfully and work inwardly with the awareness that our current "decision is a factor in the continual emergence or evolution of that situation [or story] as it exists through time" (Huebner, 1966/1999b, p. 120), and become responsibly responsive.

While on the biological level the distinction between self and others is essential for the survival of our physical bodies, when it is overgeneralized into areas that have nothing to do with basic survival, problems begin (Mingyur, 2007, p. 119). As discussed in Chap. 3, by means of locking ourselves into the dualistic mode of perception, we become unable "to recognize the infinite potential, clarity, and power of our own mind" (Mingyur, 2007, p. 117) and "begin looking [outwardly] at other people, material objects, and so on, as potential sources of happiness and unhappiness" (Mingyur, 2007, p. 117). By relying exclusively on external sources to give us happiness, we gradually "lose the ability to distinguish between the bare experience of happiness and whatever objects temporarily make us happy" (Mingyur, 2007, p. 119). As a result of this confusion, life becomes an endless struggle to pursue and defend happiness. However, as revealed in the dialogue between Buddhism and quantum physics, contrary to what we might believe based on our everyday experiences of the deceptive phenomenal world, "the truth is that all the causes of our problems are inside ourselves, in the qualities of our own minds" (Sopa, 2005, p. 2). By means of pretending, either consciously or unconsciously, that external reality has nothing to do with us, we, like the shackled prisoners in Plato's allegory of the cave, see no relationship between ourselves and the world. Being ignorant of what create the shadows on the wall, we mistake these mere shadows as the sources of our happiness and unhappiness and, as a result, mistake activities that only lead to more sufferings as the means to happiness.

This mistaken view based on an overly generalized distinction between the self and the others is known in Buddhism as *attachment* or *desire* (Mingyur, 2007, p. 119). "Craving" is the general form of attachment, and "grasping" is a more intense form (Sopa, 2005, pp. 332–333). According to Mingyur (2007), attachment, akin to addiction, is "a compulsive dependency on external objects or experiences to manufacture an illusion of wholeness" (p. 119), and it becomes more intense over time (p. 119). Attachment is like "drinking salt water from an ocean. The more we drink, the thirstier we get" (Mingyur, 2007, p. 119). Echoing Adam

Smith's caution explored in Chap. 7, by placing our happiness in winning the stake, we expose ourselves to perpetual fear and uneasiness (as cited in Ahmed, 2010, p. 208). Mingyur (2007) also indicated that "every strong attachment generates an equally powerful fear that we'll either fail to get what we want or lose whatever we've already gained" (p. 121). In other words, our attachment and selfish desire—the blind outward pursuing, grasping, and defending of hypostatized happiness rooted in the ignorance of the ultimate truth of emptiness—rather than bringing about happy and blissful experiences and leading to ultimate liberation, only perpetuates our fear and uneasiness, imprisons us in cyclic forms of suffering and blinds us to infinite possibilities. Yet, as Ahmed (2010) emphasized,

> if we do not assume that happiness is what we must defend, if we start questioning the happiness we are defending, then we can ask other questions about life, about what we want from life, or what we want life to become. Possibilities have to be recognized as possibilities to become possible. (p. 218)

The recognition of possibilities *as possibilities* is vital for becoming responsibly responsive particularly in the moment of vision. Ahmed (2010) made clear that to recognize possibilities other than defending our own happiness requires us to overcome our craving and grasping rooted in the ignorance of the true nature of human existence, to stop the outward pursuit and defense of reified objects of happiness, and to recognize the infinite potential, clarity, and transformative power intrinsic in our consciousness. Otherwise—even if we are willing to take our own suffering as a point of departure, to take both personal and historical responsibilities for the continual creation of the world, and to be answerable for the consequences of any responses made—if we mistake the causes of suffering and sources of happiness as simply external, we are bound to lose spiritual discernment and head off in the wrong direction. Becoming responsibly responsive, therefore, is, first of all, an inner work of overcoming the habitual force of craving and grasping and the sharp subject–object dichotomy in the self–world dialectic grounded on a non-dualistic worldview that knows properly the nature of consciousness, self, and reality.

Based on the above discussion, we begin to see how becoming responsibly responsive is closely related to the cultivation of selflessness. In the following chapter, therefore, I proceed to investigate more deeply the concepts of self and selflessness, and to explore the conception, approach, and educational significance of cultivating selflessness.

Note

1. Heightened consciousness might be understood as what Bucke (1905) called Cosmic Consciousness—a higher form of consciousness than Simple Consciousness (possessed commonly by human and animals) and Self Consciousness (possessed exclusively by humans and enabling one to treat his own mental states as objects of consciousness). The Cosmos Consciousness is "a consciousness of the cosmos, that is, of the life and order of the universe" (Bucke, 1905, p. 2). "Along with the consciousness of the cosmos there occurs an intellectual enlightenment or illumination which alone would place the individual on a new plane of existence" (Bucke, 1905, p. 2). According to Bucke (1905),

   > this consciousness shows the cosmos to consist not of dead matter governed by unconscious, rigid, and unintending law; it shows it on the contrary as entirely immaterial, entirely spiritual and entirely alive; it shows that death is an absurdity, that everyone and everything has eternal life; it shows that the universe is God and that God is the universe, and that no evil ever did or ever will enter into it; a great deal of this is, of course, from the point of view of self consciousness, absurd; it is nevertheless undoubtedly true. (p. 14)

References

Ahmed, S. (2010). *The Promise of Happiness.* Durham: Duke University Press.
Bohm, D. (1980). *Wholeness and the Implicate Order.* New York, NY: Routledge.
Boler, M. (1999). *Feeling Power: Emotions and Education.* New York, NY: Routledge.
Bucke, R. M. (1905). *Cosmic Consciousness: A Study in the Evolution of the Human Mind.* Philadelphia, PA: Innes & Sons.
Choi, D. (2011). *Mechanism of Consciousness During Life, Dream and After-Death.* Bloomington, IN: AuthorHouse.
Dorje, L. Y. (2005). Kangyur Rinpoche's Commentary on the Letter to a Friend. In Padmakara Translation Group (Trans.), *Nagarjuna's letter to a friend: With commentary by Kangyur Rinpoche* (pp. 79–155). Ithaca, NY: Snow Lion Publications.
Dreyfus, H., & Wrathall, M. (2005). Martin Heidegger: An Introduction to His Thought, Work, and Life. In H. Dreyfus & M. Wrathall (Eds.), *A Companion to Heidegger* (pp. 1–15). Malden, MA: Wiley-Blackwell.
Hsuan-Tsang (1973). *Ch'eng Wei-shi Lun: The Doctrine of Mere-Consciousness* (T. Wei, trans.). Hong Kong, China: The Ch'eng Wei-shih Lun Publication Committee. (Original work published 659). Retrieved from http://www.dhalbi.org/dhalbi/html_t/authors/author_main.php?p_id=8

Huebner, D. E. (1999a). New Modes of Man's Relationship to Man. In V. Hillis (Ed.), *The Lure of the Transcendent: Collected Essays by Dwayne E. Huebner* (pp. 74–93). New York, NY: Routledge. (Original work published 1963).

Huebner, D. E. (1999b). Facilitating Change as the Responsibility of the Supervisor. In V. Hillis (Ed.), *The Lure of the Transcendent: Collected Essays by Dwayne E. Huebner* (pp. 118–130). New York, NY: Routledge. (Original work published 1966).

Huebner, D. E. (1999c). Curriculum as Concern for Man's Temporality. In V. Hillis (Ed.), *The Lure of the Transcendent: Collected Essays by Dwayne E. Huebner* (pp. 131–142). New York, NY: Routledge. (Original work published 1967).

Huebner, D. E. (1999d). Education and Spirituality. In V. Hillis (Ed.), *The Lure of the Transcendent: Collected Essays by Dwayne E. Huebner* (pp. 401–416). New York, NY: Routledge. (Original work published 1993).

Kumar, A. (2013). *Curriculum as Meditative Inquiry*. New York, NY: Palgrave Macmillan.

Lief, J. (2019, February). What Are the Eight Worldly Concerns? Retrieved from https://www.lionsroar.com/buddhism-by-the-numbers-the-eight-worldly-concerns/

Lusthaus, D. (2002). *Buddhist Phenomenology: A Philosophical Investigation of Yogacara Buddhism and the Ch'eng Wei-shih Lun*. New York, NY: RoutledgeCurzon.

Mingyur, Y. (2007). *The Joy of Living: Unlocking the Secret and Science of Happiness*. New York, NY: Harmony Books.

Phelan, A. M. (2001). The Death of a Child and the Birth of Practical Wisdom. *Studies in Philosophy and Education, 20*(1), 41–55.

Pinar, W. F. (1974). Heightened Consciousness, Cultural Revolution, and Curriculum Theory: An Introduction. In W. F. Pinar (Ed.), *Heightened Consciousness, Cultural Revolution, and Curriculum Theory* (pp. 1–15). The Proceedings of the Rochester Conference (Rochester, New York, May 3–5, 1973).

Sedgwick, E. K. (2003). Pedagogy and Buddhism. In *Touching Feeling: Affect, Pedagogy, Performativity* (pp. 153–181). Durham: Duke University Press.

Siderits, M., & Katsura, S. (2013). *Nāgārjuna's Middle Way*. Somerville, MA: Wisdom Publications.

Sopa, L. (2005). *Steps on the Path to Enlightenment: A Commentary on Tsongkhapa's Lamrim Chenmo. Volume II: Karma*. Somerville, MA: Wisdom Publications.

CHAPTER 9

Cultivating Selflessness

9.1 INTRODUCTION

In the earlier exploration of the concepts and process of consciousness transformation in Buddhism, afflictive barriers and noetic barriers were identified as the main barriers to be overcome in the process of consciousness transformation. Since afflictive barriers and noetic barriers refer to barriers originating respectively from the attachment to a subjective self and the attachment to an objective universe as absolute, essential, and independent existence, cultivating selflessness and learning to embody a non-dualistic worldview are crucial for the transformation of consciousness. The cultivation of selflessness and the embodiment of a non-dualistic worldview are not essentially different, and are mutually inclusive and supportive—both require the union of wisdom-side practices based on wisdom that knows emptiness (the accumulation of wisdom) and method-side practices based on compassion, love, and *bodhicitta* (the accumulation of merits) which are embodied in the six perfections (generosity, ethical discipline, patience, joyous perseverance, meditative stabilization, and wisdom). With an emphasis on the *view* component of spiritual practices, in this chapter, I draw on the wisdom-side practices (including the perfections of wisdom and meditative stabilization) and investigate the concepts of self and selflessness, and explore how we might cultivate selflessness in an educational context. The embodiment of a non-dualistic worldview (with an emphasis on the *deeds* component) will be explored in Chap. 10.

9.2 The Concepts of Self and Selflessness

In exploring the two truths and the Middle Way doctrine taught by Buddha, in Chap. 3 we discussed the preliminary concepts of the empty and dependently arising nature of self and reality. We will now delve more deeply into these concepts. Rather than denying the existence of the self, the emptiness of self refers to the lack of an absolute, essential, and independent substantial self. Drawing on the Middle Way doctrine explicated by Nargajuna, Thompson (2015) introduced an enactive understanding of the self (p. 324). Akin to Huebner's (1967/1999a) elucidation of human temporality that emphasizes the dynamic and emerging nature of human existence, Thompson (2015) considered the everyday self as a subject of experience and an agent of action and maintained that the self is a dependently arisen series of events; in other words, the self is an enacted process (p. 323). For Thompson (2015), "the self isn't a thing or an entity at all; it is brought forth or enacted in the process of living" (p. 324). Similar to Bohm (1980) who emphasized the oneness of the thinking process and the content of thought (p. 24) (as discussed in Chap. 3), Thompson (2015) maintained that "the self is a process of 'I-ing,' a process that enacts an 'I' and in which the 'I' is no different from the I-ing process itself, rather like the way dancing is a process that enacts a dance" (Thompson, 2015, p. 325). He quoted Stephen Batchelor's assertion that "you are unique not because you possess an essential metaphysical quality that differs from the essential metaphysical qualities of everyone else, but because you have emerged from a unique and unrepeatable set of conditions" (as cited in Thompson, 2015, p. 323). In the same vein, Newland (2009) indicated that "our uniqueness arises from our distinctive, ever-shifting, and infinite array of connections with other things. We are unique… but we do not *own* our uniqueness. We have no intrinsic core. We owe our uniqueness to all of our conditions" (p. 96).

Nonetheless, the problem is that we seldom experience our *self* as an emerging and dependently arising process. Habitually, we "experience our self as if it were a unified agent that functions as the executive controller of what we think and do, and that has a permanent inner essence distinct from our changing mental and physical characteristics" (Thompson, 2015, p. 324). This fundamental cognitive error by which we "mistake something that's dependent and contingent—and hence 'empty' of substantiality—for something that's independently existent" (Thompson, 2015, p. 324) is, for Nargajuna, comparable to taking the illusory images in a dream to be independently real objects of perception with their own inner essence (Thompson, 2015, p. 324). As revealed in Chap. 3, this ancient dream metaphor is now well supported by the holographic computer-simulation model of the participatory universe. Yet Thompson (2015) cautioned that this analogy does not mean that there is no self at all or that any sense of self is mistaken: "after all, dreams exist as genuine experiential phenomena, yet they lack the independent being that we take them to have when we do not realize we're dreaming" (p. 324). Similarly, our sense of self does exist as genuine experiential phenomena although these lack the absolute, independent, and substantial essence that we take them to have. Even in the deep and direct penetrating experiential realization of the emptiness of self, akin to "becoming lucid in a dream or waking up from a dream—the subject of experience still exists but is no longer deluded about its nature" (Thompson, 2015, p. 324). The direct experience of "No-Self" or selflessness is well described by Austin (2009), who clarified that the phrase No-Self

> does not mean that the person stops witnessing... It means that witnessing happens with none of the old intrusive, Self-conscious *I-Me-Mine* standing in the way. It means that no former veils of Self obscure or distort everything in that outside environment. Once these old concepts drop off, the anonymous observer is finally graced by the glimpse of an unimaginably "objective vision." This fresh reality sees clearly *into* the eternal perfection of "all things as THEY really are." Coming out of this state of oneness, the person finally grasps the error inherent in the old Self/other mode of dual perception. (p. 117)

Austin (2009) thus made clear the meaning of No-Self, selflessness, or the emptiness of self and the transformative power of the direct non-dualistic experience of emptiness and oneness for recognizing the erroneousness of the self–other dichotomy. Cultivating selflessness, therefore, is cultivating toward the direct realization of the ultimate nature of human existence, unobscured by the erroneous cognition of an egoistic self that is entrenched in the dualistic self–other perception. The attainment of the direct experience of emptiness, according to the five-stage gradual path of consciousness transformation, signifies the perfection of the first two stages, the mundane path. On this basis, practitioners then develop further spiritual faculties and attain deeper meditative experiences. However, as discussed earlier, since most of us remain caught in a dualistic mode of perception and can hardly attain this state all at once, at the very beginning, cultivating selflessness in an educational context requires the approach of negation and the union of method-side and wisdom-side practices grounded on a proper conceptual understanding of the emptiness of self.

Conceptually, the meaning of emptiness, as explored in Chap. 3, is coterminous with dependent origination, which involves three levels of meaning: causal dependence, whole/part dependence, and conceptual dependence (Newland, 2009, pp. 69–70; Thompson, 2015, p. 330). The causal level of dependence reveals how a phenomenon is dependent on causes and conditions for its existence and its ceasing to exist (Thompson, 2015, p. 330). Whole/part dependence refers to how the part and whole of a phenomenon co-arise and depend on each other for existence (Thompson, 2015, p. 330). The conceptual level of dependence—the subtlest level of dependent origination, according to the sub-school of *Madhyanaka* called *Prasangika Madhyamaka*, refers to the fact that "the identity of something as a single whole depends on how we conceptualize it and refer to it with a term" (Thompson, 2015, pp. 330–331). This means the identity of something also depends on the scale of observation (Thompson, 2015, p. 331). Taking the cell as a metaphor for the self, Thompson (2015) illustrated that "the cell has no intrinsic identity independent of a conceptual schema and scale of observation that individuate it as a unit" (Thompson, 2015, p. 331). When observed from different conceptual and observational perspectives, the cell either dissolves into a self-organized dance of smaller molecules or loses observational validity (Thompson, 2015, p. 331). Employing the concepts of a self-specifying system, Thompson (2015) further illustrated that

> the identity of the interlocking network as one self-specifying system depends on how we cognitively frame things, that is, on our decision to focus on those conditioning relations that mutually specify each other in a recursive way. Depending on our interests or explanatory purposes, we could decide to frame things differently by focusing on other conditioning relations. What we mark off as a system depends on our cognitive frame of reference and the concepts we have available. (p. 331)

However, as was noted in Chap. 3, "this doesn't mean that nothing exists apart from our words or concepts" (Thompson, 2015, p. 331). According to *Prasangika Madhyamaka*, the full meaning of conceptual dependence is that "whatever is dependently arisen depends for its existence on a basis of designation, a designating cognition, and a term used to designate it" (Thompson, 2015, p. 332). Utilizing this formulation of dependent arising as a conceptual ingredient, which Thompson (2015) referred to as a self-designating system—meaning "one that conceptually designates itself as a self and where changing body-mind states serve as the basis of designation" (p. 332)—Thompson developed the I-making system, which he defined as a system "that has a sense of itself as an I who endures through time as a thinker of thoughts and a doer of deeds" (p. 332). Together, the three levels of meaning of dependent origination, Thompson's illustration of the concept of self as an enacted I-ing process, and the theory of the I-making system provide us with not only deepened insights into how our sense of self arises dependently, but also a consolidated conceptual ground for perceiving the deviation of our sense of self and for contemplating how we might cultivate selflessness or the emptiness of self in an educational context.

According to Thompson (2015), the way our everyday sense of self appears does involve an illusion; however, as clarified above, it is not the case that there is no self at all or that the appearance of the self is merely an illusion. Rather, "the illusion—or delusion—is taking the self to have an independent existence, like taking the mirror image to be really in the mirror" (Thompson, 2015, p. 365). To undo this illusion, meaning to cultivate selflessness or the emptiness of self, does not mean destroying the appearance of the self; it means not being taken in by the appearance of the self and holding the belief that the self has an independent existence while that appearance is still there and performing its routine I-making function (Thompson, 2015, pp. 365–366). Thompson (2015) emphasized that it is "this ignorant and deep-seated belief, not the appearance of the self as such, [that] habitually deludes us into thinking, feeling, and acting as if the self were independent" (p. 365). From the perspective of conceptual dependence, our attachment to our body-mind aggregations as our "self" that is independent of the world is in actuality an attachment to the conceptual schema and scale of observation that neglect the relationships between the self and world and confine that observation to a small scale. The cultivation of selflessness, thus, also requires us to break the boundary of the scale of observation and to include our *relationships* to the world in our conceptual schema of our self. Such a realization helps us understand Huebner's (1987/1999c) statement that "we are our relationships. Our so-called personalities and habits of language and thinking are the fabric of yesterday—the way we are in relationship with the people of our past" (p. 390). As Smith (2000) indicated, "claim an Identity, whether racial, tribal, or gendered, and quickly it can be seen how it emerges through a web of relationships" (p. 23). Pitt (2000) also emphasized that "the personal is constituted within a web of relations that includes relation of time (how the past works on the present) and relations with others, knowledge and authority" (p. 69). However, this "is not to ignore the obvious fact that we each have an explicit (but transient) physical self or to pretend that it doesn't exist" (Austin, 1999, p. 79). Rather, it is a shift of the scale of observation and conceptual schema to include our web of relationships and thus enable us to experience our self as a being-in-the-world from an expanded scale of observation. As Japanese Zen Master Dōgen said: "To study your own self is to forget yourself. To forget yourself is to have the objective world prevail in you" (as cited in Austin, 1999, p. 79).

9.3 The I-Me-Mine Complex

In practice, however, given the habitual force of our ignorance entrenched in a dualistic perception and the elusive nature of our sense of self, various conceptual tools are required for recognizing and overcoming our illusion and attachment. Given the slippery nature of our secret self, Pitt (2000) described the process of engaging with the self as a game of hide and seek. For the purpose of scrutinizing the subtle aspects of our deluded implicit self, Austin (1999) developed a descriptive system by means of separating the sensitive implicit self into three different operational components with *I*, *Me*, and *Mine* as their operative words (p. 79). Let us briefly examine their individual descriptions, beginning with the *I*. According to Austin (1999), "the *I* is, and acts. No one of us can appreciate how big our own *I* is. Other persons know" (p. 80). Austin described that, "this *almighty I is* virtually perfect. It is also vain. It monograms and polishes its self-image. Can it ever, even rarely, fall into error? No. It makes excuses and shifts the blame" (p. 81). Besides, in the repertoire of our *I*, there are also many masks, or personas (Austin, 1999, p. 81). According to Austin (1999),

> each rigid mask took many decades to construct or to conceal. The roles our persona assume stemmed not only from parents, siblings, friends and teachers but increasingly from media personalities. Collectively, they now form the mosaic of our personal identity, our self-image. We shift from one role model to another depending on the circumstances. We also adopted the attitudes of each persona. These shape how each "role model *I*" *should* behave... Each of us has an agenda of highly personal biases which distort what we perceive and shape what we then think is true. (p. 81)

The pronoun *Me* stands for our self as an object that likes to be praised, is bothered by all the "bad" events that threaten to harm, to expose, or to embarrass, and is "on the receiving end of every self-inflicted, psychic wound generated by the inappropriate activities of its two other partners, the *I* and the *Mine*" (Austin, 1999, p. 81). Austin (1999) called it the *vulnerable Me*. Lastly, "the adjective, *Mine*, stands for our grasping, greedy, possessive self" (Austin, 1999, p. 81). *Mine* represents our attachment, and (echoing our discussion of attachment in the preceding chapter) Austin (1999) described it as clutching and clinging. It is also "self-indentured, because whatever is possessed, possesses. The more it gets, the less satisfied it is, and the more it covets. But the more it possesses, the more it stands to lose" (p. 82). Similar to Lusthaus's (2002) analysis of the appropriational circuit between grasper and grasped, Austin (1999) indicated that "our *Mine* starts out in deceptively simple fashion. It proceeds from the basic premise of the self/other split in perception. But this then implies that anything around the core of *Mine*, including my thoughts and opinions, must be defended" (p. 82). Usually, not until late in the direct experience of emptiness "does one realize how pervasive was this insidious, intrusive, grasping process. Then, astonished, the experiant discovers the extent of the *Mine*" (Austin, 1999, p. 83).

This brief explication of the selfish *I–Me–Mine* complex not only provides with us clues as to how our deluded implicit and egoistic self works, particularly in our web of relationships, but also shows us traits to be negated by the approach of negation. Once again, however, this does not mean that all of our *I–Me–Mine* thoughts should be denied. Rather, the overcoming of our selfish *I–Me–Mine* complex means not being taken in by it and holding that the self has an independent and essential existence. For Austin (1999), the overcoming of one's selfish *I–Me–Mine* complex "involves reaching down through one's own efforts to pull out its prolific roots..., abdicating the sovereign *I*, abandoning the ramparts defending the *Me*, and abolishing the enslavement to the *Mine*" (p. 83). In Huebner's (1991/1999d) words, it is "a dying to oneself that we may find ourselves" (p. 397), and for Huebner, this is education. In Adam Philip's reading of Winnicott, this is development—"a growing capacity to tolerate the continual and increasingly sophisticated illusionment–disillusionment–re-illusionment process throughout the life-cycle" (as cited in Pitt, 2000, p. 68). This process can also be understood from the perspective of "the Christian experience: creation, fall, and recreation; from 'greatness' to 'wretchedness' to 'renewal' and transformation" (Huebner, 1985/1999b,

p. 317). The increasingly sophisticated cycles of illusionment–disillusionment–re-illusionment illustrate the process of overcoming our *I–Me–Mine* complex and cultivating selflessness toward the ultimate truth of human existence. As Smith (2000) put it, "truth calls me to human maturity" (p. 21). To facilitate this process, scrutinizing the fabric of our relationships is crucial. As Huebner (1987/1999c) pointed out, the agenda for religious education "is one of scrutinizing the fabric of relationships that we have, those of intimacy and those of community, and of asking how God is present or absent in those relationships" (p. 392). For Huebner (1987/1999c), God is Love, unfathomable and ineffable. If we begin, then, with an understanding of God as the ultimate nature of human existence that is identical with the non-dualistic and uncontaminated original state of human consciousness wherein love is a given, then scrutinizing the fabric of our relationships and bringing our awareness to the emerging of our dualistic selfish *I–Me–Mine* complex will help us recognize how God or love is absent in these relationships. Such scrutiny and awareness not only prevent us from being taken in by our *I–Me–Mine* complex but also provide us with opportunities to pull out its prolific roots, a process which is essential for facilitating the cycles of illusionment–disillusionment–re-illusionment and for transcending our current forms of existence.

9.4 Meditative Stabilization and Selflessness

Our exploration of the concepts of self and selflessness provides us deepened insights into how the perfection of wisdom that knows emptiness facilitates the cultivation of selflessness. Given the significance of meditative stabilization as another essential wisdom-side practice for consciousness transformation, we will now turn to exploring how meditative stabilization can be conducive to the cultivation of selflessness. The relationship between meditative stabilization and the cultivating of selflessness is highlighted by Thompson (2015) by means of introducing the concept of *self-projection*, which refers to the perspective-altering process by which one mentally projects oneself into an alternative situation of personal past or imaged future that usually includes both the first-person and third-person perspectives of the mental representation of oneself (p. 348). According to Thompson (2015), in a kind of self-projection known as mental time travel, "every memory or expectation you encounter normally represents itself as yours, as belonging to you, where you feel as if you're one and the same self who endures through time as the subject of these experiences" (p. 348). Self-projection, similar to our earlier discussion of movie consciousness, thus "exemplifies the sense of self that consists in the feeling of being a distinct individual with a unique personal identity and a protracted existence in time" (Thompson, 2015, p. 348). Neuroscientist Antonio Damasio called this sense of self the *autobiographic self*, while phenomenologists call it the *narrative self* (Thompson, 2015, p. 348).

Thompson (2015) indicated that self-projection, meaning the autobiographical or narrative sense of self, depends on a network of brain areas that overlaps closely with the *default network* of the brain; when the default network is active during resting or passive situations, spontaneous self-projection thoughts, or mind wandering, are at their peak (pp. 348–349). During meditation, such mind wandering, along with self-related thoughts and emotions, arises spontaneously, yet, according to Thompson (2015), at the moment you notice it, "you have the opportunity to disengage from identifying with the contents of these thoughts—specifically, from identifying with the mentally imaged 'I' who is the central character—and to shift your attention to the thoughts simply as thoughts" (pp. 349–350). Moreover, with repeated experience of the dynamic between being taken in by the self-related thinking that occurs in mind wandering and waking up to what our mind is doing, not only does the frequency of the arising of self-related thoughts lessen, but we also "feel the difference between identifying with the content of a self-related thought—with the 'I' as you mentally represent it—and identifying that a thought is occurring while experiencing the larger field of awareness in which it arises" (Thompson, 2015, p. 350). This difference is similar to the difference between telling and living, or between movie consciousness and heightened consciousness, as discussed in Chap. 8.

Drawing on the work of various researchers, Thompson (2015) pointed out that negative moods tend to lead to mind wandering, and that when the mind is wandering, people are less happy than when they are focusing on what they are doing (p. 350). Given the close association between mind wandering, the default network of the brain, and the self-projection network of the brain, this finding suggests that during the period of self-projection or self-related processing, including the operations of the selfish I–Me–Mine complex, people are less happy than when they are living in the here and now. Moreover, given such association, "it's not surprising that focused attention and open awareness forms of meditation, which involve stabilizing awareness while developing meta-awareness of ongoing mental activities, affect the brain's default network" (Thompson, 2015, p. 350) and therefore affect the network of self-related processing and the autobiographical or narrative sense of self. This means such meditation helps us transcend our conditioned default mode of self-projection.

A research project conducted by Judson Brewer and his colleagues at Yale University revealed that, compared to novices, experienced meditators reported less mind wandering, and the main nodes of their default network were less active during meditation periods across three types of meditation (Thompson, 2015, p. 353). Moreover, when their default network was activated, experienced meditators co-activated different brain regions (Thompson, 2015, p. 353). This implies that experienced meditators might be more likely to recognize new possibilities than novices or non-meditators. This study also suggested that the mental processes supported by the default network, including mind wandering and self-related processing, "may be more accessible to monitoring and control in experienced meditators than in novice meditators" (Thompson, 2015, p. 353). The increased accessibility to monitoring and control of self-related processing suggests that the cultivation of selflessness is easier for experienced meditators than for novice meditators or non-meditators.

In another study, Norman Farb and Adam Anderson of the University of Toronto uncovered "the relationship between mindfulness practice and the neural systems underlying two different modes of self-experience— present-moment awareness of the body versus the narrative or autobiographical sense of self" (Thompson, 2015, p. 355). Their findings suggest that with the kind of present-centered awareness training provided by mindfulness practices such as Mindfulness-based Stress Reduction (MBSR), it is easier for us to disengage from our narrative self (e.g., worrisome rumination about ourselves in memory or prospection, mentally elaborated stories with attachment to certain mental representation of ourselves, etc.), and we are also more likely to adopt an experiential focus, meaning present-centered embodied awareness that anchors our attention to our bodily being in the here and now (Thompson, 2015, pp. 354–355). This means mindfulness training is also conducive to the cultivation of selflessness. Moreover, a quasi-experimental study evaluating the effectiveness of Mindfulness Education (ME) conducted by Schonert-Reichl and Lawlor (2010) also showed significant improvements in teacher-rated social and emotional competence and the positive emotion of optimism for both pre- and early adolescents, and improvement in general self-concept for early adolescents.

The findings of the studies cited above reveal the interrelationships of meditation, self-related processing, and positive emotion, and provide us substantial evidence regarding how meditative practices can be conducive to the cultivation of selflessness and therefore to consciousness transformation, particularly when meditative practices are motivated by *bodhicitta* and grounded on wisdom that knows the emptiness of self and reality. Given their positive influences on social and emotional competence and their existential significance for cultivating selflessness and for attaining various spiritual goals, meditative practices are indispensable to curriculum for consciousness transformation.

In the following chapter, based on our deepened understanding of the concepts of self and selflessness and how we might cultivate selflessness in an educational context, I investigate the educational significance of learning to embody a non-dualistic worldview.

REFERENCES

Austin, J. H. (1999). *Zen and the Brain: Toward an Understanding of Meditation and Consciousness*. Cambridge, MA: MIT Press.

Austin, J. H. (2009). *Selfless Insight: Zen and the Meditative Transformations of Consciousness*. Cambridge, MA: MIT Press.

Bohm, D. (1980). *Wholeness and the Implicate Order*. New York, NY: Routledge.

Huebner, D. E. (1999a). Curriculum as Concern for Man's Temporality. In V. Hillis (Ed.), *The Lure of the Transcendent: Collected Essays by Dwayne E. Huebner* (pp. 131–142). New York, NY: Routledge. (Original work published 1967).

Huebner, D. E. (1999b). Babel: A Reflection on Confounded Speech. In V. Hillis (Ed.), *The Lure of the Transcendent: Collected Essays by Dwayne E. Huebner* (pp. 312–320). New York, NY: Routledge. (Original work published 1985).

Huebner, D. E. (1999c). Practicing the Presence of God. In V. Hillis (Ed.), *The Lure of the Transcendent: Collected Essays by Dwayne E. Huebner* (pp. 388–395). New York, NY: Routledge. (Original work published 1987).

Huebner, D. E. (1999d). Educational Activity and Prophetic Criticism. In V. Hillis (Ed.), *The Lure of the Transcendent: Collected Essays by Dwayne E. Huebner* (pp. 396–400). New York, NY: Routledge. (Original work published 1991).

Lusthaus, D. (2002). *Buddhist Phenomenology: A Philosophical Investigation of Yogacara Buddhism and the Ch'eng Wei-shih Lun*. New York, NY: RoutledgeCurzon.

Newland, G. (2009). *Introduction to Emptiness: As Taught in Tsong-kha-pa's Great Treatise on the Stages of the Path* (2nd ed.). Ithaca, NY: Snow Lion Publications.

Pitt, A. (2000). Hide and Seek: The Play of the Personal in Education. In *The Play of the Personal: Psychoanalytic Narratives of Feminist Education* (pp. 83–95). New York: Peter Lang.

Schonert-Reichl, K. A., & Lawlor, M. S. (2010). The Effects of a Mindfulness-Based Education Program on Pre-and Early Adolescents' Well-Being and Social and Emotional Competence. *Mindfulness, 1*(3), 137–151.

Smith, D. G. (2000). The Specific Challenges of Globalization for Teaching and Vice Versa. *The Alberta Journal of Education Research, XLVI*(1), 7–26.

Thompson, E. (2015). *Waking, Dreaming, Being: Self and Consciousness in Neuroscience, Meditation, and Philosophy.* New York, NY: Columbia University Press.

CHAPTER 10

Learning to Embody a Non-Dualistic Worldview

10.1 Introduction

As indicated in the previous chapter, cultivating selflessness and learning to embody a non-dualistic worldview are mutually inclusive and supportive, and both require the union of wisdom-side and method-side practices. In this chapter, with an emphasis on the deeds component of spiritual practice, I explore the method-side practices to gain insights into how we might learn to embody a non-dualistic worldview for consciousness transformation in an educational context. In our earlier exploration of the concepts and process of consciousness transformation, we saw the significance of the cultivation and embodiment of a non-dualistic worldview for the suppression and eradication of contaminated karmic seeds of afflictive and noetic barriers which hinder the transformation of consciousness. As revealed earlier, the wisdom-side practices for consciousness transformation are vital for the cultivation of selflessness and a non-dualistic worldview, and for preventing us from abiding in the extreme of the phenomenal aspect of reality (*samsara*). Yet for the purpose of avoiding the inconsistency between the view component and the deeds component of our practices, and of preventing us from abiding in the other extreme of the ultimate aspect of reality (*nirvana*), we also need the method-side practices (or the accumulation of merit) which aim for the embodiment of a non-dualistic worldview in everyday existential situations motivated by compassion, love, and *bodhicitta*.

© The Author(s) 2019
E. L. Chu, *Exploring Curriculum as an Experience of Consciousness Transformation*, Curriculum Studies Worldwide,
https://Doi.org/10.1007/978-3-030-17701-0_10

10.2 The Six Perfections and the Embodiment of a Non-Dualistic Worldview

While there are countless methods for embodying a non-dualistic worldview and achieving various spiritual goals, in *The Great Treatise*, Tsong-kha-pa (1402/2004) convincingly demonstrated that the six perfections (perfections of generosity, ethical discipline, patience, joyous perseverance, meditative stabilization, and wisdom), along with the arrangement of their order, constitute the best way of categorizing these methods (pp. 103–111). This categorization serves as a concise framework for understanding and applying various methods in Buddhism and in various religious and spiritual traditions. According to Tsong-kha-pa (1402/2004), the order of the six perfections reflects their arrangement in terms of arising, inferior and superior, and coarse and subtle: each of the perfections produce or influence the arising of the subsequent one, and each is inferior to, easier, and coarser than that which follows it (p. 111). Tsong-kha-pa (1402/2004) explicated the order of the arising of the six perfections as follows:

> When you have a generosity that is disinterested in and unattached to resources, you take up ethical discipline. When you have an ethical discipline, which restrains you from wrongdoing, you become patient with those who harm you. When you have patience wherein you do not become dispirited with hardship, the conditions for rejecting virtue are few, so you are able to persevere joyously. Once you persevere day and night, you will produce the meditative concentration that facilitates the application of your attention to virtuous objects of meditation. When your mind is in meditative equipoise, you will know reality exactly. (p. 111)

It is important to bear in mind that, as indicated in Chap. 3, each of the six perfections is a complex combination of methods and wisdom, and each supports, and is part of, the others; therefore, the order of the six perfections, rather than suggesting that each should be practiced one by one, is intended to provide practitioners (particularly novice practitioners) a focus of proficiency at each stage of practicing the dynamic and recursive matrix of the six perfections, and a sensible order of focus for making consolidated progress that will lead to the genuine transformation of consciousness. The order of the six perfections is thus of great significance and has important implications for the design of curriculum as an experience of consciousness transformation.

For the purpose of demonstrating how each of the six perfections should be practiced with all six perfections present, Tsong-kha-pa (1402/2004) offered the example of how to practice generosity in conjunction with all the other perfections when giving the gift of the teachings:

> When you are giving the teachings... it is extremely powerful if you practice all six perfections. You have ethical discipline when you restrain yourself from the consideration from *Śrāvakas* and *pratyekabuddhas* [meaning dedicating the merit of generosity only to one's own emancipation or happiness]; patience when you bear any hardship while you aspire to the qualities of omniscience and when you are patient with abuse from others; joyous perseverance when you yearn for the ever-greater increase of your generosity; meditative stabilization when you dedicate to complete enlightenment the virtue that you cultivate with one-pointed attention unmixed with Hīnayāna considerations [meaning considering one's own liberation only]; and wisdom when you know that the giver, gift, and recipient are like a magician's illusion. (p. 121)

This example instantiates how each of the six perfections supports, and is part of, the others, and exemplifies how in an educational context, the first four perfections (method-side practices) can be handy and powerful conceptual tools for examining our motivation for and practices of teaching, learning, studying, and decision-making. It also illustrates how the first four perfections can help prevent us from being taken in by our *I–Me–Mine* complex rooted in dual perception within the fabric of our relationships and thus provide us opportunities of transcending and redefining our sense of self—as, in Huebner's (1987/1999b) words, "we are our relationships" (p. 390). In this way, the first four perfections, which aim to embody a non-dualistic worldview, when applied in an educational context, have the potential to open formerly unseen possibilities; recover value and dignity; facilitate mutual love and reverence; enact genuine conversation and truthful knowing; return spiritual significance and existential meaning to everyday teaching, learning, studying, and decision-making; and dispel the formulaic logic of the market and the language of global competitiveness that currently permeate the educational landscape.

When understood from the perspective of the three trainings (ethical conduct, meditative stabilization, and wisdom), the perfections of generosity, ethical discipline, and patience serve respectively as the precondition, the nature, and the aid of the training in ethical conduct, and the perfection of joyous perseverance is included in each of the three trainings

(Tsong-kha-pa, 1402/2004, p. 109). Since the trainings in meditative stabilization and wisdom both rely on the establishment of a firm foundation of ethical conduct, the first four perfections constitute the preconditions for the perfections of meditative stabilization and wisdom (Tsong-kha-pa, 1402/2004, p. 110). The order of, and interrelationships among, the six perfections explained above not only help us recognize the significance of the first four perfections as training in ethical conduct and how these first four perfections relate to the other two perfections, but also remind us of the issues that could arise in an educational context with the growing popularity of meditative practices that are not necessarily grounded on a substantial training in ethical conduct and guided by wisdom that knows emptiness. In the absence of the training in ethical conduct (i.e., the first four perfections or the method-side practices motivated by compassion, love, and *bodhicitta* in everyday existential situations), the training in meditative stabilization loses its grounding; in the absence of the training in wisdom that knows the emptiness and oneness of self and reality, meditative stabilization risks being deprived of its existential significance and being trivialized by instrumentalists as merely another tool for enhancing their competitiveness or for nurturing their superiority. In short, in the absence of the training in ethical conduct and wisdom, meditative stabilization risks being degraded into a form of objectifying practices that only perpetuate suffering-laden *samsaric* experiences. Preventing such potential danger, as discussed in Chap. 2, should be of continuous concern to educators, particularly to curriculum theorists who recognize the significance of spirituality for education and seek the potentiality of the revival and renewal of the intimate relationship between spirituality and education.

10.3 The Meanings, Practices, and Educational Implications of the First Four Perfections

Let us now consider the meanings of the first four perfections. According to Tsong-kha-pa (1402/2004), in Buddhism, *generosity* is "an intention accompanying bodhisattvas' disinterested non-attachment to all their possessions and their body, and motivated by this, the physical and verbal actions of giving the things to be given" (p. 114); there are three types of generosity corresponding to three types of gift: the gift of the teachings, the gift of fearlessness, and material gifts. *Ethical discipline* is defined as "an attitude of abstention that turns your mind away from harming others and from the sources of such harm" (Tsong-kha-pa, 1402/2004, p. 143);

the coarsest factors that are incompatible with ethical discipline are the ten non-virtues: covetousness, malice, wrong view, lying, slander, harsh speech, senseless speech, killing, stealing, and sexual misconduct (Sopa, 2005, pp. 45–46). *Patience* is defined as "(1) disregarding harm done to you, (2) accepting the suffering arising in your mind-stream, and (3) being certain about the [Dharma] teachings and firmly maintaining belief in them" (Tsong-kha-pa, 1402/2004, p. 152). *Joyous perseverance* is defined as "a flawless state of mind that is enthusiastic about accumulating virtue and working for the welfare of living beings, together with the physical, verbal, and mental activity such a state of mind motivates" (Tsong-kha-pa, 1402/2004, p. 182).

While the transformative power of the first four perfections defined above relies on a proper understanding of the details of the teaching of the six perfections, given that this detailed teaching is not our current focus, only points that are of particular educational significance are selected for discussion. Firstly, rather than being intended as dogmatic moral tenets to be observed via a dual perception that sees the world as outside and independent of us, the first four perfections are practices that are in accordance with a non-dualistic worldview that sees the "objective" world as an essential part of our own existence. The meaning of the first four perfections as training in ethical conduct for embodying a non-dualistic worldview is illuminated in Smith's (2000) explication of the word "discipline," which he understands as

> the act of following a task to its true end, a kind of obedience to the call of truth as it speaks out to me from the task at hand. When I respond in a way true to the thing itself, I find my estrangement from it slowly melt away such that I become one with it, and it with me, and something new is brought into the world from out of us both. (pp. 24–25)

As Smith (2000) indicates, in pedagogical situations, the labor of overcoming our primal sense of estrangement from the world (i.e., subject–object or self–world duality) is best understood through the practice of discipline (p. 24). For Smith (2000), "Self implies Other. If there is to be truth in the world, it will be only truth as shared, something between us. Such is the foundation for ethics in the age of globalization" (p. 23). This observation reveals the ethical and pedagogical significance of the first four perfections as a kind of obedience to the call of truth as it speaks out to us here and now, calling forth the dissolution of the self–other dichotomy and the rebirth of the self.

In practicing the first four perfections, it is important to note that the completion of the first four perfections refers to the fulfillment of the mental aspect of the perfections rather than the physical and verbal aspects, such as completely removing sentient beings' poverty by giving gifts, or perfectly establishing sentient beings in a state free of all harm (Tsong-kha-pa, 1402/2004, p. 366). The educational implication of this realization is profound as it suggests that the perfection of various educational practices should be considered as mainly the fulfillment of the mental aspect of educational practices and processes rather than the mere measurable outcomes of testing, learning, competition, etc. This is not to say that the measurable outcomes are insignificant. Rather, it places the highlights, recalling Adam Smith's words, "in playing well, in playing fairly, in playing wisely and skillfully, in the propriety of our own conduct" (as cited in Ahmed, 2010, p. 208). This emphasis can be found in Mr. McNab's practices. Mr. McNab, as Aoki 1992/2004 described,

> was the one who on the annual district sports day insisted on taking all the students, the athletic and the not so athletic, breaking with the tradition of sports days for elite athletes. For us, the event was something special. It mattered little whether we won or lost. All of us were grateful that Mr. McNab took us—swift ones and slow ones, dumpy ones and lean ones, tall ones and short ones. (p. 194)

Whether his class won or lost, Mr. McNab perfectly fulfilled a genuine educational practice.

In addition, in practicing the four perfections, it is very important to bear in mind that we should not practice with arrogance. This kind of mindset is usually caused by taking a positive approach that grasps at desired ideals in contrast to the approach of negation. In the case of the perfection of generosity for example, Tsong-kha-pa (1402/2004) reminded us, "you do not despise the person who asks for something, you do not compete with others, and after you give something, you do not conceitedly think, 'I am so generous; no one else can do like this'" (p. 125). Drawing on a sutra, Tsong-kha-pa (1402/2004) explained that when ordinary beings make a gift, observe ethical discipline, maintain patience, etc., they get angry with, lose faith in, or speak disparagingly of those who do the opposite, and as a result of such contaminated karma rooted in dualistic perception, they obstruct their own practices of the six perfections and can possibly fall into miserable realms (p. 125). In the absence of impartial love and compassion, it is easy for us to fall into such pitfalls and forget that the oppressors are themselves oppressed by their own ignorant conduct. In an educational context, if we want to facilitate genuine transformation of consciousness, avoiding such pitfalls in both our discourse and practice is extremely important.

10.4 THE CURRICULUM OF WITNESSING

The first four perfections as training in ethical conduct and as a kind of obedience to the call of the truth of oneness can also be understood through the concept of *witnessing*—a concept similar to objectless or non-perceptual practices, or acting without "falling into objectifying" (Sopa, 2008, p. 217) discussed earlier. Boler (1999) explained that, in contrast to spectating, which "permits a gaping distance between self and other" (p. 184), witnessing "is a process in which we do not have the luxury of seeing a static truth or fixed certainty" (p. 186); rather, "as a medium of perception, witnessing is a dynamic process, and cannot capture meaning as conclusion" (p. 186). In other words, in positioning oneself as a witness, one defines and experiences oneself as one's relationships with the world based on the realization of the non-duality of self and world and the transcendent nature of human existence and, in this dynamic process, harkens and responds to the world in ways that correspond with this realization. The concept of witnessing is similar to Bowers' theory of *ecological intelligence* that abandons "the Cartesian representation of the individuals as spectator of an external world" (as cited in Riley-Taylor, 2002, p. 15) and considers the individual as "an interactive member of the larger and more complex… culture/environment relationship" (as cited in Riley-Taylor, 2002, p. 15). The concepts of both witnessing and ecological intelligence emphasize "the relational embeddedness of individuals" (Riley-Taylor, 2002, p. 15). As Eppert (2008) observed, "witness participates in a search for, engagement with, and communication of an inner and outer experience that is intimately linked with larger struggles for fuller connection and with the question of how to live (and die) in the world" (p. 59). For Boler (1999), ethical questions do exist in spectating. Ethical issues arise when someone is suffering yet we choose to keep a comfortable and safe distance without doing anything. Such issues indicate ethical complexities and the need to go beyond the moral binary of guilt vs. innocence—a binary that, according to Boler (1999), "severely constrains educational possibilities" (p. 186). For Boler (1999), spectating vs. witnessing provides a useful tool for learning how positionalities shift and slip in complex, unpredictable, and precarious ways. Through learning to see how and when one spectates or bears witness it becomes possible, at least provisionally, to inhabit a more ambiguous sense of self not reduced to either guilt or innocence. In this process one acknowledges profound interconnections with others. (p. 187)

Becoming aware of our positioning as spectator or witness is thus conducive not only to learning to go beyond moral binaries and cultivate morality as a response that is true to the thing itself inspired by non-dual perception, but also to learning to embody a non-dualistic worldview. In the positioning of witnessing, we stop watching the world from an outsider perspective, learn to overcome what Huebner calls the subject–object attitude, and transform the sense of human estrangement from the world that usually distorts our vision of others with the paranoia of the narcissistic and egoistic *I–Me–Mine* complex. By means of adopting the "subject–subject attitude" (Huebner, 1963/1999a, p. 88) from an insider perspective, in witnessing, we include our relationships to the world in our sense of self and become aware of how in these interrelationships, *you* and *me* co-arise concurrently and interdependently, not as separate identities but as a dyad that brings about new transcendental possibilities. In this kind of self–world dialectic, there is no longer an "other" to compete with, to fight against, or to grab from, but rather an equal to love and give to with generosity, ethical discipline, patience, and joyous perseverance based on meditative insights and wisdom that knows emptiness. Witnessing, therefore, in Eppert's (2008) words, "carries within it dimensions of relationship and the seeds of social change within the context of walking a spiritual path" (p. 59).

Nonetheless, Eppert (2008) reminded us that "it's hardly likely that change can simply be thought, spoken, or written and then spontaneously acted upon. Structural changes [or shifts of positioning] initiated without deep and sustained, long cultivated attentiveness, wisdom, and compassion are likely to reflect *samsaric* reactions rather than responses" (p. 101). Eppert's reminder makes evident the requirement of the union of method-side practices (generosity, ethical discipline, patience, and joyous perseverance rooted in compassion) and wisdom-side practices (meditative stabilization and wisdom) in witnessing. Drawing on Thich Nhat Hanh, who shed "light on dynamics of engaged (Buddhist) witnessing in contexts of advocating and acting for nonviolence, equality, ecological sustainability" (Eppert, 2008, p. 100), Eppert (2008) cautioned us via Nhat Hanh's reflection upon antiwar protests that "even though activists sought peace, to a great degree their emotions, language, and actions reflected aggression" (p. 100). For Nhat Han, "a more original paradigm shift… involves loosening the tightness of our views and notions about what is 'right.' It is attachment—grasping and clinging—that is the deep structure of discord" (Eppert, 2008, pp. 100–101). Nhat Hanh's reflection echoes with our earlier discussion of the approach of negation and of Kumar's (2013) explication that "the positive—be it love or non-violence—is not born through following ideals, which are opposite to the present state, but through negatively thinking and observing the present state of the mind" (p. 89) and that "the negative approach is not reactionary in nature. It is not a mere replacement of one approach for another" (p. 89). Echoing our discussion of the approach of negation in Chaps. 4 and 8, Nhat Han considered these positive ideals as merely like the finger that points to the Moon and reminded us of Buddha's advice: "Do not get caught in thinking that the finger is the Moon" (Eppert, 2008, p. 101). The philosophy of this negative approach, which negates the grasping of any positive ideals, is well reflected in an excerpt of T. S. Eliot's poem "East Coker":

> I said to my soul, be still, and wait without hope
> For hope would be hope for the wrong thing; wait without love
> For love would be love of the wrong thing… (Eliot, as cited in Pinar, 1974, p. 128)

Such a negative approach, for Eppert (2008), advised educators "away from rigid and too tightly enforced pedagogical agendas, whether agendas based on testing and reproduction of the status quo or on sociopolitical transformation" (p. 101) and encouraged "student-directed (un)learning and educators to sustain learners as they follow their own course/way" (Eppert, 2008, p. 101). In other words, in curriculum of witnessing, educator and learner co-arise interdependently as a dyad and "lay down a path in walking" (Varela 1987, as cited in Thompson, 2007, p. 13) together. However, given our deep-seated fear and anxiety rooted in a dualistic worldview, it is never easy to simply wait without hope and love. In the face of our fear, Eliot's poem continued:

> … there is yet faith
> But faith and love and the hope are all in the waiting.
> Wait without thought, for you are not ready for thought:
> So the darkness shall be the light, and the stillness the dancing. (Eliot, as cited in Pinar, 1974, p. 128)

This extract reveals another significant aspect of the negative approach that points to the significance of meditative insights—insights that transcend reified, idealized, and fixed kinds of hope, love, and faith rooted in fear and duality—for curriculum of witnessing.

As discussed earlier, curriculum of witnessing requires the union of method and wisdom. In consonance with our discussion in Chap. 9 regarding the significance of meditative stabilization for cultivating selflessness, in considering new possibilities for a curriculum of witnessing, Eppert (2008) addressed issues of fear and anxiety and underscored the significance of meditative insights for the overcoming of deep-seated fear and anxiety rooted in a dualistic worldview. Witnessing, as Simon and Eppert (1997) described, calls for "embodied cognizance within which one becomes aware of, self-present to, and responsive to something/someone beyond oneself" (p. 183). For Eppert (2008), "cognizance refers to insight rather than knowing or being aware as the product of thought and analysis alone" (p. 98) and "the beyond that can be witnessed is 'interbeing'" (p. 99) (interdependent being) attained through meditation (p. 99). She emphasized, "critical thinking and analysis are vital but not enough to address fear, greed, and hatred, to heal, and to live in the world nondualistically, connectedly, compassionately, and transformationally" (Eppert, 2008, p. 98). She explained, by quoting Packer and Swaebe, "to solve the problem of ego there has to be direct insight into the whole movement of thought that is creating the ego" (as cited in Eppert, 2008, p. 98). Therefore, in curriculum of witnessing, "insight and embodied experience walk hand-in-hand" (Eppert, 2008, p. 98).

Drawing on Buddha's teaching that recommended "before trying to guide others, be your own guide first" (as cited in Eppert, 2008, p. 99), Eppert (2008) stressed that witnessing "addresses the educator first and foremost" (p. 99). She cited Krishnamurti:

> Surely, the teacher himself must first begin to see. He must be constantly alert, intensely aware of his own thoughts and feelings, aware of the ways in which he is conditioned, aware of his activities and his response; for out of this watchfulness comes intelligence, and with it a radical transformation in his relationship to people and to things. (as cited in Eppert, 2008, pp. 99–100)

Similarly, Pinar discussed "the curriculum theorist/practitioner as on an educational journey or pilgrimage, rigorously engaged in questioning, studying, and reflecting upon his or her inner experience" (Eppert, 2008,

p. 100). Eppert (2008) indicated that "in his contemplation upon the nature and possibilities of autobiographical inquiry, Pinar also attends to Zen's early influences upon him, linking processes of *currere* with contemplative investigations into one's attachments, fears, and, generally, the architecture of the self" (p. 100). Addressing an issue similar to our earlier discussion of what Lusthaus (2002) called "appropriational circuit" created by projecting our theories onto our experience in form of dualistic self and others (p. 2), Pinar maintained that "only through a genuine democratization of one's interiorized elements, none of which gets deported (projected in psychoanalytic terms) to the bodies of others who then become 'others' can the body politic be reformed and the public sphere reconstructed" (as cited in Eppert, 2008, p. 100). Both Krishnamurti and Pinar prioritize autobiographical and meditative inquiries for sociopolitical reconstruction. Neither is the autobiographical inquiry of *currere* solipsistic, nor is the meditative inquiry monastic and dissociated from social concerns (Eppert, 2008, p. 100). As Eppert (2008) illuminated, what is necessary in curriculum of witnessing is an "intricate web of relationship between the personal/inner and the sociopolitical/outer" (Eppert, 2008, p. 100)—a union of wisdom (the personal/inner) and method (the sociopolitical/outer) imbued with each other.

To summarize, in this chapter, drawing on the method-side practices of the six perfections motivated by compassion, love, and *bodhicitta*, we have explored the significant educational implications of the first four perfections for learning to embody a non-dualistic worldview as an attempt to transform everyday educational planning, teaching, learning, and studying into opportunities for consciousness transformation and to return its spiritual and existential significance back to everyday life in an educational context.

In Part IV as a whole, we have considered how we might understand curriculum as an experience of consciousness transformation by means of examining six key elements: understanding the nature of consciousness, self, and reality; learning to appreciate human temporality; cultivating impartiality and *bodhicitta*; becoming responsibly responsive; cultivating selflessness; and learning to embody a non-dualistic worldview. Despite being explored separately, as we have seen, these six key elements are mutually inclusive and indivisible. Rather than being intended as a comprehensive theory, these key elements constitute a possible framework for contemplating how curriculum might become an experience of consciousness transformation.

References

Ahmed, S. (2010). *The Promise of Happiness*. Durham: Duke University Press.
Aoki, T. T. (2004). Layered Voices of Teaching: The Uncannily Correct and the Elusively True. In W. F. Pinar & R. L. Irwin (Eds.), *Curriculum in a New Key: The Collected Works of Ted T. Aoki* (pp. 187–197). New York, NY: Routledge. (Original work published 1992).
Boler, M. (1999). *Feeling Power: Emotions and Education*. New York, NY: Routledge.
Eppert, C. (2008). Fear, (Educational) Fictions of Character, and Buddhist Insights for an Arts-Based Witnessing Curriculum. In C. Eppert & H. Wang (Eds.), *Cross-Cultural Studies in Curriculum* (pp. 55–108). New York, NY: Routledge.
Huebner, D. E. (1999a). New Modes of Man's Relationship to Man. In V. Hillis (Ed.), *The Lure of the Transcendent: Collected Essays by Dwayne E. Huebner* (pp. 74–93). New York, NY: Routledge. (Original work published 1963).
Huebner, D. E. (1999b). Practicing the Presence of God. In V. Hillis (Ed.), *The Lure of the Transcendent: Collected Essays by Dwayne E. Huebner* (pp. 388–395). New York, NY: Routledge. (Original work published 1987).
Kumar, A. (2013). *Curriculum as Meditative Inquiry*. New York, NY: Palgrave Macmillan.
Lusthaus, D. (2002). *Buddhist Phenomenology: A Philosophical Investigation of Yogacara Buddhism and the Ch'eng Wei-shih Lun*. New York, NY: RoutledgeCurzon.
Pinar, W. F. (1974). In the Stillness Is the Dance. In W. F. Pinar (Ed.), *Heightened Consciousness, Cultural Revolution, and Curriculum Theory* (pp. 1–15). The Proceedings of the Rochester Conference (Rochester, New York, May 3–5, 1973).
Riley-Taylor, E. (2002). *Ecology, Spirituality, Education: Curriculum for Relational Knowing*. New York: Peter Lang.
Simon, R. I., & Eppert, C. (1997). Remembering Obligation: Pedagogy and the Witnessing of Testimony of Historical Trauma. *Canadian Journal of Education*, 22(2), 175–191.
Smith, D. G. (2000). The Specific Challenges of Globalization for Teaching and Vice Versa. *The Alberta Journal of Education Research*, XLVI(1), 7–26.
Sopa, L. (2005). *Steps on the Path to Enlightenment: A Commentary on Tsongkhapa's Lamrim Chenmo. Volume II: Karma*. Somerville, MA: Wisdom Publications.
Sopa, L. (2008). *Steps on the Path to Enlightenment: A Commentary on Tsongkhapa's Lamrim Chenmo. Volume III: The Way of the Bodhisattva*. Somerville, MA: Wisdom Publications.
Thompson, E. (2007). *Mind in Life: Biology, Phenomenology, and the Sciences of Mind*. Cambridge, MA: Harvard University Press.
Tsong-kha-pa (2004). *The Great Treatise on the Stages of the Path to Enlightenment* (Vol. 2, The Lamrim Chenmo Translation Committee, trans.). Ithaca, NY: Snow Lion Publications. (Original work published 1402).

PART V

Conclusion Without Conclusion

CHAPTER 11

The Metamorphosis and the Confounded Speech

11.1 Retrospection

This study was motivated by a deep concern over education's de-spiritualization and its inappropriate reliance on classical science, which seems to me to have come at the cost of spiritual wisdom and to be the root cause of the radical commercialization of human values and various global crises. Over the course of the preceding chapters, I have investigated the possibilities for imbuing curriculum with spiritual wisdom by drawing mainly on the work of curriculum scholar Dwayne Huebner, Martin Heidegger's interpretation of Plato's allegory of the cave, Buddhism, and quantum physics, and explored how we might understand curriculum as an experience of consciousness transformation. In the past several decades, while there has been a growing appreciation of the spiritual in the educational landscape, the concepts of spirituality found in the educational literature remain largely vague and elusive; questions regarding the nature of the spiritual and the meaning of "being on a spiritual path" remain largely unaddressed. Huebner's phenomenological and theological discourses have eloquently ruled out absolutism and objectivism, which I recognize as the main epistemologies that hinder two of the most significant aspects of spiritual truth: openness to the transcendent and a non-dualistic worldview. However, given the long-standing reliance of educational enterprises upon scientific traditions and the fact that curriculum development or the systematic tradition of curriculum—which is largely in keeping with Ralph Tyler's framework—is still thriving despite being the subject of consistent criticism (Null, 2008), I see the imperative to scrutinize spiritual wisdom from a scientific perspective and to resolve the prevailing myth of the incompatibility between spiritual wisdom and scientific ways of thinking.

My religious background inspired and enabled me to incorporate the spiritual wisdom and teachings of Buddhism into this research. By means of conducting a dialogue between Buddhism and quantum physics, I have illustrated a dramatic convergence and compatibility of the two branches of thought regarding the nature of consciousness, self, and reality; the resonances between the Buddhist concepts of the two truths (the ultimate truth of emptiness and the phenomenal truth of the daily phenomenal world) and the two distinct realities depicted respectively by quantum physics and classical physics are particularly striking. The convergence of these branches of thought provides insights into the essence of spirituality—which is all about piercing the deceptive shadowy phenomenal aspect of reality and attaining the realization of the ultimate nature of consciousness, self, and reality that brings about ultimate liberation. This deepened understanding of the nature of consciousness, self, and reality also helps us apprehend the four-stage transition of the essence of truth presumed or realized by an individual that, for Heidegger, constitutes the essence and purpose of education as well as the essence of the transformation of consciousness.

For the purpose of gaining a panoramic view of the whole spiritual path for educational use, as well as avoiding various potential pitfalls and deviations along the way, I have drawn on the five-stage gradual path of consciousness transformation into four transcendental wisdoms as prescribed in *Yogacara*, the Consciousness-Only school of Buddhism. I have explored how we might understand curriculum as an experience of consciousness transformation from the perspectives of six key elements: understanding the nature of consciousness, self and reality; learning to appreciate human temporality; cultivating impartiality and *bodhicitta*; becoming responsibly responsive; cultivating selflessness; and learning to embody a non-dualistic worldview.

In this journey, we witness the beauty and hermeneutical power of the dialectic between science and religion, or between reason and faith, in a broader sense. The convergence of new science and religious doctrines, it seems to me, heralds the coming of the historical moment for human beings to complete the metamorphosis toward a new spirit of faith, or what Paul Ricoeur called "a postreligious faith" (as cited in Quinn, 2001, p. 26)—a new religion that is not a religion.

11.2 THREE METAMORPHOSES OF THE SPIRIT: CAMEL, LION, AND CHILD

At the beginning of this book, I address the issue of de-spiritualization in education, its dire consequences, and its roots in the inappropriate reliance on classical science—a reliance on something that might be understood as what Quinn (2001) called "faithless reason" (p. 22). On the basis of Dwayne Huebner's and Martin Heidegger's works and the dialogue between Buddhism and quantum physics, I contend for the imperative of integrating spiritual wisdom and existential knowledge—essential doctrines of various religious and spiritual traditions and renewed understanding of the nature of consciousness, self, and reality unveiled by new science—into the school and university curricula.

With similar concern and contention, Quinn (2001) drew on Nietzsche's On the Three Metamorphoses from Zarathustra's Speeches in *Thus Spoke Zarathustra*, as well as Paul Ricoeur's related work, and argued for the need of "coming to a new kind of faith" (Quinn, 2001, p. 42). Quinn (2001) opened her retelling of "On the Three Metamorphoses" with the introduction that "I tell you of three metamorphoses of the spirit: how the spirit becomes a camel; and how the camel becomes a lion; and how the lion, finally, becomes a child" (p. 25). She continued:

> I tell you of the spirit first that would bear much, whose way is hard, for this spirit strong and reverent, and its strength requires the difficult and the most difficult. "O heroes, what is difficult, and most difficult?" the spirit that would take all upon itself asks, kneeling to the ground like a camel ready to be fully loaded. "I shall take such upon myself that I may exult in my strength," it declares. (Quinn, 2001, p. 25)

The spirit, thus, like a well-burdened *camel*, "would bear much and the most difficult things speeds into its desert" (Quinn, 2001, p. 25). In the lonely desert, the second metamorphosis—a *lion*—occurs (Quinn, 2001, p. 25). The lion "would master his own freedom and overcome his own desert... Here searches out his last lord and god with whom he wishes to fight to the death" (Quinn, 2001, p. 25). However, the ultimate triumph for which the lion longs is in the battle with the great dragon—a dragon named "Thou shalt" (Quinn, 2001, p. 25). The lion, with the spirit of "I will," would see "Thou shalt" as an immoveable obstacle—a gold beast with scales over its body (Quinn, 2001, p. 25). Quinn (2001) continued that

> The lion, though he cannot himself create, with the "I will" of his spirit prepares way for invention, for new values. For without the creation of freedom for oneself, new creation is not possible. Thus, the lion is the spirit of a sacred "No," that realizes illusion and caprice in "Thou shalt." (p. 25)

Then, once again, the spirit moves from the preying lion to a *child*, and "with the child comes the game of creation. The child, a new beginning, innocence and forgetting, utters now a sacred 'Yes.' The spirit wills its own will, and having been lost to world, now triumphs over its own world" (Quinn, 2001, p. 25).

Through retelling the allegory of three transformations of human spirit, Quinn (2001) intended to "illumine humanity's history with the sacred and trace the evolution of spirit wrought in its people and culture" (p. 13). For Quinn (2001), "each metamorphosis can be seen as a pivotal moment in the human history and consciousness of Western Civilization, each image a representation of the tenor and spirit of the times, of the dominant human stance taken in and toward life" (p. 13). She juxtaposed Nietzsche's allegory with Paul Ricoeur's essay "Religion, Atheism, and Faith" that presented "something of an ontological history of humanity's relation to the sacred... in Western civilization" (Quinn, 2001, p. 26) and paralleled Nietzsche's three metamorphoses—camel, lion, and child—with Ricoeur's religion, atheism, and faith (postreligious faith) (Quinn, 2001).

As "a response to Nietzschean critique of religion and the hermeneutics of suspicion, Ricoeur boldly advocates a path, or eschatological metamorphosis, from religion through atheism on the way to what he calls 'faith'" (Quinn, 2001, p. 26). What Ricoeur meant by the spirit of religion, as Quinn (2001) explicated, parallels the spirit of camel—"reverent and submissive, exults in such exhibition of virtue as it serves to assuage guilt and deliver comfort" (p. 26). In this sense, religion "is a primitive form of life rooted in the fear of punishment [of the God] and the desire for [his] protection" (p. 26), but "the edicts of 'Thou Shalt,' commandments eventually found too difficult to bear" (p. 27). Like the lion discovering the illusion in the "Thou shalt" and roaring a sacred "No," "atheism—ferocious, majestic, free, in the spirit of critique, dismantles and rips away at the foundations of religion" (Quinn, 2001, p. 27). Atheism, Ricoeur claimed, however, "is not limited to the mere negation and destruction of religion but... rather, it opens up the horizon for something else, for a type of faith that might be called... a postreligious faith or a faith for a postreligious age" (as cited in Quinn, 2001, p. 26). According to Quinn (2001), Ricoeur believed that there is a religious meaning in atheism, and "that meaning is found in its movement toward faith of a new and different kind" (p. 30). This religious meaning of atheism is also found in philosopher Simone Weil's teaching (Quinn, 2001). In the Introduction to Weil's book *Waiting for God*, Fiedler (1951) stated:

> To those who consider themselves on the safe side of belief,... [Weil] teaches the uncomfortable truth that the unbelief of many atheists is [perhaps] closer to a true love of God and a true sense of his nature, than the kind of easy faith which, never having *experienced* God, hangs a label bearing his name on some childish fantasy or projection of the ego. (p. 5)

However, while atheism might be "closer to a true love of God and a true sense of his nature" (Fiedler, 1951, p. 5) than the kind of easy, childish, fearful, or egoistic faith, like Ricoeur, Quinn (2001) cautioned that "atheism, too, is insufficient, unable to enter the game of creation, to begin anew" (Quinn, 2001, p. 13), and emphasized the significance of following the sacred "No" with the sacred "Yes" to life (p. 30).

Quinn (2001) linked atheism with reason and indicated that "the kernel of Western Civilization can be most accurately depicted as the relentless pursuit of reason and an unwavering faith in it as humanity's hope for achieving the knowledge of the good and the good itself" (p. 19). Since the development of classical science, we have heard of lions roaring sacred "No" and "I will" not only in the West, but all over the world; as we have seen, however, "the lion's reign, too, is an unsatisfactory conclusion" (Quinn, 2001, p. 31). In finding our way to the sacred "Yes," Ricoeur believed that we are "incapable of returning to an order of moral life which would take the form of a simple submission to commandments or to an alien or supreme will, even if this will were represented as divine" (p. 31). Also, for Ricoeur, while "Nietzsche has these sprinkles of the 'sacred "Yes"' throughout his work, it is dominated by rebellion and critique" (Quinn, 2001, p. 31). Ricoeur argued:

> This positive Nietzschean philosophy, which alone is capable of conferring authority on his negative hermeneutics, remains buried under the ruins that Nietzsche has accumulated around him... His aggression against Christianity remains caught up in the attitude of resentment; the rebel is not, and cannot be, at the same level as the prophet. Nietzsche's work remains an accusation of accusation and hence falls short of a pure affirmation of life. (as cited in Quinn, 2001, p. 31)

The sacred "Yes" to life, or the affirmation of a new kind of postreligious faith, therefore, cannot be attained through "a meager reconciliation of a hermeneutics of suspicion, which seeks to slay generations of idols, and a restorative hermeneutics, which works to resurrect the original living symbols behind those idols" (Quinn, 2001, p. 31); and apparently, neither could it be attained through mere accusation or rejection of either religion or atheism (reason). For Ricoeur, working toward the sacred "Yes" to life lies in "a dialectic between religion and atheism" (Quinn, 2001, p. 31), and the spirit of the new kind of faith, which Quinn (2001) likened to Nietzsche's spirit of child, is "a movement and future hope through which we might traverse the dialectical relationship between religion, or camel-spirit, and atheism, the spirit as lion" (p. 13). Faith, therefore, Quinn (2001) explicated, is *not* "a linear conclusion following on the heels of the human evolution from religion, in its primitive sense, to atheism, which for Ricoeur is inclusive of more than its literal sense" (p. 13); rather, it is "forward-looking, a kind of synthesis involving religion and atheism, and yet also a metamorphosis moving humanity beyond them" (p. 13).

It seems to me, the insufficiency of atheism lies in that in the preying lion's roars, the lion, while rejecting an extrinsic God who commands "Thou shalt," remains caught up in a sharp inner–outer (subject–object, or self–world) duality. Being ignorant of the ultimate nature of consciousness, self, and reality that signifies infinite possibilities and the dependently arising nature of all phenomena, particularly the inner–outer correlations, the preying lion grasps at the phenomenal aspect of reality as the only reality, confuses the mirror with the origin, shadows with the source, and pursues or fights outwardly. In other words, the insufficiency of atheism lies in its lack of *inwardness* and in that it is, borrowing Quinn's (2001) words, a *faithless reason* that refers merely to the phenomenal aspect of reality.

Regarding the problem of religion, I believe, the issue is not religion in itself per se, but mainly in the confusion between its essence and its expediency shaped by historical and political contexts, and in our dogmatization, reification, distortion, overgeneralization, and misinterpretation of its disciplines and doctrines. In short, the problem of religion emerges only when it becomes a kind of *reasonless faith* (borrowing Quinn's (2001) term). With this realization, it becomes clear that the rejection of religion and spiritual wisdom as a whole and the killing of the God can only be considered as acts of *reasonless reason*. Quinn (2001) retold the Judeo-Christian "Story of Creation" and the "Fall of Man" and remarked that it seems Durkheim is right: "We have no more gods, thus eventually, we ourselves become as gods and attempt our own salvation. The echo of the serpent sounds through the corridors of history: 'Ye shall be as gods'" (p. 61). Quinn (2001) lamented, "where God is dead,... so begins the languishing of all things" (p. 16), and by killing the God ourselves, "we are also effecting the death of the world, of humankind itself, of ourselves" (p. 16). What are indispensable toward a sacred "Yes" to life, toward the confirmation of the spirit of child as a being-in-the-world, toward the enjoyment of the game of creation and the transformation of consciousness into transcendental wisdoms, I believe, are *faith with reason* and *reason with faith*, or, in terms of the Buddhist Middle Way, wisdom imbued with method and method imbued with wisdom—the union of method (rational methods motivated by compassion, love and *bodhicitta*) and wisdom (meditative wisdom that knows emptiness)—that refers simultaneously to both the phenomenal and ultimate aspects of reality.

In literature, the emphasis of equal validity of faith and reason is also found in the works of Robert Musil (1880–1942). Musil was named in 1949 by an article in the *Times Literary Supplement* as the most important writer in German of his time (Pinar, 2015, p. 201). David Luft also suggested that Musil probably is "the equal of anyone since Nietzsche in his intelligence and insight in the realm of the soul" (as cited in Pinar, 2015, p. 201). Pinar suggested the significance of Musil's works for our time by quoting Stefan Jonsson: "The parallels between our time and Musil's are so striking that it is no longer possible not to read his writings historically and politically" (as cited in Pinar, 2015, p. 201). One significant feature of Musil's works is his acknowledgment of "the necessity of both reason and religion (understood as mysticism) [for inner life]; they are simultaneously operating functions of the human mind in its efforts to apprehend reality" (Pinar, 2015, p. 204). For Musil, "both poles of experience and perception possess equal validity; one must resist the temptation of positioning only one at the center of one's life" (Pinar, 2015, p. 204).

Similar to Ricoeur's emphasis on the need of "a dialectic between religion and atheism" (Quinn, 2001, p. 31), "Musil believed that the process of balancing these poles [of reason and religion] probably involved a thorough, even dialectical investigation first of the one and then of the other" (Pinar, 2015, p. 204). Musil called the synthesis of reason and religion (mysticism) "'*das rechte Leben*', the creative or right life" (Pinar, 2015, p. 204). The language he used for articulating the creative or right life was "precision and soul" (Pinar, 2015, p. 207) and such language was embodied in Musil's essayism—"an intellectual strategy that extended the methodological rigor of the natural sciences into the sphere of singularity, that domain represented by art (especially fiction) and ethics" (Pinar, 2015, p. 207). However, "rather than looking for laws and regularities, essayism seeks the understanding of lived experience in individual and particularistic ways that rely on *metaphor* [emphasis added] rather than upon nomological relations among numerically represented variables" (Pinar, 2015, p. 207). The power of the Musilian language is in that it "communicates a multiplicity of apparently irreconcilable perspectives, creating fissures through which intellectual breakthrough becomes possible" (Pinar, 2015, pp. 208–209), and it "bridges incommensurate realities via juxtaposition, creating a 'cacophony of rivaling perspectives'" (Pinar, 2015, p. 209). Pinar drew on Peters' assertion that, for Musil, "the *synthesis of reason and mysticism* [emphasis added] had to be regarded as the most urgent task facing mankind in the twentieth century" (as cited in Pinar, 2015), and this remains true for our time.

While, according to Quinn (2001), in 1969 Ricoeur suggested that in this interim "before the emergence of a new spirit, the recognizable metamorphosis from lion to child, atheism to faith" (p. 32), what the philosophers can do are only to think and question, and "the rest is the job of the prophet, perhaps" (p. 32), I believe that our time is privileged time, and each of us can do what the "prophet" do on our way toward the spirit of child and new faith, toward the transformation of consciousness, or toward what Musil called "creative or right life" (Pinar, 2015, p. 204). As revealed in the dialogue between Buddhism and quantum physics, thanks to the breakthroughs of new science, we are granted profound opportunities to get closer to the ultimate nature of human existence and reality. We are privileged to witness the convergence of religion and science (faith and reason), and the hermeneutical power of their synthesis. This means we are privileged and obligated to take actions, to take on the most urgent task facing mankind in our time, rather than merely thinking and questioning. Wallerstein (2007) reminded us that while for more than 200 years, we have been living in a structure of knowledge in which science and philosophy have been considered as distinctive and virtually antagonistic forms of knowledge and this division implicates the entire realm of knowledge, this is not always so—before the middle of the eighteenth century, such division was virtually unknown anywhere in the world (p. 130). Noë (2010) also stressed that "the idea that science and philosophy, or the humanities more generally, are separate spheres with their own standard and criteria is itself a bit of questionable ideology, a relic of enthusiasm of an earlier modern age" (p. xv). As he indicated, physics actually used to be known as natural philosophy, and natural science was never considered to be discrete from broader human concerns (Noë, 2010, p. xv). Given their joint goal—the unveiling of the ultimate nature of human existence and reality for the benefits of mankind—it would be unsurprising if they eventually find and join each other.

In our efforts toward the metamorphosis from lion to child that embrace faith with reason and reason with faith, and in our contemplation of how we might understand curriculum as an experience of consciousness transformation, Huebner's (1963/1999a) reminder is particularly helpful:

> The compartmentalization of human thought into religious, philosophical, and scientific sections, without attempting consciously to compare and evaluate the differing language and symbol categories for the same phenomena or situations, cannot be justified. Such comparison and evaluation does not imply that one thought or language system must predominate over the others, for each has its own values. But the values can only be realized if their respective powers and limitations can be identified. (p. 91)

Similarly, Aoki (1980/2004a) was concerned about the monodimensional effect of the dominance of scientific method in curriculum inquiry (pp. 93, 96), and underscored the need to increase our vision through employing "as many perspectives as we can find appropriate" (Aoki, 1980/2004a, p. 96). During this journey, we have seen how Huebner's phenomenological and theological discourses, Buddhism, and quantum physics shed light on each other and deepen our understanding of spirituality. This gives us a glimpse of the hermeneutical power of cross-discourse studies. While encouraging the employment of differing language and symbol categories and many perspectives, both Huebner (1963/1999a) and Aoki (1980/2004a) cautioned us from the predomination of one single thought or language system in curriculum. In the next section, I explore further Huebner's reminder and its related issues through the allegory of The Blind Men and the Elephant.

11.3 The Blind Men and the Elephant

The Blind Men and the Elephant is an ancient allegory that is traceable to the Buddhist text, but it is likely older and may well have a Jain origin (Wang, 1995) as "it does illustrate well the Jain doctrine of *Anekanta*, the manysidedness of things" (Wang, 1995). Ireland (1997) suggested that the allegory "is probably older than both [Buddhism and Jainism] and is still used today by modern Hindu teachers" (p. 9). In the following is a summary of this allegory from the Buddhist canon *Udana*.

> One day, a number of bhikkhus went to the Buddha and said,
> Sir, there are living here in Savatthi many wandering hermits and scholars who indulge in constant dispute, some saying that the world is infinite and eternal and others that it is finite and not eternal, some saying that the soul dies with the body and others that it lives on forever, and so forth. What, Sir, would you say concerning them? (Udana 68–69, as cited in Wang, 1995)

In response, the Buddha told an allegory: Once upon a time, there was a king who asked his servant to gather together all the men of Savatthi who were born blind and show them an elephant (Ireland, 1997; Wang, 1995). These blind men were led to the head, the ears, a tusk, the trunk, the foot, back, tail, and tuft of the tail of the elephant respectively (Ireland, 1997; Wang, 1995). After the blind men had felt the elephant, the king asked them to describe the elephant (Ireland, 1997; Wang, 1995).

> Thereupon the men who were presented with the head answered, "Sire, an elephant is like a pot." And the men who had observed the ear replied, "An elephant is like a winnowing basket." Those who had been presented with a tusk said it was a ploughshare. Those who knew only the trunk said it was a plough; others said the body was a granary; the foot, a pillar; the back, a mortar; the tail, a pestle, the tuft of the tail, a brush. (Udana 68–69, as cited in Wang, 1995)

Then these blind men started to quarrel, shouting "'Yes it is!' 'No, it is not!' 'An elephant is not that!' 'Yes, it's like that!' and so on, till they came to blows over the matter" (Udana 68–69, as cited in Wang, 1995). After telling this allegory, the Buddha remarked: "Just so are these preachers and scholars holding various views blind and unseeing... In their ignorance they are by nature quarrelsome, wrangling, and disputatious, each maintaining reality is thus and thus" (Udana 68–69, as cited in Wang, 1995). The Buddha then rendered the implication of this allegory into a verse:

> O how they cling and wrangle, some who claim
> For preacher and monk the honored name!

11 THE METAMORPHOSIS AND THE CONFOUNDED SPEECH 189

> For, quarreling, each to his view they cling.
> Such folk see only one side of a thing. (Udana 68–69, as cited in Wang, 1995)

In resonance with Plato's allegory of the cave wherein human beings are likened to chained prisoners seeing nothing but the shadows on the wall as the whole reality, this allegory also points to the finitude of human cognition and suggests the multi-sidedness of things and reality. The finitude of human cognition is now well recognized by contemporary science. In *The Future of the Mind*, Kaku (2014) drew on his interviews with prominent scientists and proposed a new model of the brain. One of the peculiar features of this model is that "most of our mental processes are subconscious" (Kaku, 2014, p. 39), that is, "our choice of politicians, marriage partners, friends, and future occupations are all influenced by things that we are not conscious of" (Kaku, 2014, pp. 39–40). Based on a variety of empirical studies, Kaku (2014) further indicated that "what we consider to be 'reality' is only an approximation that the brain makes to fill in the gap. Each of us sees reality in a slightly different way" (p. 40). In quantum physics, the uncertainty principle (as briefly mentioned in Chap. 3) also points to this human limitation. According to Greene (2011),

> the uncertainty principle establishes that regardless of what equipment you use or what techniques you employ, if you increase the resolution of your measurement of one property, there is an unavoidable cost: you necessarily reduce how accurately you can measure a complementary property. As a prime example, the uncertainty principle shows that the more accurately you measure an object's position, the less accurately you can measure its speed, and vice versa. (Greene, 2011, p. 31)

Using the photographing of an impish fly as a rough analogy, Greene (2011) illustrated:

> If your shutter speed is high, you'll get a sharp image that records the fly's location at the moment you snapped the picture. But because the photo is crisp, the fly appears motionless; the image gives no information about the fly's speed. If you set your shutter speed low, the resulting blurry image will convey something of the fly's motion, but because of that blurriness it also provides an imprecise measurement of the fly's location. You can't take a photo that gives sharp information about position and speed simultaneously. (p. 31)

Thus, "the more precise your knowledge of a feature from one list [of properties], the less precise your knowledge can possibly be about the corresponding feature from the [other]... list" (Greene, 2004, p. 96). According to Greene (2004), this principle applies to everything rather than merely to the microscopic world, although sometimes the degree of uncertainty is too tiny to be noticed (p. 97). In the realm of biology, drawing on systems biology and complexity theory, Theise and Kafatos (2013) revealed an inherent biological uncertainty that is *explicit* in *all* of our descriptions of biological systems (p. 15). The systems biology approach suggests that "biological systems can be described as nested or overlapping levels of organization whose definition depends on the scale of observation" (Theise & Kafatos, 2013, p. 13)—"what appears to be a unitary (however mobile) entity at one level of scale (a flock of birds, a school of fish, and a green grass prairie) resolves at a lower scale into interacting component organisms" (Theise & Kafatos, 2013, p. 13). Thus, "as in the quantum realm, experimental observations themselves limit our capacity to understand a biological system completely because of scale-dependent 'horizons of knowledge,'... Specifically, observational selection is inherently, irreducibly coupled to observed biological systems (Theise & Kafatos, 2013, p. 11). This implies that "no single technique or perspective allows comprehensive viewing of all of a biological entity's complete qualities and behaviors" (Theise & Kafatos, 2013, p. 11).

Fully recognizing this human finitude, Gadamer (1960/2004) maintained that "all understanding inevitably involves some prejudice" (p. 272) and it is this recognition that "gives the hermeneutical problem its real thrust" (p. 272). By "prejudice," Gadamer does not mean iniquitous judgement, but "something that anticipates our judgments: the preconceptions, presuppositions, predispositions, and other meaning inherited from that past that always initially shape and orient our inquiry and action" (George, 2016, p. 58). While the contemporary meaning of the hermeneutic circle emphasizes "the idea that we always understand or interpret out of some presuppositions" (Grondin, 2016, p. 299), in ancient rhetoric and hermeneutics, the hermeneutic circle is of the whole and its parts—"we can only understand the parts of a text, or any body of meaning, out of a general idea [or pre-understanding] of its whole, yet we can only gain this understanding of the whole by understanding its parts" (Grondin, 2016, p. 299). It's evident that both the ancient and the contemporary meanings of the hermeneutic circle can be found in the allegory of The Blind Men and the Elephant and can be applied to the understanding and creation of the meaning of life as well as the communication between differing languages and discourses in our exploration of the nature of human existence and reality. In comparison to the spiritual wisdom of various religious and spiritual traditions that point to the panorama of reality (the whole), our ordinary dualistic mode of cognition and reasoning is as finite as the blind men's touch (the parts). By excluding spiritual wisdom from curriculum, we have deprived generations of human beings of the vision of a general understanding of the whole. In lack of the vision of "the whole," we, like the blind men, lose the required hermeneutic circle in our search of meaning and purpose of life. In this hermeneutical sense, I again argue for the equal validity and necessity of religion and science, or faith and reason, and contend for the imperative of the re-spiritualization of curriculum—integrating spiritual wisdom and existential knowledge into the school and university curriculum. Only by means of maintaining a double vision—keeping both the whole and its parts, faith and reason, wisdom and method, or the ultimate and phenomenal aspects of reality in sight, can we create a hermeneutic circle that allows multiple meanings of life to emerge, to unfold, and to play creatively, in the middle, in between.

In addition to the whole, maintaining a double vision and the hermeneutic circle for understanding and creating meanings, however, also involves keeping in sight the singularities or particularities of "the parts." Like a text as a whole is constituted by its parts—the sentences, human life as a whole is constituted by its parts—lived experiences. Understanding and creating the meaning of a text requires a back-and-forth play between the whole and its parts; understanding and creating the meaning of one's life requires a back-and-forth play between spiritual wisdom and existential knowledge that provides a panoramic view to a general meaning of human life (the whole) and the singular lived experiences of the person (its parts). Yet, to have lived experiences does not mean to merely have undergone experience "in the sense of the cliché 'Been there, done that, bought the t-shirt'" (Davey, 2016, p. 32); neither is it a kind of narrow psychological process that, as discussed in Chap. 5, "can easily be reduced to a form of solipsism" (Boler, 1999, p. 177) and does not result in any measurable change to oneself (Pinar, 2012, p. 47). Rather, as Davey (2016) put it, to have lived experiences or to be "experienced" is "to have reflected on, to have learned, and to have been changed by a series of experiential involvements and practices" (p. 32). Like an alchemical elixir that turns iron into gold, it is spiritual wisdom that makes possible the revelation of spirituality, singularity, and meaning intrinsic in seemingly trivial everyday experiences and brings about genuine transformation; these singular transformative lived experiences in turn deepen our understanding of spiritual wisdom, in a back-and-forth play. While the singularities of one's lived experiences are essential for maintaining a hermeneutic circle for understanding and creating specific meaning of life for an individual, the dominance of the technical language of the scientific method has gradually blinded human beings to the singularities of their own lived meanings and deprived them of the rich opportunities to reflect, to learn, to be transformed, and to make meaning. As discussed earlier, when lived meanings are hidden or silenced by objective meanings, we become "heedless of this silence" (Aoki, 1991/2004b, p. 381). Getting lost in this oblivion and blindly taking up the general societal norms, logic, and values "as if they somehow revealed the ultimate truth about how one should live" (Dreyfus & Wrathall, 2005, p. 7), humans end up living a diminished half-life with values and meanings that are not their own.

The above discussion exposes how the predominance of scientific language and the exclusion/neglect of spiritual wisdom, existential knowledge, and lived experiences from curriculum have undermined human beings' capacities to understand and create the meaning of life. In the Prologue of this book, I express my profound concerns about how the relentless power of the machinery of the education system drove everyone forward and left deeper questions of meaningfulness to the individual youngsters as "their own business" and I posed the question: Is this really none of our business? Here, I think we find the answer.

In our efforts to employ "as many perspectives as we can find appropriate" (Aoki, 1980/2004a, p. 96) on the same phenomena, situations, or issues, it is also crucial to keep in sight the singularities or particularities of different discourses. Similar to Musil, for Aoki, "coming to know how to communicate cross-paradigmatically at the level of deep structure" (Aoki, 1980/2004a, p. 110) was an urgent task. In cross-paradigmatic communication, particularly in the dialectic between science and humanities (including religions), understanding is of primary significance. For Gadamer, "the 'prejudiced' nature of our understanding should be recognized as that which makes understanding possible" (Grondin, 2016, p. 300), and therefore can be employed "to fight against the false ideal of a presupposition-less type of knowledge which would have been imposed upon the humanities by the objectivity requirement of exact science" (Grondin, 2016, p. 300). The significance of attending to the singularities of, and differences between, science and humanities is also emphasized by Pinar (2015). In his discussion of Musil's essayism, he quoted Luft:

> the characteristic fault of bourgeois reason was its misapplication of the model of natural science; in its drive for uniformity, bourgeois reason had lost track of the capacity to create value and enhance life. In its yearning for truth, concept and abstraction, it had lost respect for the flesh, for the concrete lives of individual human beings. (as cited in Pinar, 2015)

For Aoki, the differences between knowledge of science and humanities are the sort of what Deleuze called "differences in kind" (Aoki, 1993/2004c, p. 206). Seeing only differences in degree while neglecting the differences in kind, for Aoki (1993/2004c), might be one of the most general errors or irrationalities common to science and metaphysics (Aoki, 1993/2004c, p. 206) that makes cross-paradigmatic and cross-cultural conversation and understanding difficult.

11.4 The Tower of Babel

In cross-paradigmatic and cross-cultural communication, the singularities of the parts exist not only at the level of deep structure of discourses, but also at the individual level with a dynamic nature. In his reflection on the Tower of Babel, the symbol of confounded speech, Huebner (1985a/1999b) reminded us that

> as more and more people seem capable of understanding people of other cultures, other types of strangers and foreigners appear on the scene. The scattering process appears to be constitutive of human kind. As we become unified in some aspects, we become scattered in others. (p. 313)

Huebner's insights remind us of the empty and transient nature of all phenomena and prevent us from positively pursuing hypostasized, reified, or fixed kind of ideals of unification or uniformity in the process of cross-cultural and cross-paradigmatic communication. Recalling Bohm's (1980) reminder that unity or oneness is already the nature of reality—in a sense similar to what Rancière (2010) would call "an axiom to be verified" (p. 5), given the "whole in every parts" property of hologram in the holographic universe, or what Theise and Kafatos (2013) termed the "scale-dependent horizons of knowledge" (p. 13) that suggests we are already a whole from a much larger scale of observation than our egoistic perception—and the attempt to unify people is itself only an act of fragmenting or scattering, as the unifying of a group of people simultaneously separates this group of people from the rest of the world (p. 20). Like the blind men holding various views blind and unseeing, our views are finite and prejudiced in nature. Rather than grasping at our own views and quarreling with others or trying to unify various views that would generate only another set of reified or fixed kind of prejudiced views or "conclusion," in cross-cultural and cross-paradigmatic communication, creating a hermeneutical situation and maintaining an ongoing process of hermeneutical understanding are of greatest significance not only for communication, but also for bringing about experiences of consciousness transformation. As Gadamer (1960/2004) indicated, "understanding becomes a scholarly task only under special circumstances and that it is necessary to work out these circumstances as a hermeneutical situation" (p. 305). Also, it is important to keep in mind that

> a hermeneutical situation is determined by the prejudices that we bring with us. They constitute, then, the horizon of a particular present, for they represent that beyond which it is impossible to see. But now it is important to avoid the error of thinking that the horizon of the present consists of a fixed set of opinions and valuations, and that the otherness of the past can be foregrounded from it as from a fixed ground. (Gadamer, 1960/2004, pp. 304–305)

Davey (2016) explicated Gadamer that

> hermeneutic understanding is… not a question of fixing the inherent meaning of a text as if it were somehow "there," present before us on the page to be deciphered. It is, rather, a matter of engaging with and negotiating the meanings set in play when the horizons of a literary tradition, of a specific text, and of an individual reader meet. In essence, hermeneutic understanding is dialogical, an ongoing self-transforming participatory process. (p. 329)

Such a process inevitably involves the experience of tensions between the horizons of the past and the present (Gadamer, 1960/2004, p. 305) and the fusion of these horizons. However, it is important to note that the fusion of horizons "does not imply melding different horizons of meaning into one" (Davey, 2016, p. 329). As Gadamer (1960/2004) indicated, "the hermeneutic task consists in not covering up this tension by attempting a naive assimilation of the two but in consciously bringing it out" (p. 305). According to Davey (2016), "following Heidegger, Gadamer conceives of the frameworks of meaning embodied in different religious, political, and linguistic traditions as being essentially open… Their inherent openness permits the possibility of transformation" (p. 329). Gadamer's insights bring us back to Huebner's (1985b/1999c) eloquent articulation that is worthy of revisiting:

> Education is the lure of the transcendent—that which we seem is not what we are for we could always be other. Education is the openness to a future that is beyond all futures. Education is the protest against present forms that they may be reformed and transformed. Education is the consciousness that we live in time, pulled by the inexorable Otherness that brings judgment and hope to the forms of life which are but the vessels of present experience. (p. 360)

Huebner also quoted Hans Küng that "understanding someone properly involves learning from him, and learning from someone properly involves changing oneself" (as cited in Huebner, 1985a/1999b, p. 319). The above discussion reveals the interrelationships between human finitude of cognition, human temporality, otherness, openness, the transcendent, hermeneutical situation, hermeneutical understanding, ongoing conversation, education, and consciousness transformation. Given these interrelationships, I agree with Huebner (1985a/1999b) that "the confounding of our language could indeed be God's work" (p. 319) as when we try to understand and accept others, we "necessarily bring under question our taken-for-granted ways [and views]" (p. 319).

This study employs various languages—including educational, philosophical, religious, and scientific—for understanding spirituality and education. Rather than attempting to unify, this study, as an enthusiastic response to Huebner's (1993/1999d) invitation, aims for participating in, and hopefully enriching, the continuing "symbolic process whereby reality is produced, maintained, repaired, and transformed" (Carey, as cited in Pinar, 2012, p. 1). With full awareness of my own limitations of scope of knowledge, wisdom, and language, I wish to present this book to the readers as a cordial invitation to join, expand, and enrich this ongoing "spirited and informed communication" (Pinar, 2012, p. 1), which is the characteristic of curriculum (Pinar, 2012, p. 1).

References

Aoki, T. T. (2004a). Toward Curriculum Inquiry in a New Key. In W. F. Pinar & R. L. Irwin (Eds.), *Curriculum in a New Key: The Collected Works of Ted T. Aoki* (pp. 89–110). New York, NY: Routledge. (Original work published 1980).

Aoki, T. T. (2004b). Taiko Drums and Sushi, Perogies and Sauerkraut: Mirroring a Half-Life in Multicultural Curriculum. In W. F. Pinar & R. L. Irwin (Eds.), *Curriculum in a New Key: The Collected Works of Ted T. Aoki* (pp. 377–388). New York, NY: Routledge. (Original work published 1991).

Aoki, T. T. (2004c). Legitimating Lived Curriculum: Toward a Curricular Landscape of Multiplicity. In W. F. Pinar & R. L. Irwin (Eds.), *Curriculum in a New Key: The Collected Works of Ted T. Aoki* (pp. 200–215). New York, NY: Routledge. (Original work published 1993).

Bohm, D. (1980). *Wholeness and the Implicate Order.* New York, NY: Routledge.

Boler, M. (1999). *Feeling Power: Emotions and Education.* New York, NY: Routledge.

Davey, N. (2016). Lived Experience: Erlebnis and Erfahrung. In N. Keane & C. Lawn (Eds.), *The Blackwell Companion to Hermeneutics* (pp. 326–332). John Wiley & Sons Inc.

Dreyfus, H., & Wrathall, M. (2005). Martin Heidegger: An Introduction to His Thought, Work, and Life. In H. Dreyfus & M. Wrathall (Eds.), *A Companion to Heidegger* (pp. 1–15). Malden, MA: Wiley-Blackwell.

Fiedler, L. A. (1951). Introduction. In S. Weil, *Waiting for God* (E. Craufiird, trans.). New York, NY: Harper & Row.

Gadamer, H. G. (2004). *Truth and Method* (J. Weinsheimer & D. G. Marshall, trans.). New York: Continuum. (Original work published 1960).

George, T. (2016). Gadamer and German Idealism. In N. Keane & C. Lawn (Eds.), *The Blackwell Companion to Hermeneutics* (pp. 54–62). John Wiley & Sons Inc.

Greene, B. (2004). *The Fabric of the Cosmos: Space, Time, and the Texture of Reality.* New York, NY: Alfred A. Knopf.

Greene, B. (2011). *The Hidden Reality.* New York, NY: Alfred A. Knopf.

Grondin, J. (2016). The Hermeneutical Circle. In N. Keane & C. Lawn (Eds.), *The Blackwell Companion to Hermeneutics* (pp. 299–305). John Wiley & Sons Inc.

Huebner, D. E. (1999a). New Modes of Man's Relationship to Man. In V. Hillis (Ed.), *The Lure of the Transcendent: Collected Essays by Dwayne E. Huebner* (pp. 74–93). New York, NY: Routledge. (Original work published 1963).

Huebner, D. E. (1999b). Babel: A Reflection on Confounded Speech. In V. Hillis (Ed.), *The Lure of the Transcendent: Collected Essays by Dwayne E. Huebner* (pp. 312–320). New York, NY: Routledge. (Original work published 1985a).

Huebner, D. E. (1999c). Religious Metaphors in the Language of Education. In V. Hillis (Ed.), *The Lure of the Transcendent: Collected Essays by Dwayne E. Huebner* (pp. 358–368). New York, NY: Routledge. (Original work published 1985b).

Huebner, D. E. (1999d). Education and Spirituality. In V. Hillis (Ed.), *The Lure of the Transcendent: Collected Essays by Dwayne E. Huebner* (pp. 401–416). New York, NY: Routledge. (Original work published 1993).

Ireland, J. D. (1997). *The Udana and the Itivuttaka: Two Classics from the Pali Canon*. Kandy: Buddhist Publication Society.

Kaku, M. (2014). *The Future of the Mind: The Scientific Quest to Understand, Enhance, and Empower the Mind*. New York, NY: Anchor Books.

Noë, A. (2010). *Out of Our Heads: Why You Are Not Your Brain, and Other Lessons from the Biology of Consciousness*. Hill and Wang.

Null, J. W. (2008). Curriculum Development in Historical Perspective. In F. M. Connelly, M. F. He, & J. Phillion (Eds.), *The SAGE Handbook of Curriculum and Instruction* (pp. 478–490). Thousand Oaks, CA: Sage Publications.

Pinar, W. F. (2012). *What Is Curriculum Theory?* (2nd ed.). New York, NY: Routledge.

Pinar, W. F. (2015). *Educational Experience as Lived: Knowledge, History, Alterity: The Selected Works of William F. Pinar*. New York, NY: Routledge.

Quinn, M. (2001). *Going Out, Not Knowing Whither: Education, the Upward Journey, and the Faith of Reason*. New York, NY: Peter Lang.

Rancière, J. (2010). On Ignorant Schoolmasters. In C. Bingham & G. J. J. Biesta (Eds.), *Jacques Rancière: Education, Truth, Emancipation* (pp. 1–24). London: Continuum Publishing Group.

Theise, N. D., & Kafatos, M. C. (2013). Complementarity in Biological Systems: A Complexity View. *Complexity, 18*(6), 11–20.

Wallerstein, I. (2007). The Structures of Knowledge or How Many Ways May We Know. In B. de Sousa Santos (Ed.), *Cognitive Justice in a Global World: Prudent Knowledges for a Decent Life*. Lexington Books.

Wang, R. (1995). The Blind Men and the Elephant. Retrieved from http://dsh.cs.washington.edu/rywang/princeton/berkeley/258/parable.html

Index

A
Absolutism, 10, 11, 25, 26, 29–32, 35, 36, 55, 66, 67, 179
absolutistic (worldview), 4–6, 8, 9, 25, 85, 90, 107, 110
Ahmed, Sara, 133, 144, 145, 150, 170
Alaya, 45, 64, 72n9, 81
Alienation, 30, 32, 109, 110
Anxiety, 118, 146, 173, 174
Aoki, Ted T., 105, 170, 187, 192, 193
Approach
 of negation, 10, 12, 14, 25, 89–93, 107, 128, 133, 141, 142, 156, 159, 170, 173
 of science, 12, 107
Appropriational circuit, 13, 137, 145–150, 159, 175
Atheism, 14, 182–184, 186
Austin, James H., 155, 158, 159
Authenticity, xxi, 12, 18, 118–121, 131
 inauthenticity, 119
Authority, 72n6, 128–130, 158, 183

B
Bardo, 121
Being-in-the-world, xx, 103, 119, 122n1, 133, 158, 185
The Blind Men and the Elephant, 187–193
Bodhi, 81
Bodhicitta, xviii, 10, 51, 73n12, 82, 83, 85, 87, 93, 101, 111, 122, 125–134, 139, 140, 153, 163, 165, 168, 175, 180, 185
Body-mind aggregations, 157
Bohm, David, xx, 57–61, 65, 70, 107, 140–142, 193
Boler, Megan, 110, 145, 171
Borrows, John, xx, 6
Brain, 7, 59, 111, 112, 161, 162, 189
Buddha, 43–46, 48, 50–52, 56, 65, 82–84, 86–89, 93, 96n2, 97n3, 107, 108, 116, 119, 144, 154, 173, 174, 188

[1] Note: Page numbers followed by 'n' refer to notes.

200 INDEX

Buddhism, vii, xv, xxi, 6, 8–12, 20, 36, 41–70, 79, 101, 117, 138, 166, 179
Buddhahood, 52, 81, 82, 85–87, 93, 125, 134–135n1
Buddha Nature, 81, 82, 91, 127–129

C

Care, 4, 5, 21, 26, 28, 29, 31, 32, 104, 110, 133
Cartesian, 27, 171
Causal dependence, 73n11, 156
Change, 6, 19, 22, 24, 25, 27, 30, 34, 35, 45, 48, 67, 72n5, 74n16, 88, 103, 104, 109, 110, 137–139, 145–147, 172
Changelessness, 137, 145, 146
Christian, xxi, 4, 17, 117, 159
  Christianity, 183
Classical science, 3–6, 9, 11, 28, 36, 179, 181, 183
Commercialization, 5, 9, 179
Compassion, xviii, 13, 85, 87, 111, 112, 126, 127, 129, 153, 165, 168, 171, 172, 175, 185
Complicated conversation, vii
Conceptual dependence, 46, 73n11, 156, 157
Conceptual designation, 46
Conformism, 119
Confounded speech, 11, 14, 179–195
Consciousness, vii, xviii, 6–8, 10–12, 17, 42, 79–95, 101–112, 115, 125, 137, 153, 165, 179
Consciousness-Only, 42, 43, 46, 49, 53, 56, 58, 60, 66, 70, 71n2, 79, 81, 83, 85, 93, 102, 180
  See also Yogacara
Consciousness transformation, vii, 9–13, 70, 79–95, 101, 112, 116, 122, 140, 153, 155, 160, 163, 165, 166, 175, 179, 180, 194, 195

Conversation, vii, viii, xxi, 5, 11, 20, 28, 29, 31, 95, 104, 130, 131, 133, 167, 193, 195
Cosmic religious feeling, 24, 132
Currere, xv, 175

D

Dasein, 116, 118–120, 122n1, 144
Death, xviii, 12, 13, 45, 50, 65, 108, 116–122, 122n2, 146, 151n1, 181, 185
Dehumanization, 13, 137, 147
Dependent origination, 44–46, 49, 53, 54, 56, 60–62, 66, 89, 116, 117, 119, 156, 157
  dependent arising, 44–46, 48, 73n11, 119, 156–157
  three levels of, 73n11, 156, 157
  twelve links of, 44, 45, 117
Dialectic, xx, 23, 26, 92, 150, 172, 180, 184, 185, 192
Dialogue, 10–12, 17, 28, 32, 36, 41, 79, 90, 95, 101, 102, 122, 138–140, 149, 180, 181, 186
Dichotomy, 13, 28, 80, 91, 92, 105, 106, 119, 125, 131, 133, 137, 139, 140, 150, 155, 169
Dogmatization, 184
Double vision, viii, 128, 191
Dreyfus, Hubert, 118–120, 192
Duality, 13, 51, 84, 89, 110, 128, 169, 174, 184
  dualistic, 14, 47, 50–52, 80, 84–86, 88, 90–94, 107, 125, 127, 128, 130, 133, 143, 144, 147–149, 155, 158, 170, 173–175, 191

E

East Coker, 173
Education, xi, xviii, xxi, 3–14, 17–36, 41, 46, 66–70, 79,

90, 93–95, 101–103, 106–112,
117, 128–130, 132, 133, 138,
142, 159, 160, 168, 180, 181,
192, 195
Ego, 73n9, 89, 91, 133, 147, 148,
174, 183
egoism, 125
egoistic, 51, 159, 172, 183, 194
Eight negations, 89, 91
Eight worldly concerns, 148
Einstein, Albert, xix, 24, 53, 55, 62,
106, 115, 132
Emancipation, 51, 73n14, 130, 167
Emancipatory teachers, xiii, 129–131
Emptiness, 42–53, 55, 56, 66, 70,
72n4, 79, 80, 84, 86–88, 90,
91, 104, 106, 109–111,
116–118, 120, 125, 127, 131,
132, 134, 134n1, 138, 144, 150,
153–157, 159, 160, 163, 168,
172, 180, 185
Enslavement, 22, 105, 159
Epistemology, 27
epistemological, 11, 20, 25–30,
35, 92
Eppert, Claudia, 171–175
Equality, xii, 13, 82, 125, 126,
128–132, 172
Essayism, 186, 193
Estrangement, 137, 147, 169, 172
Ethical discipline, 51, 83, 87, 88,
166–170, 172
Experience, xix, 20, 31, 61, 68, 94,
117, 149, 174, 179, 187

F
Faith, viii, xvi–xviii, 10, 14, 27, 28,
83–85, 170, 173, 174, 180,
182–187, 191
Faithless reason, 181, 184
Fear, 88, 92, 106, 109, 110, 133, 148,
150, 173–175, 182

Fearlessness, xvi, 168
Fenwick, Tara, 17–20
Finitude, 189, 190, 195
Five spiritual faculties, 84
Five-stage gradual path, 10, 12,
81–85, 90, 93–95, 96n2, 101,
122, 140, 155, 180
Four exact realizations, 13, 84, 137,
140, 143
Four noble truths, 13, 42, 50–53,
137, 140, 143–145
Four reflections, 13, 84, 137, 140, 143
Four-stage transition, 10, 33, 68, 70,
82, 180
Fourteen difficult questions, 107, 108
Four transcendental wisdoms, 10,
12, 81–82, 85, 87, 93, 125,
135n1, 180
Fragment, 57, 105, 140, 141
Fragmentation, 57, 58, 88, 91, 106,
107, 109, 140, 141
Frozen futurism, 12, 104
Fuchs, Christopher A., 63, 64
Fusion of horizons, 194

G
Gadamer, Hans-Georg, 190, 192,
194, 195
Gamma waves, 111
Generosity, 51, 52, 83, 87, 89, 153,
166–168, 170, 172
Genuine conversation, 104, 130,
131, 167
Global competitiveness, 5, 13,
132–134, 167
Global crises, 3–6, 8, 68, 93, 103,
109, 110, 134, 179
God, 21, 69, 86, 91, 106, 117, 128,
129, 135n3, 151n1, 160,
181–185
Gore, Al, 6, 8, 110
Great mirror wisdom, 81, 82

Index

Greene, Brian, xix, xx, 7, 8, 53–60, 62, 63, 65–67, 69, 90, 115
Grondin, Jean, 190, 192
Guanyin bodhisattva, xiii, xvi–xix, 122n2

H
Half-life, 12, 105, 192
Happiness, 50, 51, 53, 81, 112, 126, 133, 134, 137, 144, 148–150, 167
Heidegger, Martin, xx, 10–12, 14n1, 20, 28, 33–35, 68–70, 85, 105, 107, 118, 119, 180, 195
Heightened consciousness, 148, 161
Hermeneutic circle, 10, 14, 190–192
Hermeneutics, 182–184, 190
Hidden curriculum, 27, 103, 109
Historicity, 8, 116, 138
Holistic education, 18
Holographic principle, xix, 53, 56–61, 63, 65–67
Hope, xxi, 24, 31, 32, 43, 95, 132, 173, 174, 183, 184, 195
Hsuan-Tsang, 43, 60, 73n13, 80–84, 125, 140
Huebner, Dwayne E., vii, xx, xxi, 4, 17, 18, 22, 23, 25, 28, 48, 103, 116, 138, 147, 160, 195
Human temporality, 3, 8, 10, 12, 13, 101, 102, 112, 115–122, 134, 138, 140, 154, 175, 180, 195

I
Ignorance, 45, 46, 50, 51, 80, 81, 84, 86, 87, 95n2, 125, 128, 129, 144, 148, 150, 158, 188
I-ing, 14, 154, 157
Illusion, 7, 52, 57, 59, 149, 157, 158, 167, 182
I-It, 28
I-making, 157
I-Me-Mine, 14, 155, 158–161, 167, 172
Impartial love, 126, 127, 129, 131, 171
Implementation, 104, 105
Improvisation, 82, 105
Inequality, 13, 128–132
Infinite possibilities, 28, 29, 32, 47, 49, 66, 88, 89, 94, 104, 137, 184
Innovation, 138, 139
Instrumentalism, 105
instrumental, 105
Interconnectedness, 6, 19, 24, 29, 30, 49, 58, 62, 73n16
interconnected, 30, 61
Interdependence, 6, 27, 47, 62, 119
Interiority, 20
Irrationality, 193
I-Thou, 28

J
Joyous perseverance, 51, 73n14, 83, 153, 166, 167, 169, 172

K
Kaku, Michio, 54, 55, 63, 106, 112n1, 189
Karmic seeds, 45, 64, 65, 69, 73n10, 80, 81, 90, 91, 93, 107, 117, 148, 165
Knowledge, 26, 27, 32, 102, 109, 120, 128, 183, 191, 195
Krishnamurti, Jiddu, 89, 92, 104, 105, 142, 174, 175
Kumar, Ashwani, xx, 88, 89, 91, 92, 105, 106, 142, 143

L
Lamrim Chenmo, 84, 97n3
Language, 5, 94, 105, 137, 185, 187, 195

Liberation, 10, 13, 22, 50–53, 68, 70, 79, 82, 85, 87, 88, 101, 110, 125, 127, 132, 134, 138, 144, 150, 167, 180
Lived experience, xx, 10, 14, 30, 48, 186, 191, 192
Lived meanings, 105, 192
Love, 5, 13, 21, 24, 26–29, 31, 32, 47, 86, 87, 91, 92, 104, 109–111, 117, 126, 127, 129, 131–133, 153, 160, 165, 167, 168, 171–175, 183, 185
Lure of the transcendent, xx, 31, 32, 35, 130, 195
Lusthaus, Dan, 13, 60, 71n2, 95n2, 137, 138, 145–147, 159, 175

M

Madhyamaka, 46, 73n11, 80, 95n2, 156
 See also Middle Way
Mahabodhi, 81
Mahaparinirvana, 81
Maharaj, Nisargadatta, 109, 110
Mahayana, 51, 72n6, 73n12, 73n13, 84, 86, 132
Maitreya, 73n14, 84, 143
Manas, 72–73n9, 81
Manysidedness, 187
Market logic, 109, 110, 132–134
Meditation, 43, 47, 49, 66, 83–87, 95–96n2, 111, 112, 121, 134n1, 143, 144, 161–163, 166, 174
Meditative stabilization, 14, 51, 52, 83, 111, 153, 160–163, 166–168, 172, 174
Metamorphosis, 10, 14, 179–195
Method, viii, 12, 14, 85–90, 92, 93, 96n2, 103–106, 109–111, 126, 134n1, 135n4, 175, 185, 187, 191, 192

Method-side practices, 10, 12, 52, 85–88, 91, 94, 96n2, 111, 112, 132, 153, 165, 168, 172, 175
Middle Way, 13, 46, 71n1, 80, 91, 93, 95n2, 96, 128, 130, 142, 154, 185
 See also Madhyamaka
Miller, John P., 11, 18, 20, 29, 30, 32, 33, 48, 86
Miller, Ron, 18
Mindfulness, 19, 84, 162
Mindfulness-based Stress Reduction (MBSR), 162
Mingyur, Yongey, 45, 49, 50, 111, 112, 125, 127, 128, 144, 149, 150
Mirror, 82, 147, 157, 184
Mortality, 13, 73n13, 118, 120, 122
Movie consciousness, 13, 137, 145–150, 161
Multiplicity, 186
Musil, Robert, 185, 186, 192, 193
Musilian, 186

N

Nargajuna, 154
Narrative self, 161, 162
Near death experiences, xviii, 121
Newland, Guy, 42–47, 54, 91, 154, 156
Nietzsche, 14, 181–185
Nirvana, 47, 73n13, 80, 86, 165
Noë, Alva, 186, 187
Non-change, 137, 138, 145, 147
Non-dualistic worldview, 10, 11, 14, 28–32, 35, 41, 49, 55, 58, 66, 89, 101, 122, 140, 142, 150, 153, 163, 165–175, 179, 180
Non-objectifying, 131
Non-perceptual, 89, 171
No-Self, 155

O

Object, 28, 42, 46, 52, 57, 63, 71n1, 73n9, 80, 84, 88, 89, 105, 112, 125, 128, 159
Objectifying, 88, 89, 92, 105, 110, 121, 132, 168
objectification, 109
Objective meanings, 105, 192
Objectivism, 10, 11, 25–27, 29–32, 35, 36, 55, 66, 67, 103, 134, 179
objectivistic (worldview), 4–6, 8, 25, 28, 85, 90, 107, 110
Objectless, 89, 171
Observed, xx, 5, 7, 51, 54, 55, 57, 58, 63, 92, 130, 132, 138, 143, 156, 188, 190
Observer, xx, 5, 54, 55, 57, 58, 92, 143, 155
Observe without observer, 89
Omniscience, xvii, xviii, 13, 51, 125, 127, 132, 167
Oneness, 47, 66, 70, 84, 88, 104, 141, 142, 155, 168, 171, 193
Openness, viii, xx, 10, 11, 14, 28–32, 35, 49, 87, 131, 132, 179, 195
Otherness, vii, 21, 31, 91, 131, 194, 195

P

Palmer, Parker, 11, 18, 20, 21, 26, 27, 32, 92, 134
Partiality, 13, 126, 127, 131, 147
Participatory universe, 53, 62–66, 155
Path of application, 83, 84, 140
Patience, 31, 51, 83, 153, 166, 167, 169, 170, 172
Perennial philosophy, 18, 29, 30, 47, 48, 68, 79
Perfect achievement wisdom, 81
Perfect transcendental wisdom, 81

Phelan, Anne, viii, xi, xv, xx, xxi, 143
Pilgrimage, 174
Pinar, William, vii, xi, xv, xxi, 3, 13, 14n1, 18, 110, 137, 147, 148, 173–175, 185, 186, 193, 195
Pitt, Alice, 158, 159
Plato, 41, 43, 49, 52, 53, 66–70, 79, 80, 82, 85, 101, 107, 149, 179, 189
Plato's allegory of the cave, 10, 11, 20, 31–36, 43, 49, 52, 67, 68, 82, 85, 101, 149, 179, 189
Play, xviii, 14, 132, 141, 191, 194
Positivism, 4, 25, 67
Prejudice, viii, 190, 192, 194
Profound contemplation wisdom, 81
Pure Land, 121, 122–123n2
Pure observation, 89, 142, 143

Q

Quantum physics, vii, xxi, 6–11, 20, 36, 41–70, 90, 95, 101, 102, 138–140, 149, 179–181, 186, 187, 189

R

Rancière, Jacques, xiii, 13, 128–131, 193
Reason, vii, viii, 10, 14, 23, 126, 180, 183–187, 191, 193
Reasonless faith, 184
Reasonless reason, 184
Reification, 13, 89, 133, 137, 142, 184
Reincarnation, xvi, xviii, 45, 121, 135n2
Religion, xv, xviii, 3, 10, 11, 14, 17–21, 23, 30, 180, 182, 184–186, 191, 192
Responsibly responsive, 10, 13, 101, 134, 137–150, 175, 180

INDEX 205

Reverence, xv, 5, 13, 117, 122, 167
Ricoeur, Paul, 14, 180–186
Right view, 13, 42, 45, 48, 51, 70–71n1, 80, 122

S

Scale of observation, 14, 156–158, 190, 194
Science
 scientific approach (methods), 12, 103–107, 121, 187, 192
 scientific validity, 104
Sedgwick, Eve K., 143
Self, 154–163
 self-knowledge, 109–111
 self-other, 155, 169
 self-projection, 160–162
 self-protection, 125
 self-specifying system, 156
 self-transformation, 110
Selflessness, xviii, 10, 13, 14, 101, 150, 153–163, 165, 174, 175, 180
Shadows, 10, 33, 35, 36, 36n1, 49, 69, 85, 107, 120, 148, 149, 180, 184, 189
Siderits, Mark, 60, 89, 142
Singularities, 89, 186, 191–193
Six perfections, 14, 51, 52, 73n14, 83, 84, 87–89, 128, 132, 144, 153, 166–170, 175
Six realms, xvi, 127, 135n2
Smith, David G., xv, 5, 104, 109, 133, 134, 157, 160, 169
Solipsism, 110
 solipsistic, 175
Sopa, Lhundub, 42–45, 48, 50–52, 64, 65, 82–84, 86–89, 95n2, 102, 117, 125–127, 132, 143, 144, 149, 169, 171

Spirituality, vii, 7, 9, 11, 12, 17–36, 67, 68, 92, 95, 96n2, 168, 179, 180, 187, 195
Spiritual truth, 10–12, 29–32, 35, 36, 41, 42, 49, 53, 67, 68, 85, 107–109, 125, 179
Spiritual wisdom, xx, 4–12, 14, 25, 36, 87, 88, 102–104, 106–112, 120, 121, 129, 131, 132, 179–181, 184, 191, 192
Subject, 28, 52, 64, 80, 105, 112, 115, 125, 140, 147, 154, 155, 160, 180
Subjective, 13, 26, 27, 63, 64, 80, 90, 91, 119, 121, 146, 153
Subject–object, 13, 28, 51, 80, 84, 85, 89–94, 95n1, 105–107, 110, 119, 125, 131, 133, 140, 141, 143, 147, 150, 169, 172, 184
Subject–subject, 28, 29, 172
Supramundane paths, 83, 94, 96n2

T

Talbot, Michael, xviii, 56, 57, 59, 62
Teleology, 106
Ten non-virtues, 83, 169
Ten virtues, 83
Thompson, Evan, 13, 46, 121, 154–157, 160–162, 173
Three Metamorphoses, xiv, 14, 181–187
Three Saints of the West, 123n2
Three spheres, 88, 89
Three trainings, 51, 52, 83, 144, 167
Time, xix, 9, 12, 31, 49, 53, 56, 59, 65, 72n5, 108, 115–118, 122n2, 127, 129, 139, 149, 157, 158, 160, 161, 185, 186, 195
Tower of Babel, 193–195

Transcendent, xv, 10, 11, 21, 22, 25–32, 35, 41, 48, 49, 66, 94, 102, 104, 129, 130, 138, 148, 171, 179, 195
Transformation, xviii, 85, 88, 95, 101, 110, 138, 145, 148, 159, 173, 174, 182, 195
  of consciousness, vii, 6, 9–13, 43, 70, 79, 81–82, 93, 94, 101, 103, 107, 109, 111, 112, 116, 122, 125, 132, 138, 140, 153, 155, 160, 163, 165, 166, 171, 175, 179, 180, 185–187, 194, 195
Truth, 8, 17–36, 41, 79, 101, 115, 125, 137, 154, 169, 180
Truth force, 8, 110
Truthful knowing, 27, 28, 32, 47, 49, 89, 92, 104, 130, 131, 167
Tsong-kha-pa, 44, 47, 51, 65, 84, 86, 88, 166–170
Two barriers, 80, 81, 94
  afflictive (barrier), 80, 81, 90–93, 107, 153, 165
  noetic (barrier), 80, 90, 104, 153, 165
Two fruits, 81
Two truths, 42–50, 52, 61, 70, 83, 96, 115, 130, 154, 180
Tyler, Ralph, 180

U
Uncertainty, 53–56, 189, 190

Uniformity, 193
Universal equality wisdom, 81, 82, 125, 132

V
Verbalization, 142, 143

W
Wei, Tat, 42, 43, 71n2, 72n9
Wholeness, xx, 19, 22, 24, 31, 49, 57–59, 105, 149
Whole/part dependence, 73n11
  See also Hermeneutic circle
Wisdom, viii, xvii, xviii, xx, xxi, 3, 4, 6, 10, 12, 14, 18–20, 29, 48, 51, 52, 79, 81–90, 92, 104, 105, 107–112, 126, 128, 134, 135n1, 153, 160, 163, 166–168, 172, 174, 175, 180, 185, 191, 195
Wisdom-side practices, vii, 10, 12, 13, 52, 91, 94, 96n2, 111, 112, 144, 153, 156, 160, 165, 172
Witnessing, 14, 155, 171–175
Worldly paths, 83, 96n2
Wrong views, 71n1, 80, 81, 83, 108, 116, 169

Y
Yogacara, 42, 44, 45, 71–72n2, 72n3, 72n9, 79–82, 91, 95n2, 180
  See also Consciousness-Only